U.S. Occupation and Human Rights Issues:
Special Reference to Iraqi Women

U.S. Occupation and Human Rights Issues:
Special Reference to Iraqi Women

Dr Vinitha Varghese
Dr C Vinodan

KALPAZ

ISBN: 978-93-5128-245-7

Price: ₹ 1080

First Published, 2017

Published by

Kalpaz Publications
C-30, Satyawati Nagar,
Delhi – 110052
E-mail: kalpaz@hotmail.com
Ph.: 9212142040

Printed at: G. Print Process, Delhi

Cataloging in Publication Data—DK

Courtesy: D.K. Agencies (P) Ltd. <docinfo@dkagencies.com>

Varghese, Vinitha, author.

U.S. occupation and human rights issues : special reference to Iraqi women / Dr Vinitha Varghese, Dr. C Vinodan.

pages cm

Includes bibliographical references.

ISBN 9789351282457

1. Women—Violence against—Iraq. 2. Women's rights—Iraq. 3. Human rights—Iraq. 4. Humanitarian intervention—Iraq. 5. Iraq War, 2003-2011—Social aspects. I. Vinodan, C., author. II. Title.

HQ1236.5.I72V37 2017 DDC 323.3409567 23

Contents

List of Tables and Figures

Abbreviations

CAT	:	Convention Against Torture
CEDAW	:	Convention on the Elimination of All Forms of Discrimination against Women
COM	:	Council of Ministers
CPA	:	Coalition Provisional Authority
CRC	:	Convention on the Rights of the Children
CRPD	:	Convention on the Rights of Persons with Disabilities
CWIHP	:	Cold War International History Project
DGS	:	Directorate of General Security
DIA	:	Defence Intelligence Agency
DOD	:	Department of Defence
DRL	:	Democracy, Human Rights, and Labour
EAFORD	:	Elimination of All Forms of Racial Discrimination
ECOSOC	:	Economic and Social Council
FGM	:	Female Genital Mutilation
GFIW	:	General Federation of Iraqi Women
HRC	:	Human Rights Council
HRW	:	Human Rights Watch
IBC	:	Iraq Body Council
ICCPR	:	International Covenant on Civil and Political Rights
ICERD	:	International Convention on the Elimination of All Forms of Racial Discrimination
ICESCR	:	International Covenant on Economic, Social and Cultural Rights
ICRC	:	International Committee of the Red Cross
IGC	:	Iraqi Governing Council

IKR	:	Iraqi Kurdistan Region
ILPS	:	Introducing a Personal Status Law
IRCS	:	Iraqi Red Crescent Society
IRMO	:	Iraq Reconstruction and Management Office
IRRF	:	Iraq Relief and Reconstruction Fund
ISMUN	:	International Youth and Student Movement for the United Nations
ITAO	:	Iraq Transition Assistance Office
KRG	:	Kurdistan Regional Government
MAD	:	Mutually Assured Destruction
NATO	:	North Atlantic Treaty Organisation
NGO	:	Non-Governmental Organisation
NHRI	:	National Human Rights Institutions
NWI	:	Nobel Women's Initiative
NWSA	:	National Women's Studies Association
OAS	:	Organisation of American States
OCHA	:	Office for the Coordination of Humanitarian Affairs
OLC	:	Office of Legal Counsel
ORB	:	Opinion Research Business
ORHA	:	Office of Reconstruction and Humanitarian Assistance
OSCE	:	Organisation for Security and Cooperation in Europe
PCO	:	Project Contracting Office
PHR	:	Physicians for Human Rights
RCC	:	Revolutionary Command Council
SCIRI	:	Supreme Council for Islamic Revolution in Iraq
TAL	:	Transitional Administrative Law
UN	:	United Nations
	:	Untied States
USA	:	United States of America
UDHR	:	Universal Declaration of Human Rights
UNAMI	:	United Nations Assistance Mission for Iraq
UNDP	:	United Nations Development Programme

UNDRIP : United Nations Declaration on the Rights of Indigenous Peoples

UNESCO : United Nations Educational Scientific and Cultural Organisation

UNHCR : United Nations High Commissioner for Refugees

UNICEF : United Nations Children's Fund

UNSC : United Nations Security Council

WHO : World Health Organisation

WILPF : Women's International League for Peace and Freedom

WMD : Weapons of Mass Destruction

Preface

The concept of 'Human Rights' has undoubtedly emerged as the most dominant idea of the contemporary world because of the increasing tendency of modern nations to incorporate rights and duties into their constitutions amidst the continued violence and marginalisation in different part of the world. The process of globalisation and the information communication revolution has opened many new challenges to human rights. Human rights, as a concept, seem to be very simple, but it has wider and complex ramifications on account of its philosophical foundations getting mixed up with political expediency. For, all political purpose, the genesis of human rights is not older than the Second World War, though the concept of an individual having certain inalienable rights against the state had its origin in the past. Human rights can be broadly defined as "those minimum rights that every individual must have against state or public authority by virtue of being a member of human family, irrespective of any other consideration." The concept of human rights has been evolving in the previous centuries but rapidly expanding due to the tremendous impact in raising the status of the individual under modern international law and in providing a criterion of legitimacy for government and civilised status for a society. Today, human rights have become a subject of intense discussion, not only at the international level but also in national jurisdiction. Every country, whether developed or developing, expresses genuine concern over promotion and realisation of human rights. The world will not easily accept an inhuman treatment in any context, which seriously undermines even legitimate security operations. Failure in respecting universal human rights and norms undermines the international cooperation and public support. It is, therefore, very important to restore the balance between liberty and security by reassuring the human rights framework. A grave and systematic violation of human rights and fundamental freedom is being carried out against the entire population of Iraq, in different forms and dimensions, without any precedent. The right to life, the most basic right, is being denied to millions by the continued war, occupation and the sanctions policy, implemented by the United States. Iraqis, in general, and Iraqi women, in particular, have complained that the volatile security situation and continuing insurgency have contributed to deterioration in their status.

Statement of the Problem

Despite the common rhetoric of democratisation, women's rights and inclusion, Iraqi women turned out to be the biggest losers in the political and social map of Iraq. Having already suffered from the steady erosion of socio-economic rights, violations gained momentum in the early years of the Saddam Hussein regime. Moreover, women and gender relations have been particularly hard-hit by economic sanctions (1990-2003), as well as by the war in 2003 and its ongoing violent aftermath. *This work focuses on analysing the human rights violations in Iraq, especially during the U.S. occupation of the country, with special emphasis on the violations against Iraqi women within the framework of the theory of human rights.* Serious accusations have been raised against the insurgents, the U.S. led coalition forces and the Iraqi government for their extensive human rights abuses during the course of the war. The war has created a deep political crisis in the international system and a deeper humanitarian crisis in Iraq. The issue of human rights, particularly that of women's rights in Iraq, has taken up new relevance, following the U.S. occupation of Iraq since 2003. One of the major questions the international community faces today is the extent to which the Iraqi women are being isolated and threatened by both the occupation forces and the violent uprisings. There are serious concerns regarding the inadequacy of efforts to facilitate their entry in to the mainstream of Iraqi life by reintegrating them into the political, educational and economic spheres after a long period of decline-exacerbated by three major wars and economic sanctions. The military action not only aggravated the humanitarian crisis, but also endangered major economic, political, legal, military and strategic repercussions.

In this context, the present study attempts to analyse the causes and consequences of the U.S. war on Iraq through the democratic and human rights' perspectives. This study raises some questions like what are the changing perceptions of human rights in the contemporary world and to what extend the U.S. interventions are responsible for the violation of human rights and sufferings of the Iraqi women. These issues did not acquire visibility until recently, but a concern over human rights that has grown gradually in the post-war period accelerated a significant change in the international dialogue in human rights in the last decade. The reasons for the current prominence of the issue are primarily political, although economic conditions also have their specific role. Changes in the top political hierarchy and the mobilisation at the grass-roots level have also contributed to this change. Even though these major political changes have made human rights a central issue on the international political agenda, progress in this area has, by no means, been universal. In some societies, there has been deterioration of the human rights situation. But that deterioration has become an important measure of the development of those societies, a reflection of the changing appraisal of the significance of human rights. As an effort to address all these questions, this study examines the evolution of rights, origin of human rights, the theory of democracy and rights, profile of Iraq, Saddam Hussein's administration in Iraq, U.S. intervention, post-Saddam era etc. The study focuses on the worst situation of Iraqi women, state's responses to the violations of human rights and the future challenges.

Background of the Problem

As we have seen, politics, economics and the social situations played their role in the abuse of human rights in Iraq. To these, we have to add the historical data for a complete picture. In the 1930s, Iraqi women played a vital role in the fight for independence from Britain. Women were particularly unhappy with British colonialists who tried to deny their request for the civil right. With the close of British indirect rule in Iraq, women's groups staged massive protests for their civil rights. After the creation of Iraq as an independent kingdom, the monarchy sought to maintain the status-quo of Sunni dominance, prompting conflict between the Arab Sunni establishment and several minorities. But the monarchy also sought solutions, compromises and certain forms of elections and democratic expressions. Saddam publicly acknowledged the moral authority of Islam and this acceptance led to an unfortunate reduction in women's rights that so often accompanies a patriarchal interpretation and implementation of the Holy Koran. Saddam perceived a kind of traditionalist patriarchal pressure from a threatened male population within Iraq and from his Islamic neighbours. Iraqis increasingly turned to religion for solace. This sharpened the division between the country's Shi'ite and Sunni Muslims. Saddam Hussein, launched a Faith Campaign in the early 1990s to co-opt the support of conservative religious leaders while eradicating Shiite leadership, rolling back women's legal protections in the process. Many of the gains of the international sanctions in the 1990s were lost during the economic depression. Men took priority in the shrinking job market. Families pulled girls out of school, to work at home and female literacy plunged. In these national circumstances, the status of the women was worsened everyday in the Muslim world. In the Muslim societies, unmarried women are often cornered. Both the stress of running a household in wartimes and the pressure of finding a husband had led many women in Iraq to commit suicide. Muslim world believes that individual freedom should not threaten the interest of the community. According to Shari, "It is the state's duty to enhance human dignity and alleviate conditions". So, human rights are not granted through individual initiative, but by state alone.

Following the U.S. invasion in March 2003, the CPA attempted to elevate Iraqi women's status through educational programmes, job-skills training, right awareness, and networking. Nevertheless, women in Iraq actually need immediate political representation to secure these long-term efforts. Unlike other post-conflict situations, wherein international bodies such as the United Nations dispatch civilian experts to handle political negotiations, Iraq has seen coalition forces take the lead in establishing and appointing local governing councils, particularly in rural areas. Non-governmental organisations have helped Iraqis to build political coalitions and take other steps toward democracy. But when it came to political appointments, the military overpowered.

In this background, this study gives special attention on the theories of human rights and its changing meaning in the present century. It also deals with the role of U.S. in Iraq and in what extent their presence violates the rights of the people, especially Iraqi women. Human rights were never a principle justification for the war. Though WMDs and Saddam Hussein's links to terrorism are said to be the causes, they were discredited due to the lack of evidence. Human Rights Watch and Amnesty International, leading human rights groups, further argued that even though human rights concerns were said to be the central reason for the invasion, military intervention could not be justified on humanitarian grounds. Heavy civilian casualties occurred as a result of U.S. military operations in Fallujah. Many of the victims were women, children and the elderly people. U.S. military officials argued that U.S. forces have taken great precaution to avoid and minimise civilian casualties. Since the U.S. led invasion of Iraq in 2003 and the formation of CPA, the Bush administration stated its interest in ensuring Iraqi women's involvement in reconstructing Iraq. Although modern Iraqi history is replete with liberal view towards women, Shi'ism and the country's wider culture may create obstacles for increasing women participation in Iraqi political and social life. Iraq's constitution does not specify who will decide which version of Islam will prevail in the country's new legal system. But the battle has already begun. Victory by the progressive would have positive implications for all aspects of the future of Iraq, since women's rights are critical to democratic consolidation in transitional and war-torn societies.

In Iraq's volatile security climate, women's empowerment was not a major concern of the military personnel who is in the front lines of nation building. Involvements of women become considerably more difficult after U.S. forces entrench conservative religious clerics and tribal leaders in positions of power. Iraqi women are reconciling the principles of their faith with the chances for new political, economic, and professional identities. Even women from the most conservative regions of the country are enthusiastic about becoming involved in public life, says Zainab Salbi, who runs women's centres across Iraq through her U.S.=based nonprofits organisation- Women for Women International. A group of Shiite women seeking funds for a centre for women in their hometown of Karbala recently told potential donors that they wanted room for a prayer along with their computer terminals and English lessons. Ultimately, greater political participation of women could provide Iraq with a stabilising force to avoid the potentially disastrous division of the country into ethnic states. Women's share in the economic and social development impels transcendence in regional, ethnic and religious divisions. Yet, it is not easy to secure meaningful political representation for Iraqi women. Success of women in Iraq would also reverberate throughout the broader Muslim world. In every country where Shari'a is enforced, women's rights have become a divisive issue due to the balance struck between tradition and equality. We recognise that women in Iraq have a critical role to play in the revival of their country and they bring skills and knowledge that will be vital to restore Iraq to its rightful place in the region and in the world. In many Islamic countries reformers have largely abandoned attempts to replace Shari' a with a secular law- a route that has proved mostly futile. Instead, they are trying to promote women's rights within an Islamic framework. This approach seems more likely to succeed, since it fights theology with theology- a natural strategy in conservative countries where religious authority is hard to challenge.

Conclusions

This work concludes with a set of findings which evolved as the product of the systematic approach to the topic. Also it explains limitations of the study and recommendations for expansion of this topic for future research projects. To do something meaningful and fruitful, one must be liberated from today's fears and able to enjoy basic human rights. Iraqi women are not in that process. They continue to be in a pathetic situation. Despite all the rhetoric about building a new democracy, Iraqis are buckled under the burdens of abuse and plunder committed by the U.S.=led occupation and its local Iraqi sub-contractors. Daily life for most Iraqis is still a struggle for survival, with tragedies and atrocities engulfing them. This is more vulnerable situation. Human rights under occupation have proved to be a mirage similar to weapons of mass destruction. Torture and ill treatment of members of political and armed groups, even the torture of children is widespread. Iraqi women were the most liberated in the Middle East. Occupation has confined them to their homes. But now a typical Iraqi woman's day begins with the struggle to get the basics: electricity, petrol or a cylinder of gas, fresh water, food and medication. It ends with a sigh of relief for surviving death. From the other point, in absence of a sustainable democracy, no one can anticipate what will happen in

Iraq. How much the civil society is powerful and how much the people will participate in the process of rebuilding state and society is still not clear. However, it seems that best way for women in Iraq is to shape their own movement, in their own local way based on the existing capacities, so that they can institutionalise their needs. Such a movement has never been self-initiated and it is time for women to move forward. The movement should find its own appropriate mechanisms to define itself. This can also affect the women's movements in the region. The role of nongovernmental organisations in Iraq can be vital in this regard.

1

Theoretical Foundations of Human Rights

Right from the dawn of human civilisation, human beings strived for the enjoyment of their *rights for a good life*, which includes the sum total of those opportunities which ensure enrichment of human personality by providing necessary conditions for development. Eventhough they are the social requirements of an individual for the development of his or her personality and society at large, these are also necessary for the development of society and social values. In the evolutionary history of human rights, mainly three aspects of human existence were safeguarded, which are human integrity, freedom and equality. Evidently these three aspects are the admiration of the dignity of every human being. The most remarkable concepts while tracing the origin of rights are: (i) rights were dictatorial in accumulation, (ii) hierarchical with diverse people being approved with special rights, and a few having more rights than others and (iii) the divine right of kings which allowed unlimited power over the subjects by leaving less room for many rights to be settled to them.[1] The history provides conceptual basics and even some practical attempts to answer the existing dilemma of rights. Yet, millions of people have faught to succeed and maintained the spirit of independence. In such conditions, rights of a human being were inconceivable to life with just honour and self-esteem (Mishra, 2007). The overt evidence of rights has differed wholly in diverse periods of narration. In many cases, the structure of rights promulgated by one group had spiky and tart inconsistency with that of other groups. In order to realise the real meaning and values of human rights one must know the origin and evolution of rights. The real meaning of this holistic development, vital to world citizenship, is essential to our human evolution. This chapter gives a brief introduction to rights and emergence of the concept of rights. It also mentions the views of different political thinkers on rights, classifications of rights, the concepts of rights in various centuries. This chapter gives an opening to the concept of human rights and human rights theory.

The Bible, the Vedas, the Quran and the scriptures of other world religions are the oldest sources that include the rudiments of duties, responsibilities, and the privileges of human beings. The values of civil rights can be established constantly in the Mauryan Empire in Ancient India and predominantly throughout the periods of Emperor Asoka, the Great. The well-known Kalinga war transferred the 'chandasoka' to 'dharmasok' as King Ashoka adopted the strategy of non-violence and defence of human rights, as his chief apprehension for the utmost contentment of his subjects. Under the leadership of Cyrus the Great, in the sixth century BC, doctrine of human rights were carried out (Mishra, 2007). Freedom of religion, abolition of slavery, freedom of movement, socio-economic rights, right to property, right to security etc.[1] are some of the human rights institutionalised by Cyrus. Infrequent thoughts never constitute a disengage draft on human rights. Marcus Tullius Cicero, the great Roman Jurist says that, "There is one eternal and immutable law which will apply to all people at all times and which emanates from God is Natural Law" (Bajwa, 1997). Kantian thought further consolidates by saying: "the right to resort, for all men are entitled to present themselves in the society for others by virtue of their right to communal possession of the earth's surface. Since the earth is globe, they cannot disperse over an infinite area, but must necessarily tolerate one another's company."[2]

If we make an effort to forecast the upcoming of rights in our world, we should constantly memorise that the account of rights has been neither linear nor fully knowable. This is almost true for the past 150 years. During this period, people entrusted the nurturing and fortification of human rights to the nation state. Rights were no longer considered as being an appearance of an individual's ability, eminence, or power, but as the state's requirement to care for its citizens. Human rights law helps to prevent violations, punish violators, and afford some relief to victims (Weissbrodt and Connie, 2007). Rights were preserved in legal documents that handed downstairs rights to the subjects of the defensive state. The result has been that both here and out of the country when states had to settle on between the rights of individual and the 'good' of the state during the twentieth century, the individual generally lost, in both terrible and predictable ways.

We live in an of human rights. It has today become a common language of humanity. The history of human rights has taken a log of poignancy today. Human rights issues are more political in nature than societal or economic. This is because of the dominance given to the political nature of rights (Azadi, 2011). On the other hand, rights are natural and God-gifted, and infringement of them leads to the call for fortification and endorsement. The concept of rights emerged with the rise of modern state and out of the criticism of the old social and political order. Its tone was radical and in its ultimate employment, was revolutionary; the demand for individual rights was made by the rising commercial or middle class which was the product of industrial revolution. It became the accepted ideology of American and French revolutionaries and was expressed in the Declaration of Independence, the Constitutional Bill of Rights on America, and in the Declaration of Rights of Man in France. Prominent liberal writers such as John Locke, Rousseau, Bentham, J.S. Mill, T.H. Green, Harold Laski, Ernest Barker and others have advocated the rights of the individual on different grounds. In the post-war period, the concept of rights has been further expanded by John Rawls, Robert Nozick, Ronald Dworkin and others. Right now the matter of 'who has what legal rights' is occasionally addressed by the constitutions of the meticulous nations. The world has witnessed a volatile expansion of the human rights progress. Human rights are privileges, which individuals are permitted to by good quality or asset of being 'human'. The rights, we denote are human rights, which is also synonymously called normal or natural rights. By human rights, we signify the rights related with our birth as a human being. Prior to going to elucidate the human rights, its violation, protection, and promotion, is necessary overthrow light on the evolution of rights. Human rights abuse still continues in the nation-states across the globe (Byrne, 2003).

I. Rights in the Various Ages

Regarding the sources of rights, primarily the origins of rights is something in the individual (Brennan, 2012).

Rights flow from the inherent fact of one's own moral personality and his or her social nature. In the case of sadaq, the first and most important portion of a bride's dowry, involves a transfer of property to both the bride and the groom separately. The woman's share was held apart from her husband's property for the duration of the marriage, and there was no legal recourse whereby husbands could force their wives to share their wealth. The sadaq therefore established a "legal and independent channel by which women could acquire property without depriving them of their share in the inheritance" (Glick, 2011). The Constitution of Medina (622 AD; Arabia) instituted a numeral of rights and duties for the Muslim, Jewish and pagan communities of Medina, establishing autonomy of worship for non-Muslims in rejoin for additional taxes (the jizya), the defence of women, a method for yielding enrichment of individuals, and an official organisation (Denny, 1977).

The Magna Carta (1215) was an appearance of the hierarchy of rights and an effort to repeat the Kings their existences. The Magna Carta (1215; England) required the King of England to relinquish certain rights and esteem certain legal process. It restricted the sovereign power of King John of England. The sixteenth century Reformation enlarged individual freedom in religious matters (Borgohain, 1999). In addition, to admit the will of the king was bound by law. English nobles and clergy rallied against King John 1's ill-treatment of power-weighty taxation to finance exclusive, ineffective wars and his denial to allow power of the Catholic Pope, which successfully set to the left churches in England closed for years. The aristocracy along with clergy subjected the king to the rule of law by enacting a great charter of liberties.

The Henrician Articles (1573; Poland-Lithuania) or King Henry's Articles were an unending bond that avowed the essential set of guidelines of pre-eminence and legitimate law in their Commonwealth. In addition to the constitutional rights of the landed gentry to elect the king, to gather together in Parliament whose approval was obligatory to levy taxes and converse out war or quiet to religious deliverance, and the right to rebel in case the king transgressed were adjacent to the laws of the republic or the rights of the affability (Chibi, 1998).

The notion of Natural Law was intricate throughout the middle ages and was established in the works of Christian theologians. They followed the conviction that the Law of God subsist on top of all human laws. In accordance with St. Thomas Aquinas, "Natural Law was the participation in the eternal law of the mind of a rational creature" (Bajwa, 1997). The nobles, on the other hand, obsessed extensive rights, including privilege to own and manage property and to exercise control over large expenses of land. Not only rights were incomplete but they were also something only granted in return for specific duties. The more rights one haunted, the more duties one was expected to perform. In fact, the increasing poverty is one of the major causes for the abuses of human rights throughout the world. Freedom from poverty is a basic human right that gives rise to the moral and legal responsibilities of governments and other actors and has obtained increased international attention in recent years (Vizard, 2006). The role of maintaining the peace, was carried out by those who were entitled to ownership of great estates. Therefore, rights were both traditional and fundamental part of the social hierarchy.

In the eighteenth century, the law of nature had begun to emphasise itself to shield the individual adjacent to the influence of the state. This culminated in the great broad-spectrum assertion of the rights of man in France in 1789 and in the U.S. Constitutional Amendment of 1791.[3] The supreme belief in natural rights went into to the hard belief of a rejection during the nineteenth century. But replaced largely by concerns with the idea of freedom, it has returned to favour in the second half of the twentieth century. A natural result of the idea that all men are born with equal rights is the belief that we must all take pleasure in equal rights. The roots of human rights to the rejection of torture are a means for finding the truth (Hunt, 2007). It was due to the influence of the early revolutionary liberal movements which were based on equality of rights. They required the elimination of the hierarchical system of rights that remained from the feudal age. They argued for a just and democratic situation where every citizen shall enjoy equal rights under the law and in their contact with government. The elementary dilemma with shielding the human rights administration in terms of natural rights thinking is the collapse of its advocates to endow with a persuasive theory of human nature on the ground of human dignity.[4]

Through the Westphalia Treaty (1648) the wars had to be ended by the parties (Gross, 1948). In some states, the agreement also leads to a religious toleration by allowing Catholic or Protestant minorities' rights to private esteem, liberty of sense of right and wrong and mass departure. The Bill of Rights in England (1689), announced that Englishmen, as represented by the Parliament, possess certain civil and political rights and collective rights (Howard, 2009). In Scotland, *The Claim of Right* declared in 1689, was different from *The Bill of Rights* in England (Lynch, 1992). Without the Parliament's approval, the bill prohibited taxation or maintenance of an army in peacetime and also prohibited excessive bail or fines, and cruel and unusual punishment.

The U.S. Declaration of Independence (1776) had a wide-ranging and lasting authority on individual rights in Western civilisation (Armitage, 2007). It was an awakening rebellion besides the South American Spanish Act and in opposition to the monarchy in France. Its most of the parts are based on Natural Right theories. The Declaration scheduled the colonists' injustices side with the British King, and other atrocities happened during the American War of Independence (1776) (Mc Donnell, 2006) and French Revolution (1789) (Doyle, 2001). All these contributed capability to the opening out of human rights. *The Untied States Declaration of Independence* had emphasised natural rights and status that all men are created equal and their creator donated them certain unalienable rights that surrounded by life, liberty and pursuit of happiness. Similarly, the French Revolution included three new terms- liberty, sameness and alliance. In particular, the class distinctions were abolished within the society through the French Revolution (Mishra, 2007). *The Declaration of the Rights of Man and of the Citizen* (1789) was one of the most important recommendations of the French Revolution, momentous to set both the individual rights and mutual rights of the community. The U.S. Bill of Rights (1789-1791; U.S.), the first ten amendments of the U.S. Constitution (1787), summarised the precise rights of individuals in which government could not get in the system, together with the rights of free assembly, self-determination of religion, assessment by adjudicators, and so on.

Following to the French Revolution, the principle of Natural Law was an attitude of intangible and unassailable values of infinite and indestructible human rights in Germany. The reactions aligned with the philosophy of natural law came out with "historical school of jurisprudence, but in India the canon of civilised arbitration has been taken on adaptation of Nationals or residents of unfamiliar countries" (Bajwa, 1997). Humanitarian intrusion is very important to preserve human rights ('humanitarian' implies 'a man with guaranteed values'). The more difficult task was to put an end to slavery and the slave trade which arouse during the nineteenth century. Moreover, the late eighteenth and nineteenth centuries saw the codification of human right guarantees in national constitutions. The term 'human rights' was introduced in the *U.S. Declaration of Independence* (1776) and in the U.S Constitution came into life a Bill of Rights. French Revolution gave birth to the *Declaration of Human Rights of Man and Citizen* (1789). In 1929, Institute of International Law, New York, set a *Declaration of Human Rights and Duties*. In 1945, the inter American Conference conceded a resolution looking for concern of an International Forum for the preservation of human rights.[5] Throughout the twentieth century, equal rights with an increased ample to women, was the most fundamental issue for liberal thinkers. The Preamble to the *Universal Declaration of Human Rights* (1948) states that the detection of the innate self-esteem and the equal and immutable privileges of all members of the human folks is the institution of autonomy of justice and stillness in the world (Cassese, 1990). The Roman Catholic Church in Europe, though was the sole of Christian authority, failed to convince its followers the sacred requests because of corruption and powerlessness. In the twenty-first century, there exists an elemental consciousness to esteem human dignity giving importance to all cultures and religions of the world (Friedman, 2011). As assorted global human demographic division might be, it ruins to see if there exists any religion or culture that certainly and obviously denies the crucial appreciation of human dignity.

Definitions of Rights

There is huge variance about what is meant accurately by the term 'rights'. "Human rights could be generally defined as those rights which are inherent in our nature and without which we cannot live as human beings" (Rajwat, 2001). Different groups and thinkers have worn it for diverse purposes, with particular and sometimes contrasting definitions, and the accurate definition of the principle, has something to do with normative rules. It has got different shades understandings but the term 'right' has to be looked upon the ways in which it is utilised.

The religious universalists, for instance, St. Augustine and Thomas Aquinas talked about the impartiality of people before God, thus affirming the worldwide laws but yet again, not overtly in the framework of rights. The law is a universal command of the governing element in a community, although it may be oppressive, immoral and irreligious. Augustine did not go so far as this, but he realised the distinction which exists between a state permeated by justice, and a despotism or democracy which is still a state, though far removed from justice. He saw that state, reduced to its lowest terms, might be people without manners and their customs beastly, associated for bad ends, yet still a state, because of internal peace. The distinction between legal and moral right can be derived out of this definition which allows to the community the full rights of a commonwealth, irrespective of its moral character (Sanlon, 2014). And, therefore, it leads to what we call a life of captivity in this earthly city as in a foreign land, although it has already received the promise of redemption" (Joanne *et. al.*, 1992). He argues that the states can make certain a degree of tranquillity and precautions, which is required for requirement of social continuation. The earthly city has thus got assistance indirectly to the awareness of Christian values.

St. Thomas Aquinas (1225-1274) believed that human self-esteem and worth are inborn properties, validated according to natural law. He based this argument on his perceptive of the Christian faith (Bigong, 1997; Finnis, 1998). A vital point is that government is seen as a way of nurturing efficient human assistance, rather than a suppressive institution which is emotional while dealing with sin and its penalty. Aquinas' Christian faith opens up new landscapes and possibilities for philosophical inquiry and insights into ethics and politics (Keys, 2008).

The Dutch jurist Hugo Grotius (1583-1645) is the one who made the first noteworthy case for the concern of international laws to defend all citizens of the world. He began with the concept of natural law which is the starting point of all positive law or written law. All rules were ascertainable by the submission of right motive and did not depend on any advanced force (God) for its legality. Relocating natural rights in such a spectrum was widespread in the seventeenth century. Individual rights were thus deriving at once from the natural right theory that afterward accustomed the dispute over the questions of rights throughout the seventeenth and eighteenth centuries. During these centuries, the rights indicated that one's own good takes precedence over the good of another person. Grotius developed his understanding of the civil community and its right through sophisticating a theory of the unity of the city (Brett, 2002).

Two English philosophers'of the epoch, Hobbes and Locke, both asserted that these rights come into the way of life when the individual enters the world. For Hobbes, they consisted at the right to life, to liberty, and to the quest of happiness. Locke added the enjoyment of property to Hobbes list (McNaughton, 1996). Thomas Hobbes (1588-1679) argued for rights in dreadfully partial way. According to him, rights were imperfect to the material right to life of the individuals, especially the right to peace and substantial defence. He claimed that humans are, essentially, violent and greedy animals, and that in their natural state, they live in a world of anarchism (Zagorin, 2009). On the other hand, out of a strong yearning for self-preservation in order to protect themselves and make certain their personal security, they come together to ascertain a set of rules. The king (in fact the modern state) is the demonstration of these rules. Individuals submit their special freedoms to the state in return the security it offers. As a result, the King (or the state) is yielding the right to rule, at the same time as the deprived, subjects (or the citizens) have the duty to obey. This is the centre of 'the social contract'. As Hobbes said, "not fear about any power or to cause them, are divergent to natural, are but words and of no strength to save a man at all."[6]

Another English philosopher John Locke (1632-1704), first recommended that there are such belongings as natural rights, which are ours by asset of the fact that we are human (Grant, 2010). John Locke promoted credence in natural law. He also argued that, all people share these rights; they are immutable, and cannot be done away with by any political ability. In his Second Treatise of Government (1690), he used the same slant as Hobbes but reversed his antecedent's conclusions. He maintained the situation that individual was imparted with three crucial and natural rights- right to life, liberty and property, and hence he is considered as the founder of modern liberalism. These rights are innate with every human being as the gift of nature and so those rights could not be removed by the state, under any circumstance or compulsions. Locke described human rights as:

> "The natural liberty of man is to be free from any superior power on earth, and not to be under the will of legislative authority of man, but to have only the law of nature for his rule. The liberty of man in society is to be under no other legislative power but that established by consent in the commonwealth."[7]

Jean Jacques Rousseau (1712-1778), the Swiss philosopher, comprehended the social bond ritual beyond the unsophisticated individualism of Hobbes and Locke to add in the role of the community in his famous tome *The Social Contract*. In it, he argued that the community must be a symbol of the general will of the people. He implies that the government concurs that they can rule only if the rights, property and happiness of the people are looked after by their rulers. If the state fails to defend the concern of the ruled, the social contract is broken and the ruled are free to prefer their substitute governments. Rousseau believed that freedom could not be achieved through unknown states, in which democracy meant only irregular contribution in the election of representatives, except from side to side smaller communities participatory democracy could not be accomplished in such situations (Bertram, 2004). In his view, the rights in a civil society sanctified: "But the social order is a sacred right which serves as a basis for other rights. And as it is not a natural right, it must be the one founded in covenants."[8] Rousseau then elaborated a numeral of rights of citizens and confines on the sovereign's power.

Immanuel Kant (1724-1804) visualised this 'Core of the common good' in these terms: "Putting aside all greed, which is always country to the public interest and choosing universal peace with liberty, this holy people, pious and renewed, is seen to have neglected their own advantage to care for the public safety of the human race."[9] Freedom is central to Kantian conception of right action; he did not regard it as a sufficient condition for morality or for the pursuit of perfection. He argues, 'each individual believes of himself that he would by all means maintain the sanctity of the concept of right and obey it faithfully, if only he could be certain that all the others would do likewise, and the government in part guarantees this for him; thus a great step is taken towards morality (although this is still not the same as a moral step) towards a state where the concept of duty is recognised for its own sake, irrespective of any possible gain in return' (Strathern, 2012). Edmund Burke (1729-1797) defined rights as something "derived from their forefathers and it is also an inheritance. These rights are transmitted to their posterity, that belonging to the people at any reference prior right."[10] It is a particular to each society. Being particular to each culture, it could not make any universal claims (Norman, 2013). His point of view on rights was the traditional British view.

The scientific and rational achievements of the seventeenth century include the discoveries of Galelio and Sir Isaac Newton, the materialism of Hobbes, rationalism of Rene Descartes, pantheism of Benedict de Spinoza, and the empiricism of Francis Bacon. In the seventeenth century came the first conception of natural rights, opening the door to an entirely new world of political ideas. Until the seventeenth century the concept of 'rights' was somewhat limited to feudal rights. Thus, slaves and medieval serfs had very few rights in their movements, work and personal lives (Mc Naughton, 1996).

Eminent philosophers like Thomas Paine, (1737-1809) John Stuart Mill and Hegel (1770-1831) too tried to explain human rights during the eighteenth and nineteenth centuries. Thomas Paine thought that individual human being enjoyed self-determination and natural rights, proceeding to the derivation of formal governance. Thomas Paine, a devotee of the revolutions in America and France, was essentially a democratic republican who whispered entirely in the dominion of the individual person (Conway, 2010). We could observe in support of Paine that the formal accomplishment of rights within the political field was crucial for the establishment of social justice. Like Locke, he necessarily his defends immutable rights- rights of mind, personal happiness and freedom, being inveterate to a pre-social time, in his case was the act of Creation. According to Thomas Paine, natural rights are those that are appertain to man in right of his subsistence (Paine, 2004):

> "Natural rights are those which appertain to man in right of his existence. Of this kind are all the intellectual rights or rights of

the mind, and also all those rights of acting as an individual for his own comfort and happiness, which are not injurious to the natural rights of others..."[11]

Jeremy Bentham (1748-1832) scoffed at the idea of natural law, and of rights in wide-ranging. He perceived it from a utilitarian point of view in which it can only be valid if they are seen to have emerged out of the hunt for the utmost happiness. According to utilitarian perspective, human rights are not, therefore, theoretical pre-social phenomena, rooted in natural law, but the products of human decision-making. He argued that by escalating the quantity of contentment and diminishing the level of pain, this demanded the theory of 'greatest happiness to the greatest number'. By going to the concept of utility and thus maximising happiness to maximum number of people, he tried to split law, and thereby to bring it from the natural law to an autonomous sphere of scientific force. Bentham says that a natural right is a misrepresentation of language. These rights are vague, metaphorical and had chaotic after-effects (Mill, 2008). He adds that these rights cannot serve as a legal restriction on what we can or cannot do. It advises that there are general rights- that means rights over no specific object-so that one would have a claim on whatever one chooses. Natural rights become ambiguous. In such a broad conception, no legal system could properly function. So there could not be any general rights in the sense suggested by the French declarations.[12]

The German philosopher, George William Hegel (1770-1831), who was the founder of modern idealism, developed the idea that realisation and material objects are in fact unified. In his major work Philosophy of Right (1821), Hegel depicts the importance of state, which was a moral and the highest expression of human freedom (Heywood, 2002). He clarified the legal history in which the development of the spirit of legal philosophy was "the march of freedom in civil relations." His ideal of 'freedom as an idea' was the highest manifestation of law. The realisation of this idea co-existentially generalised is the existence of general will. It was the synthetic co-existence of the political idea with the legal idea as they were unfolded in juristic rules, doctrines and institutions (Mogi, 1989)

John Stuart Mill (1806-1873) is the most significant intellectual among the British philosophers and political theorists in the nineteenth century, who both shaped the climate of opinion in twentieth century British politics and provided one of the most influential defenses of the ideal of personal liberty (Matthews, 2012). He says that rights are institutionally protected interests or in the case of moral rights, those interests that ought to be protected by law. He attacks a great deal of weight to individual liberty. He writes:

> "The sole end for which mankind is warranted, individually or collectively, in interfering with the liberty of action of any of their members, is self-protection. That the only purpose for which power can be rightfully exercised over any member of a civilised community, against his will, is to prevent harm to others. His own good, either physical or moral, is not a sufficient warrant." (Rawls, 1971).

For Karl Marx (1818-1883) the rights are the property of a coherent subject- contestable though that might be- essentially presupposes that they are assets of an individual. The Western philosophical discussion on human rights has always emphasised individualism, and advocated that human rights are open to disapproval if they carry on basing their thoughtful of rights on Western individualism. According to Marx, there are no pre-social rights, since we become people only in society. Thus, rights are political and social, and are achieved through historical development and struggle (Hargaden, 2013). While applauding the possibilities contained within the new discourse on citizenship, he dismissed the egoism and individualism of the *Declaration of the Rights of Man in France* as insubstantial in terms of true empowerment. The rights of equality, liberty, security, and property, addresses private individuals and not humanity as a species society. It is one thing to recognise in law as an individual with certain highly individualised rights (From, 1981). Karl Marx stated that, "None of the so-called rights of man goes beyond egoistic man.... an individual withdrawn behind his private interests and whims and separated from the community."[13]

Thomas Hill Green (1836-1882) insisted on the general nature of the good and the call for rights to be recognised by all members of the community. Sovereignty was as imperative to Green. He implicit it in relation to the role it plays in creating an order that enables human beings to deal with their behaviour realising their essential social aspirations (Brooks, 2003). In this regards, he comments, "A right is a power of acting for his own ends-secured to an individual by the community on the supposition that it contributes to the good of the community" (Mohanthy, 2010).

Mohandas Karamchand Gandhi (1869-1948), a constructive philosopher and visionary has observed human rights as: "Affection cannot be manufactured or regulated by law. If one has no affection for a person or system, one should be free to give the fullest expression to his disaffection, so long as he does not contemplate, promote, or incite to violence (Shepard, 2014). In my humble opinion, non-cooperation with evil is as much a duty as is cooperation with good. However, in the past, non-cooperation has been deliberately expressed in violence to the evil doer. Gandhi says that, "he is endeavouring to show to his countrymen that violent non-cooperation only multiplies evil and that as evil can only be sustained by violence, withdrawal of support of evil requires complete abstention from violence" (Farnham, 2014).

Modern critics say that, people who had no birthright of democracy or freedom from the ancestors had no habitual right to them. Freedom and rights are necessary part of being human but in the case of inheritance that is handed down to the British people as a piece of property might be."[14] If Burke's opinion is correct, in Africa or Asia, which lack the culture for the emergence of democracy, Westminster-style democracies will never flourish.

John Bordley Rawls (1921-2002) described about the concept of state of nature. His confrontation of the idea of a just society, was based on usually decided moral values' mendacity. People if given the choice, would decide on for a society governed by the concept of state of nature because this would be the most useful to all. This principle is ground in equality and justice. In *A Theory of Justice*, Rawls invokes two key concepts of ethics- the right and good. He claims that ethics is mainly settled on by how it defines and connects these two vital thoughts. (Rawls, 1999). He distinguishes the two ways of involving the right and the good. The initial method is to classify the good in competition from the right and then the rights as that, which maximises the good (Wolf, 1977). He observed about human rights as: "Each man, in realising his own interest, is certainly free to balance his own losses against his own gains. We may impose a sacrifice on ourselves now for the sake of a greater advantage later. A person quite properly acts, at least when others are not affected, to achieve his own greatest good, to advance his rational ends as far as possible."[15]

Ronald Dworkin (1931-2013) has advanced further on the issue of rights in his book *Taking Rights Seriously* (1978). He has tried to put up a new theory of politics, based on the primacy of moral rights (Ripstein, 2007). He identifies only two moral rights of the citizens to indulgence as natural or absolute (i) the right of the citizen to treat equally, and (ii) right to have respect for human dignity. He critically writes, "The idea of a right to liberty is a misconceived concept that does deserve a political thought" (Mohanthy, 2010).

According to Robert Nozick (1938-2002), the theory of rights originated from the principle of natural right of 'self-ownership' which means treating people as they are an end in themselves. According to Nozick "the individual have rights and there are no things a person or groups may do to them (without violating their rights") (Nozick 1974). For him an individual is a holder of himself and his aptitude, and ranking to make use of his powers as he wished. Every individual has an exclusive domain, which must not breach without his consent. Rights are prior to the civil law from which the latter derived.

At the wake of twentieth century, the contemplation of human rights has got a new component mutually in the international and national levels. One of the major reasons was the Nuremberg Trial after the Second World War, where the Nazi war criminals and their aggression directed to the Jews were questioned and punished. This swayed the U.N. to convene 'Genocide conventions and pass resolutions against crime beside humanity'. All the members of the U.N. accepted that resolution and India is a signatory to it.[16] The term 'Human Rights' has developed since the last 50-60 years. Though the discourse on 'Human rights' may be somewhat modern creation, the ideas that authenticated it, can be traced back at least as far as the classics, if not prior to. On the other hand, in certainty most ancient religions include codes of that might be elucidated as suggesting certain rights, still if these were largely stratified. Ancient and classical philosophers also contributed much to this discourse. Human rights is a twentieth-century name for what had been traditionally known as natural rights or more in an exhilarating phrase, the rights of man. Perhaps the best, definition of natural rights begins with the claim which everybody naturally makes. Nobody wants a violent death, or to suffer an injury and to be uncared without treatment, or undergo an arrest and imprisonment without fair trial and defence and being heard, or to be deprived of expressing his thought and publishing his opinions and views in protest against any authoritarian action. All rights are inherited by man because of his birth in the species and therefore he is reasonable and rational and also moral. These rights are, therefore, also called fundamental and moral (Kumar, 1998). The Enlightenment, which permitted a revival of secular moral universalism, provides the roots from where we can trace the growth of the idea of human rights. On the very first human rights day, 10 December 1948, the General Assembly of the U.N. adopted the Universal Declaration of Human Rights (UDHR) whose opening preamble states: "recognition of the inherent dignity and of the equal and inalienable rights of all members of the human family is the foundation of freedom, justice and peace in the world" (Sacino, 2012). By the term 'human rights' the declaration understood a wide range of concerns, including not only civil and political rights such as right to vote and right to fair trial but also numerous economic, social and cultural rights such as the right to reasonable standard of living, the right to healthcare, and the right to education.

Nowadays the human rights are violated all over the world. Human rights are a theme of law, but they are considered largely as a matter of politics. Lawyers, politicians and governments, NGOs, men and women- the elderly as well as children, violators as well as victims- all of them are drawn in to human rights. Human rights are internationally settled values or rules for arranging the direction of states towards their own citizens and towards non-citizens. Preamble of the UDHR expresses it as a: "a common standard of achievements for all peoples and all nations" (Peter, 2001). Due to these rules, the states have obligation upon them that confines their freedom to act towards their entire population whether they are citizens or non-citizens, men or women, adults or children, whites or non-whites, believers or non-believers, married or not, heterosexuals or homosexuals. This condition is diverse from the past, when states or rather their princes were complete sovereigns who could treat their subject in any way they required. Simultaneously, human beings have rights: human rights.

Human rights are not absolute. A process of thinking about it, is needed (for example, by an independent court if different courts come into conflict with each other). Capacity to facilitate human rights more closely and effectively may alter over time. In ancient Athens, the affirmation or evidence of a slave only received if he had subjected to afflict. In spite of all, in the Middle Ages, torture considered as the *probatio probatissima,* "the proof of all proofs". Nowadays, views have wholly changed and torture is diminished to view lowly as unacceptable violation of human self-esteem (Rejali, 2009). To obtain acknowledgement by torture or any illegal manner is not accepted as a proof at present because a person, who is tortured, may confess to all kinds of things only if the pain is unbearable and death instigating.

II. Classification of Rights

Recent conceptions of rights often gives emphasis to liberty and equality as among the salient aspects of rights, though conceptions of liberty, (e.g., positive or negative) and equality (e.g., of opportunity or of outcome), may commonly differ (Clapham, 2007). The humanitarian principles embodied in the U.N. Charter and the UDHR marked the beginning of a full-blown human rights regime. Although the Universal Declaration requires states to provide subsistence needs and basic welfare provision along with a panoply of civil and political rights. In sagacity, a right is an acquiescence to do impressive or prerogative to an unambiguous examine or conduct, and these rights have been called positive rights. Conversely, in an additional logic, rights may agree to or entail effective and these are called negative rights; they consent or have need for doing nothing. It is vital to accentuate that universal human rights from the very onset encompassed unease for positive rights such as combined stipulation of education and healthcare as well as negative rights such as freedom from exploitive government policies etc. (Dunne, 1999).

In some democracies, for example, U.S. they have positive and negative freedom to vote and not to vote. But in democracies like Australia, citizens have right to vote but they do not have a negative right to not vote while non-voting citizens can be fined. One case in point of a positive right is the so-called "right to welfare".[17] At the same time negative rights are permissions not to attain belongings, or entitlements to leave alone. The positive and negative rights should not be baffle with active rights that means "privileges" and "powers" and passive rights that means "claims" and "immunities". The human rights with person's civil and political rights are a product of the last 150 years of European Enlightenment and the secularisation of thought and society (Ness, 1999).

Negative and Positive Rights

- Within the philosophy of human rights, some philosophers and political scientists see a distinction between positive and negative rights.
- Negative rights suggest the sphere where the state is not permitted to enter whereas positive rights prescribe the responsibility of the state in securing rights of individuals.
- Negative rights indicate that as to which acts of the individuals shall not be restricted by taking part in positive measures for the protection of rights of the weaker and vulnerable sections or those placed in a vulnerable position.
- According to this view, a positive right imposes a moral obligation on a person to do something for someone with a positive right, while a negative right merely obliges others to refrain interfering with someone's attempt to do something. For example, a negative right to life would require others to refrain from killing a person.
- A positive right to life would require others act to save the life of someone who would otherwise die.
- Negative rights may be used to justify political rights such as freedom of speech, property, habeas corpus and freedom from violent crime, freedom of worship, a fair trial, freedom from slavery and the right to bear arm. Whereas Positive rights may be used to justify state-provided education, health-care, social security or a minimum standard of living.

Under the speculation of positive and negative rights, a negative right is a right not to be subjected to an achievement of a person, or a group or a government, intentional for illustration generally in the form of cruelty or intimidation. Human rights along with the freedom and justice that they rest on, signify a purposely liberal or capitalist ideal that is largely alien to the political culture and irrelevant to the economic and social needs of non-Western people (Pollis, 1980).

A positive right is a right to be subjected to a deed of a different individual or cluster. Within theory, a negative right forbids others from substitute against the right possessor even as a positive right obligates others to proceed with esteem to the right possessor. In the structure of the Kantian, negative rights can be associated with the just duties and the positive rights, connected to defective duties (Gayur, 2002). Conviction in a peculiarity among positive and negative rights is generally maintained, or emphasised, by libertarians, who believe that positive rights do not subsist in anticipation because they are a 'produce by agreement'. *The U.N. Declaration of Human Rights* lists together positive and negative rights (but does not make out them by itself). The constitutions of liberal democracies mainly undertake negative rights, than embracing positive rights. Even positive rights are a lot assured by further laws, the mainstream of liberal democracies afford their citizens with widely funded education, healthcare, social security and unemployment benefits, along with the right to life, to choose, to vote, to work, to strike, to dissolve the parliament, to asylum, to equal action before the law, to exist and to sentence an offender to death etc.

Generally, the concept of human rights typically makes a distinction among three 'generations'. The first generation refers to civil and political rights- the classic human rights (Stein, 2009). Economic, social and cultural rights belong to the second generation (Leckie, 2006). The third generation contains of all collective or group rights that have to encounter with increasing attention in recent years (Narveson, 1991).

The first generations of human rights are called "civil and political rights" or "negative statute rights". They are essentially concerned with individuals or groups of individuals having political and individual freedom (Donnelly, 2003). They contain the right to fair trial, freedom of speech and religion, freedom of movement and assembly and guarantee against discrimination, slavery and torture (U.N. 1948, Art. 2-15). Civil and political rights were historically associated with the capitalist West, although this link becomes weak at the Cold War's end. They include the following rights and liberties: the right to life; prohibition of torture; equality before the law; principle of non-discrimination; independence of the judiciary; the right to a fair trial; right of ownership; freedom of expression; freedom of conscience and religion; freedom of travel; freedom of association; and the right to privacy, free will of expression, choice to assemble and association and right to participate in governmental and political process and also the equal access to the public service.[18]

Second generation of human rights goes beyond civil and political rights, by including economic, social and cultural rights. Initially, these rights were associated with socialist and developing countries, but later, it had been introduced into the mandates of some Western organisations and donor agencies.[19] They are also called 'positive rights' because it promotes the intervention of the states to assure the poor and destitute to live in a decent manner. The right to work, the right to education, decent lives etc. are the second group of rights (Aral, 2004). Each country has to provide sufficient standard of living to its citizens, based on its resources. In this generation of rights, everybody "has the right for a standard of living enough for the health and well-being including food, clothing, housing, medical care and necessary social services" (Reichert, 2006). Additionally, motherhood and childhood are also entitled to particular concern and supports. Moreover, everyone has the right to have free education at the basic level (U.N. 1948. Articles 16-27). Recognising this economic, social, and cultural rights require more government intervention than in the civil and political rights. The government and individuals must take action to preserve or satisfy these rights. In other words, government should provide these rights.

Third and final set of human rights includes: collective rights among nations. This set of human rights is the least developed among the three types of human rights. This set of rights demands that everyone is to be enabled to do something to a social and international order in which human rights can be fully realised (U.N. 1948, Arts. 28-30). Basically, promotion of collective human rights requires governmental cooperation on world issues. Collective human rights, as outlined within UNDRIP (U.N. Declaration on the Rights of Indigenous Peoples), suggests that all claims, whether political, legislative or judicial institutions must be adjudicated before nation-state. This plan of relying primarily on nation-state institutions negates the autonomy and powers of indigenous self-government. Collective human rights are meant to serve the interests of collective groups, like a group of ethnic citizens who have a common claim and have consented that their claims are appropriately adjudicated within the nation-state institutional order (Wall, 2007). Most naturalised migrant citizens and native-born citizens accept the obligations and duties of nation-state citizens. Many indigenous nations, however, do not agree fully that the institutions of the nation-state should adjudicate their claims or self-governance and territorial occupation. Rather, such issues should be negotiated and treated on a government to government basis, if not within international forum. The collective human rights that are positions presented within UNDRIP, do not recognise indigenous rights outside the institutions of the nation-state, while substituting collective human rights granted to national citizens for indigenous rights.[20] This position denies indigenous rights and reduces collective human rights to a form of minority or ethnic right.

The international standards called 'human rights' are laid down in many legally binding treaties as well as in non-binding declarations. The UDHR and the two human rights covenants of 1966 are generally refer to as the International Bill of Human Rights. At the same time, one must not be based on the reports of the U.N. themselves, of Amnesty International, and of other human rights organisation, because the international standards are often being violated. National criminal and penal laws are as often breached as international human rights standards. Crimes such as murder, theft and rape are prevented in most national societies. International standards are not usually found in laws, but in declarations and obligatory treaties. Similar to the national context but less satisfactory, international process is mournfully insufficient. In an ideal world, laws and treaties in the field of human rights would be abundant and all caring. In a world that is far from accurate, there is a greater need for such instruments.

Today we are facing a new situation,where numerous human rights violations are occurring in nation-states. In the earlier times also, the human beings faced different types of violations. Each and every human being has the rights but no one knows how to utilise these rights in a precise manner. The right discovers its broad manifestation in the liberties of the individual on one hand and the sphere of state activities on the other. As a subject, necessarily, it involves within its fold a discussion of individual as well as the development of his personality. The ultimate ground of a right is the conditions of achieving the ends which inspire and determine the whole system of rights, the highest possible development of the personality of the individual. In short, rights are the demands of the individual from the society which are secured by law because they are the condition of the development of the personality.

III. Theories of Human Rights

Several theories have been promulgated to explain the development of the concept of human rights. It is necessary to look at certain theories relating to rights during the different phases of the history in order to have basic understanding of human rights. In theory, human rights, are natural, universal and absolute, its meaning are held by everyone by asset of being human and cannot be given up or taken away. Several competing bases have been asserted for universal human rights. It is essential to understand those various foundations, since they can result in quite different understandings of the specific benefits protected by human rights. Many have argued that human rights exist in order to protect the basic dignity of human life. In poor countries, advocates of the nation recognise that some economic and social rights may only be realised progressively. Regardless of this awareness, they still maintain that basic levels of social and economic rights should always be respected.[21] The term or the phenomenon known as human rights is related not only with the protection of individual from the exercise of state but also directed towards the creation of societal conditions by the state in which individuals could develop their potentials to the fullest extent. Those human rights must be directed to protecting and promoting human dignity mainly by Western liberals. The historical developments that have lead to the expression "human rights" since the end of Second World War and the founding of the United Nations in 1945 are as fascinating as they are complicated. During the twentieth century, the term "human rights" has replaced earlier expressions such as "natural right" (*lex naturalis*) in classical Greek and Roman thought, "natural law" (*jus naturale*) and the "law of nations" (*jus gentium*) in Roman law and during the Middle Ages and since the modern era and the French and American revolutions, the "laws of nature" and the "Rights of Man." In the twentieth century, the concept of "human rights" has replaced secular "natural right" theory not only because of the decline of Western natural law doctrines, but also because the language of the "Rights of Man" failed to include the rights of women (Finnis, 2011). By First World War few theorists would or could defend the "Rights of Man" along the lines of traditional natural law or natural right. Each approach to human rights has different strengths and vulnerabilities. The theories provide an analytical tool to determine the concept upon which there may be agreement on the notion of human right. Some of the major theories that are of relevance to human rights these are the following:

Liberalism and Human Rights

The modern liberal conception of human rights is guided, generally by two different viewpoints competing between human rights' need-based morality and human rights as political commitment to individual liberty. Following Isaiah Berlin's essay *Two Concepts of Liberty*, argues that these can also be seen as 'positive' and 'negative' rights. The former is a contemporary theory and practice premised upon the interests and needs of an individual holder of rights and the necessity to protect them through 'active', or 'positive', intervention. The second is based upon the moral agency and liberty of the individual as a holder of rights, or a 'passive' recognition of the right to non-interference. Both these theories seem to rely on is external institution or agent that allows the rights to be 'given' or 'ensured' to the rights holder (Berlin, 1958 and Isaiah, 1969). Moreover, both rely heavily upon a theory of individualism. But it can be said that the contemporary human rights movement has 'lost' something from the past, classical liberal position on rights (Brown, 1986).

The conception of rights, in and of themselves, had seemed to presuppose a relationship between certain types of institutions one that can bestow or grant rights, the subjects of the rights and so on. Thus, a certain apolitical morality and ethics is created. Liberty of the individual is not a fundamental aspect of human rights. As an alternative place for the rights to be protected, it is the positive conception, while the negative conception depicts along the lines of the classical conception of liberal thought natural rights. The theory of emergence of natural rights from a specific historical condition was the time during which the most classic liberal writers emerged and propagated their theories on the conception of man. Here 'man' basically, meant white, property owning man (Clark, 2010). Women, blacks and labourers with no property had not part of the equation due to their material dependence as a situation for limiting their addition and use of reason. Theory of natural rights was simply an experiential view of the world as resisted to a natural theory. The universality of theorists like Locke, Hobbes and Hegel were the first to point out that natural rights were not really empirical, but based on preconceived, theory loaded conceptions. However, the empiricists' claim that their descriptions of the needs are not merely neutral but consistently commit them in adopting a particular view of society and the future. It may be a deceiving belief to presume that modern liberal human rights theory had in some way prevail over that era and are not themselves an expression of modern historical circumstances. When one looks beyond the revolutionary movements, certain contradictions emerge that had overthrown monarchism and feudalism. Though the reform movements included workers, women and minorities were out of the realm of rights. The recognition of their rights was that they were essentially appealing to a higher power to give them their rights, as opposed to a revolutionary movement, which sees itself as becoming that higher power. However, within the liberal human rights theory that gives opportunity to the classical rights struggle because it is instead of third-party paternalism, it is an exercise of moral agency where third-party paternalism is decidedly false. Apart from the revolutionary movements, the marginalised groups of people attained their 'rights', at all instances were through the granting by the paternal authority of the state and its legal system. The granting of rights only corresponded with the historical, economic and political stipulations that made them reasonable. In these conditions, if it were not for the change of the marginal groups, violent suppression would have continued like today in the underdeveloped countries of the world.

As John Rawls says, in the congresses of Western nations, political representations of those who advocate for slavery or feudalism never enjoy representation. But the limit of liberal theory is that, these constituents did not simply retreat from the political sphere. In most of the cases, they were powerfully suppressed and the ethical and moral coordinates of political society continued to use pressure on the social and cultural norms that made slavery and feudalism no longer part of rational, reasonable discussion (Whelan and Jack, 2007). The political module of *laissez faire* free market capitalism in the economic realm is another negative view of human rights. In other words, the liberal negative rights grasping individualist place on human rights is one of political and civil rights as opposed to material ones. The requirement of material subsistence had been achieved through self-preservation with certain political and civil rights, for example, the right to property and freedom of association. Furthermore, this position advocates a difference between those rights which are decided upon politically and those that are decided upon morally. In this sense, the contributors of rights holder emphasised the process in which rights are enforced and articulated, instead of being a passive receiver of human rights that had entitled to him from a higher moral authority. This position had been seen as largely discredited, especially because now almost no modern democratic liberal government functions on this level of rights. Although there may have been a time when non-interference was enough in respect to liberty, the conditions of industrialisation and the progression of capitalism has forced a re-conceptualising of what human rights entail. Part of the delegalisation of this position rests on the issue regarding that, in order to exercise the right to participate in the process, certain preconditions are necessary such as material security and the 'right to participation'. Furthermore, this 'individualist' position seems to be wholly incapable of taking into account and acting upon conceived morally desperate situations, especially in the international arena that has the cases of genocide and ethnic cleansing.

This, again, can be seen as a limitation of liberal human rights theory and the political institutions it entails in the face of changing historical conditions. The concept of the 'individualist' human rights theory seems entirely outdated and inadequate to deal with the problems of a world of globalisation, where interdependency, transnational corporations and a myriad of other international concerns underscore the fabric of society which was unseen or unheard during the heyday of classic liberalism. If it were to be truly enacted in practice, it would amount to a political position of sitting by and watching as one group of people committed genocide upon another and excused as an example of the rights struggle as people exercising their moral agency in a battle to claim their rights. In liberal human rights theory, state is the mediator, and however, since rights always entail a restriction on political action, there always exist a conflict with democracy. On the basis of a certain moral condition in which the liberal state is founded, monopolisation of a concept of human nature and approaches of its interference into civil society from a point of view of right legalisation is in possession of an absolute moral truth (Schopenhauer, 2012). When, below the liberal state the rights holder is seen as an individual, political institutions are, then, organised approximately under this concept of human nature and influences the types of relations that can be established. On the basis of political institutions, they are lawful as long as they secure the liberty and freedom of the individual. Within the liberalism theory, rights are given claiming against the state and develop the concept of human rights as a theory of governance and political legality.

Using the U.S. intervention in Iraq as an example: the U.S. overthrow of Saddam Hussein, legitimised in terms of ending the suffering of the Iraqi people, was not only motivated by other political-economic interests (oil), but also based on a specific idea of the political and economic conditions that should open up the perspective of freedom to the Iraqi people (Western liberal democracy, guarantee of private property, inclusion in the global market economy, and so on). Thus, the purely humanitarian, anti-political action of merely preventing the suffering amounts, in effect, to the implicit prohibition of elaborating a positive collective project of socio-political transformation. If one defends human rights the liberal perspective today, one is defending a *status quo* situation of specific types of institutions and more or less defending the highjacking of the theory in the interest of modern power relations. Liberal human rights theory was once a progressive reckoning, designed to check and eventually overthrow the unusual institutional powers of theocratic and monarchist regimes and give a voice to oppressed, but this is not the case today (Charvet and Elisa, 2008). One of the first theoretical attempts to deconstruct and transcend liberal human rights theory is Marxism.

The Legal Theory of Rights and the Legal Realist Theory of Rights

The legal theory of rights is a reaction against the theory of natural rights (Dickson, 2011). Thomas Hobbes, John Austin and Jeremy Bentham are the proponents of legal theory rights. Proponents of this theory argue that the idea of natural law and natural rights are abstract and ridiculous phenomena. Hence, the existence and enjoyment of fundamental rights of an individual could be better maintained and practiced by the state rather than by the individual himself. The legal realist theory of rights is of recent origin. The legal realist major concern is that there is no general theory of rights as such; rather, they act as an important instrument in the study of the processes and interaction of policy, law and legal institutions. Rights, then, might emerge as the end-product of such a process of interaction, thereby reflecting the prevailing moral values of society at any given time. The legal realist mainly originated in U.S. with the expansion of regulatory activities followed by 'New Deal Policy'of President Roosevelt. Karl Llewellyn, Roscoe Pound and group of jurists are the foremost among the legal realists, they discussed of rights, and the point as to what law does, rather than what law is, in a highly complex and industrialised society and as a temporary manifestation of an ongoing process. According to Thomas Hobbes, John Austin and Jeremy Bentham, rights are purely utilitarian concepts and thus the rule and regulations are necessary for the identification and protection of one's rights. Towards this end, every individual has to sacrifice certain rights and freedoms for the general welfare of the society. The problems of legal realist are that they are unable to identify 'goals', 'ends', 'purpose' of rights. Thus, rendering coherency and interconnections of rights in relation to rights *inter-se* and societal goals, makes the argument meaningless (Green, 2005). Pound's 'Social Engineering'-ordering of human relations through politically organised society, so as to secure maximum possible with the least sacrifice of the totality of interests, is 'descriptive science in the social field'[22] and deficient in assisting non-native enquiry. The legal theory of rights also has been criticised on the ground that law alone does not create rights (MacCormick, 1982). Rather it recognises and protects them. At the same time customs, traditions and morality have a basis for rights. Though, the truth in the theory lies in the fact that it enables individuals to demand certain specific and recognised rights as granted and guaranteed by the state. Though, they argue that human rights are nothing but a manifestation of an ongoing process rather than a theoretical debate. This new approach to the concept of human right does away with the problems relating to the abstract nature of the concept. Yet, this theory goes about questioning the existing laws, their values and the actions, so far enacted upon the society. In short, it questions the shortcomings and ineffectiveness of the existing laws but does not prescribe any solution in the form of super-value of a human being.

Positivist Theory and Human Rights

According to the positivists, the existence and content of rights had been derived only from the laws of the state and not from God, reason or not even from *a priori* moral assumptions or views on which law ought to be had no place and are cognitively worthless. Kant's theory, supported on non-empirical natural law and natural rights tradition, suggested that the absolute moral good, is identifiable in the exercise of virtuous will by all rational individuals. Kant calls 'categorical imperative' (Walker, 1999). David Hume argued that inquiry into social phenomenon could have two categories, fact and value. It is the fact category that matters which were empirically provable or that form the basis of valid scientific enquiry. John Austin argued that in positivism, to an extent, rights are simply those rules which the state has enacted for the protection of individuals and their property interest. The only valid laws, therefore, were the command of sovereign or the ruling political power, which were accompanied by appropriate sanctions or remedies. Indeed, positivist thinkers such as Bentham and Austin were often in the vanguard of those who sought to bring about reform in law offering flexibility to meet changing needs since it is always under human control. The positivist theory, by philosophically divorcing the legal system from the ethical and moral foundation of society, was unable to motivate human beings for future-oriented developmental actions. In fact, the anti-Semitic edicts of Nazis, the immoral *apartheid* practices in South Africa and the neo-politico-cultural nationalism in India, are the product of the sensibility of positivist theory. Positivist philosophy had been able to justify obedience to immoral laws such as Nazi Nuremberg laws on racial purity.

Positivist theories of rights and law have filled much of the vacuum left by the rejection of divine law and natural law as foundations for human rights and positive law (Waluchow, 1994). In general positivist, see law as a coercive order created by human communities to protect people from one another, and rights as entitlements granted by law.[23] Positive laws are commanded by "political superiors". According to

Austine, these superiors the "sovereign", and he defines "sovereign" as the person or persons who are not in the habit of obeying anyone else, and who everyone else is in the habit of obeying. Positive laws are general commands by people who themselves are not bound by them, and who can enforce obedience from everyone else whether a certain rule is a *law*, creating *legal* obligations to comply with it, all depends on its source. Valid laws are simply rules that come from certain people (kings, city councils, etc.), in accordance with certain procedures, that the society enforces. A rule can be a genuine, valid law even though it is grossly unjust.

Utilitarianism Theory, Anti-Utilitarian Theory and Human Rights

Utilitarianism holds to do what maximises 'utility'. Utilitarianism is one of the most powerful and influential approaches to normative ethics in the history of philosophy. Though not fully articulated until the nineteenth century, proto-utilitarian positions can be distinguished throughout the history of ethical theory (Long, 1990).The fundamental tenant of utilitarian theory is measured in pleasure and pain. Bentham developed a school of positivism known as utilitarianism[24] and gave humanitarian face to apparent amoral starkness of Hume's position. The good is prior to and independent of the right or duty. Something is a right or a duty only when it contributes to overall utility, and only when it does so to a higher extent than violating that right or duty. Bentham's utilitarian morality was derived, not from metaphysical source, but from the expression of the majority's preferences. On the other hand, human rights tell us that never do certain things, not even if doing those things would maximise overall social utility (happiness, pleasure etc.). Some human rights theories provide exceptions to this rule and don't use the qualifier "never". The central work of utilitarianism, based on self-satisfaction, was that pleasure and pain dominated human existence by increasing the former and diminishing the latter. By the improvement of pleasure, the whole mankind would be improved. For example, in a situation of extreme danger for the whole of society, these rights theories provide the possibility that some rights are temporarily suspended. But, they typically provide a very high threshold, otherwise it would become difficult to speak about "rights" and the theory would collapse into utilitarianism, if rights can be suspended regularly, they are no longer rights. In practice, however, instead of maximisation of felicity i.e. greatest happiness to the greatest number of people, it had the potential to lead to a tyranny of the majority and to the oppression of the minority in any given state. The right to life is just too important and a deterrent effect doesn't lift us above a threshold of suspension of rights. Within the state the utilitarian had given little thought to minorities or communities or individuals whose preferences are not represented by the majority and who may, in consequence, be severely disadvantaged or, in rights talk, deprived of their rights. People have rights; even if the outcome of those rights is more overall utility could be achieved when some rights are violated in some cases. Only when the utility of violating rights is very high do some rights theories allow those violations. Socio-cultural minorities, for instance, homosexuals and lesbians, whose practices are forbidden, would not be able to make an agreement to gainsay the utilitarian position since, as a minority their preference would have to give way to the wishes of the pluralistic, democratic state. Such a position would be untenable. These rights theories are threshold theories because, they allow torture if a very large number of lives is at stake, even though generally and under non-marginal conditions people have a strong right not to be tortured.

Much of modern political theorists, therefore, have a strong anti-utilitarian focus. A large variety of presentation and analyses among neo-scholastic rights oriented scholars to set their major debate on normative rights theory. Three well-known political tradition namely, liberal communitarian debates, theories of group entitlements and theories of recognition have momentous ramifications for the way in which we organise our relationship with each other in society and in polity (Scarre, 1996). There are certain theorists who strongly argue that the priority of the well-being of the majority as stated by the utilitarian is not the prime objective of the State. This theory of rights is supported by Dworkin, Nozic and John Rawls. They uphold the view that the welfare of the majority might lead to detrimental consequences as far as the welfare of a particular person or a group of persons is concerned. However, there has to be proper settlement between welfare of the majority and individual well-being for the better enjoyment of social and individual rights. Nowadays, the demand for right to development on international forum is perhaps the manifestation of this theory. When compared to utilitarianism and human rights theories, these two are the strong and threshold theories because that they are able to protect strong interests of minorities and individuals against the burden of aggregated and possibly weak interests of large majorities. To have a theory that protects individual rights against aggregate social utility. Most human rights theories claim that human rights are necessary because they generally produce good consequences and promote certain important values. There is no human rights theory that holds rights hostage to case-by-case utility accounting or that claims that all human rights have optimal consequences all of the time. From a utilitarian perspective that respecting human rights is generally most advantageous doesn't mean that is always most favourable. Violating rights once will diminish their authority and will ultimately destroy them, making it impossible to reap the generally positive benefits of rights.

Marxist View on Human Rights

The most comprehensive and theoretically sound rejection of human rights has undoubtedly come from the norm of Marxism-with its rejection of capitalism, its emphasis on collective existence its position that the institution of private property is the foundation for exploitation and alienation and the subsequent distance between 'formal rights' and real human security and fulfilment. Liberal human rights theory is individualist and property centred. According to Marx, in liberal democracies, freedom is often deceptive concept (Kolakowski, 1983). The liberal regime advocated individual value in market value, not on human dignity. Capitalism defends fundamental rights not as universal human rights but capitalists as the property of the legal structures that follow. Marxist theory views men and women not as individuals with rights developed from either a divine or inherent nature, *but* of men and women as 'specie beings'. Marx regarded the 'law of nature' approach to rights as 'idealistic'. Rights, for him, "were simply bourgeois concepts and a product of bourgeois capitalist society, designed to maintain and reinforce the pre-eminent position of the ruling class." Rights concepts are historical categories whose content is determined by the material condition of the life of the people and by their social circumstances. The essence of an individual is that of a social being who has the potential to use one's abilities to the fullest and to satisfy one's need. In capitalist society production is controlled by a few, but such a society cannot satisfy those individual needs. An actualisation of potential is contingent on the return of men and women to themselves as social beings in a society devoid of class conflict.

Crucial to the significance of human rights is the claim that they hold not simply for modern, Western society but for all societies, modern as well as ancient, Western as well as Eastern. Thus, human rights can be used to evaluate the social life and practices of all humans throughout history. Whether Marx did or could accept such a notion of human rights has been a matter of considerable dispute. Some hold that Marx criticised inadequate or mistaken conceptions of rights, but still was committed to rights (Fabian, 2011). G. A. Cohen, for instance, maintains that natural rights occupy a place of central importance in revolutionary Marxist belief. Others, however, deny this. Accordingly, Steven Lukes claims that those Marxists who believe in human rights can only be revisionists who have discarded or abandoned those central tenets of the Marxist canon, which are incompatible with such a belief Marx rejected. Those rights, claimed to be human rights, are, held, relative to capitalist society.

However, in contrast to other recent discussions, it is possible to identify a basis for Marx's views on human rights, which explains the relativism Marx attributes to human rights. Marx's theory of human rights, thus, coincided with a theory of economic development and the idea that socialism would bring about not only political emancipation of the working class but also the unfettered growth of economic abundance through a new organisation of the relations of production. In most situations where Marxists have taken power, this has not been the case. Marx views human rights with his characterisation of bourgeois distributive justice, and indicates the dialectical origin of human rights, out of earlier forms of society. What had been called human rights are simply those rights fundamental to capitalist society, which it has proclaimed to be universal (Nayar, 1980). The way in which Marxism treats human rights follows a very distinct ideology of radical social change. The first idea is that liberal human rights are premised on inequality and injustice and should be seen as simply a theory natural to capitalism, and, therefore, opens to complete rejection. The second idea is that if a movement has an emancipatory plan and ideology that conform to the rejection of capitalism and the desired setting up of socialism, then terror and abuses to human dignity can be accepted for a certain transitional period in order to suppress those who are opposed to see this plan come to fruition. The rejection of human rights is to be tolerated under the guise of necessity and a rejection of 'bourgeois morality'. Though Marx was aware of, at least, some of the major issues concerning the nature of rights which trouble philosophers today, he says very little above these topics. Thus, for example, though Marx refers to a wide variety of rights like 'human rights', 'the rights of man', 'natural rights', 'civil rights', 'political rights', 'legal rights', 'abstract rights', 'nominal rights', 'existing rights', etc., and occasionally suggests their interrelations, in general, he rarely seeks to subordinate some either conceptually or logically. He mentions various interrelations between rights and duties, but did not concern himself with the nature or acceptability of such correlation (Brekert, 1986).

In conceptual terms, human rights are themselves imitative of the concept of a right. Human rights are rights that connect to human beings and function as moral guarantees and it claims towards the enjoyment of a minimally good life. Here focuses upon the philosophical analysis of the concept of a right and also express the various constituent part of the concept from which human rights emerges (Freeman, 2002). In order to gain a full understanding of the philosophical foundations of the doctrine of human rights.

Moral rights and legal rights as two separate categories of rights, it is fundamental importance to understanding the basis and potential application of human rights. Legal rights refer to all those rights found within existing legal codes. A legal right is a right that enjoys the recognition and protection of the law. A legal right cannot be said to exist prior to its passing into law and the limits of its validity are set by the jurisdiction of the body which passed the relevant legislation (Martin, 1993 and Sumner, 1987). Legal positivists argue that the only rights that can be said to legitimately exist are legal rights, rights that originate within a legal system. On this view, moral rights are not rights in the strict sense, but are better thought of as moral claims, which may or may not eventually be assimilated within national or international law (Sumner, 1987). During nineteenth century, the legal positivist claimed, there can be no such thing as human rights existing prior to, or independently from legal codification. Positivist determining the existence of rights is no more complicated than locating the relevant legal precedent. In severe contrast, moral rights are rights that, it is claimed, exist prior to and independently from their legal counterparts. The existence of a moral right is not supposed to be dependent upon the actions of jurists and legislators. A belief that fundamental rights which may or may not have received legal recognition away, remained entirely applicable and morally compelling even, and perhaps especially, in those countries whose legal systems had not recognised these rights. Human rights are meant to apply to all human beings everywhere, regardless of whether they have received legal recognition by all countries everywhere; Human rights certainly share an essential quality of moral rights. Numerous countries that wholly or partially exclude formal legal recognition to fundamental human rights. The universality of human rights as moral rights clearly lends greater moral force to human rights. However, legal rights are not subject to difference of opinions as to their existence in quite the way moral rights are. It should be exclusively identifying human rights with moral rights otherwise it would be a mistake. Human rights are better thought of as both moral rights and legal rights. Human rights originate as moral rights and their legitimacy is necessarily dependent upon the legitimacy of the concept of moral rights. A principal aim of advocates of human rights is for these rights to receive universal legal recognition. The legitimacy claims of human rights are tied to their status as moral rights. The practical usefulness of human rights is, on the other hand, largely dependent upon their developing into legal rights. In those cases where specific human rights do not enjoy legal recognition, moral rights must be main concern with the intention that defending the moral claims of such rights as a necessary prerequisite for the eventual legal recognition of the rights in question.

To understand of the functional properties of human rights it is necessary to consider the more specific distinction between claim rights and liberty rights. W.N. Hohfeld identified four categories of rights: liberty rights, claim rights, power rights, and immunity rights (Perry, 1977). However, numerous scholars have subsequently tended to collapse the last two within the first two and hence to restrict attention to liberty rights and claim rights. The distinction between claim rights and liberty rights, are to a well-established trend in rights analysis in viewing the former as being of primary importance. A claim right as consisting of being owed a duty a claim right is a right one holds against another person or persons who be obliged a corresponding duty to the right holder. Further necessary distinctions within the concept of a claim right, between a positive claim right and a negative claim right. The former are rights one holds to some specific good or service, which some other has a duty to provide. Liberty rights as rights that exist in the absence of any duties not to perform some desired activity and thus, consist of those actions one not prohibited from performing (Jones, 2000). In contrast to claim rights, liberty rights are primarily negative in character. Liberty rights provide for the capacity to be free, without actually providing the specific means by which one may pursue the objects of one's will.

Feminist Perspectives on Human Rights

Gender equality is a human right. Gender is a primary or related factor. Because today abuses related with gender has been most neglected and offers the greatest challenge to the field of human rights. Human rights of females are violated in a variety of ways. Women are discriminated against and abused on the basis of gender. Female victims are not visible in many times because the prevailing image of the political system is male. Violations of women's human rights are distinctly connected to being female, that women are discriminated against and these violations are not given its rightful place in the priorities of the human rights (Bunch, 1990). Women sometime suffer abuses such as political repression that are similar to abuses suffered by men.

Today, in worldwide developments, the actors also accept that advancing women's rights and gender equality is a cornerstone of any successful sustainable development framework. Women are entitled to live in dignity - in freedom from war and fear (Cravioto, 2012).Women's rights as human rights can be successful only by misrecognition of the geopolitical context of human rights internationalism and the nationalisms that are sustained by it (Grewal, 1999).The term 'violations of women's rights' or 'women's human rights' is not used by the critics in a merely international law sense, but refers to the serious violations of human dignity suffered by women, whether or not they would constitute a violation of human rights guarantees under accepted interpretations. These 'violations' include violations that fall within the classical categories of civil and political rights violations such as torture and maltreatment in detention, with or without a gender-specific element; violations suffered in the hands of the state or its officials, or in the hands of private individuals acting in a private capacity; denials of access to social and economic benefits on a discriminatory basis; and a disproportionate denial of access to social benefits and opportunities because of the use of models or definitions derived from male experience and life patterns.

The term violations of women's right is apparently intended to refer to 'gender-specific' violations, that is, violations which may be suffered only or predominantly by women or which appear to be based on sex or gender. For example, rape, female circumcision, forced prostitution, trafficking in women, discrimination in nationality laws (Andersen, 2005). In public view, women and girls are recognised as the key agents in development. The term violations of women's human rights are broader in its coverage, including human rights violations where women just happen to be the victims. That is, the violations are not gender-specific and men are equally the victims of similar violations. For example, persecution of politically active women, discrimination against members of an ethnic minority, forced evictions.

Women's issues are often overlooked and post-conflict societies, because they must rebuild, are ideally poised to introduce standards that would enable and ensure the active participation of the entire population, including women, in rebuilding a more stable, fair and democratic polity (Fineman, 2013).Women suffer violations to their dignity for many different reasons and in many different ways. In some cases the reason and form of violation may appear indistinguishable from those leading to violations against men in similar circumstances. In other cases their sex or gender may be the occasion for or determine the form which the violation takes. In many other cases there may be a complex interaction between sex or gender, race, class, political activities or some other factor in explaining the origin and form of human rights violations from which women suffer. Followings are the examples of different types of violations.

- rape by State officials or by private individuals
- dowry deaths

- family and domestic violence
- forced prostitution and trafficking in women
- denial of equal rights to participate in political life (including denial of the right to vote)
- harassment of politically active women
- denial of inheritance and property rights
- sexual surgery or female circumcision
- denial of reproductive rights
- discriminatory provisions in nationality law both as to the acquisition and transmission of nationality
- unequal access to healthcare and unequal enjoyment of the right to life and right to adequate food
- discrimination against women refugees
- persecution of women because of their family relationships
- denial of access to land and economic opportunities.

The violence against women in many forms is a widespread phenomenon throughout the world and it has been documented time and time again (Lockwood, 2006). The problem has been recognised in some international level, one of the major human rights violations to which women are subject on account of their sex. The forms of violence against women include, violence in the hands of the state- as detainees, genital mutilation in state hospitals, forced abortion- as well as widespread violence in the hands of private individuals like their male relatives, pervasive domestic violence, dowry deaths, and sexual assault and harassment.

In 1946, the U.N. Commission on the Status of Women was established to secure equal political rights, economic rights, and educational opportunities for women throughout the world. However, the institutional allocation of responsibility for 'human rights issues' and 'women's issues' within a system of U.N. human rights may make it important to ask about every human rights violation is suffered by a woman and the violations of race, class or political opinion against women. The exclusion of sex and gender means that women just happen to be the victims of them and gender plays no significant role. In October 1999, the United Nations General Assembly adopted the Optional Protocol to the 1979 CEDAW otherwise known as the

Women's Convention (Leung, 2000). The United Nations Universal Declaration of Human Rights proclaims that all human beings are born free and equal in dignity and rights. Yet women's freedom, dignity and quality are persistently compromised by law and by custom in ways that men's are not. The mere extension of existing human rights protection to women is insufficient. Women's rights must be understood as human rights (Peters, 1995). Criticisms of rights have taken a variety of forms with rights being seen as too individualistic, reinforcing existing power imbalances, failing to account for women's experiences and focusing too much on the public sphere (Marshall, 2009).

Third World Approaches to Human Rights

A Third World approach to human rights arises from a geographical space and a different historical horizon of understanding from the 'exteriority' of Europe, an external that is inextricable from the inside. The decolonisation of the humanities, the social sciences and culture in general are both an intellectual and political project that emerges from the standpoint of the third world, and aims at opposing colonialism and abuse of power. The basic rights to survival and food are asserted both as qualifying civil and political rights and as depending upon them (Patnaik, 2004). In the immediate aftermath of the Second World War, Third World countries wanted to regain its human dignity and to enjoy the 'human rights' which were long denied it. These are rights because of every human being by virtue of his or her humanity, without any requirement of membership of any group or other qualification.

Human rights are not merely claims that individuals have done something against the state or other citizens, but it is the way of ordering life in a family so as to ensure dignity for all its members. In the Third World the right to self-determination, which "is an internationally recognised right of long and dubious standin", is being given a new shape. As such, they have to be distinguished from citizens' rights or the rights of the inhabitants in a specific territorial state, or the rights of a group of persons belonging to a certain race, religion, sex or nation. For example, the English Bill of Rights or the French Declaration of the Rights of Man and the Citizen, applied only to the metropolitan citizens of the colonial power. They did not apply to the citizens of third world countries which were colonised, discriminated against and oppressed by these European powers (Yusuf, 2013). Almost all

Third World states have constitutions including bills of rights on the model of the U.S. Bill of Rights, the French Declaration, the Universal Declaration of Human Rights, or the European Convention on Human Rights. Most of which were drafted after World War II.

In Third World, human rights are understood to embrace political and religious concepts as well as indigenous traditional values. Human rights are conceived as elements of the right to self-determination, which protects the rights of peoples to their cultural traditions and language, as well as their right for development. Although socialist concept may seem to be predominate in the Third World. Human rights argue that civil and political rights are not subordinated to economic and social rights. Third World countries now set out to the contest of the concept of civil and political rights as well as the universality of the human rights idea (Burke, 2010). For example, the late José W. Diokno from Philippines, former senator and presidential candidate, argues against the notion that governments in the Third World are inevitably authoritarian either because of the need for rapid economic development or because of indigenous traditions. He characterises the second justification for authoritarianism as 'racist' and the first as 'a lie', which perpetuates an unjust status quo. Religious leaders who affirm that human rights as an expression of their faith. Religious leaders see human rights not only as means of protecting the individual from oppression by the state, but as the way of creating justice and peace within the states and within the world community.

Not all human rights abuses, in the Third World are the results of historical process. Many are consequences of the internal political decisions of sovereign Third World states. Countries of the Third World must go back to the drawing board. They must begin to retrace their steps. And the sooner the better for time is running out. There is little time left before their economies become permanently distorted. Now is the time to begin to put in place sound and effective national and international policies of economic and social development. Third World is developing a conception of human rights that goes beyond both individual and social notions. Development can succeed only if economic change goes hand in hand with the extension of human rights. Global view sees rights as both inherent in the individual and socially derived by development. Political freedom is not possible primarily without the social development and conflicts which are resolved in terms of the welfare of society as a whole. The achievement of progress in the implementation of human rights is dependent on these things. The Third World must be ready to pay for development. The price may be high, but so that the stakes can get higher position. Therefore, Third World development must geared towards a larger end. The promise of a better life must, consequently, be matched with concrete development plans. The hope for survival, security, and contentment requires that our governments direct their resources to the most urgent needs. They must act together. These efforts must go beyond fake and deceptive machinations. The Third World has human and material resources which is necessary to eliminate poverty and other incidents of underdevelopment. However, to achieve this, their governments must accept certain standards of good governance, which should be based on legitimacy, accountability, competence, and respect for human rights. Countries of the Third World are presently undergoing momentous political transformations. Their citizens are yearning for democracy (Udombana, 2000).

IV. Human Rights and Democracy

Democracy and human rights are viewed as global norms. The relation between democracy and human rights is one of the most important issues occupying a dominant place in the contemporary political studies. The evolution of democracy and human rights can be considered as two parallel projects with both complementing and competitive exchanges between one another (Beetham, 2000). The dual concepts have their origins in the western liberal democratic tradition. In ideals of individualism, equality and liberty and universalism rest of the core of both the projects. The compatibility of both the concepts are beyond doubts as democracy creates the basic conditions for flourishing human rights and human rights constitute the inalienable and inviolable rights of individual that can be developed and enjoyed properly in democracy. Protecting the freedom of members of such groups to lead publicly visible lives is an essential a matter, not of seeking various sorts of state endorsement of their particular identities, but, rather of ensuring that the state guarantees egalitarian recognition by defending their civil rights. Far from requiring a homogenous public sphere, when the state relates with its citizens, primarily in the mode of respect for their rights to freedom and equality, it protects the conditions under which social difference can flourish in the informal public sphere.

Since the second half of the last century, following the success of the decolonisation movement and corollary emergence of a number of newly liberated countries, the issue of democracy and human rights has assumed newer dimensions by gaining wider scope. The prime objective of democracy is the empowerment of all. In this sense, it is collective, whereas human rights are individualistic. The new administration should place a higher priority on developing security assistance programmes and cooperative relationships with intelligence agencies that promote better human rights practices and encourage civilian democratic oversight of military and security services in some fashion (Katulis, 2009). Democracy focuses on the nature of the rulers or ruling groups and the human rights concentrate on the way of ruling and more specifically on issues of governance. It is also true that the increasing popularity of the concept of the human rights since the last half of the twentieth century has to be given credit to Noam Chomsky who defined human rights "as set of rights associated with liberalism, the U.S. sought to protect its sphere of influence over a much wider area, viz., to gain access to markets." The third wave of democratisation has influenced the human rights discourse.

The idea that any human rights violations automatically necessitate military action by Western powers has no moral basis. Such a civilising mission takes the shape of a moral duty on the part of the Western powers to enforce human rights standards as perceived and defined by them, where the focus has much more to do with the expansion of their global capital. A great majority of countries that implemented multiparty democracy in the early 1990s, with democratic institutions, such as parliaments and courts with powers of judicial review, and institutions of restraint (human rights commissions, electoral commissions, ombudsmen and others) have provided only limited 'checks' on executive power. In addition, the so-called like-minded donors (the Scandinavian countries, Canada and the Netherlands) introduced legislation and policy statements on the place of human rights in their aid programmes as far back as the 1970s. The EU has developed the promotion of democracy into one of the pillars of its relationship with other countries. The European Initiative for Democracy and Human Rights was founded in 1994.[25] Technically, one may be inclined to believe that liberal democracy and human rights are likely to be the two sides of the same coin. However, there can be a danger in a mere attempt to substitute the language of democracy with that of human rights. Often, the discourse on 'rights' and 'democracy' have become hegemonic narratives. Human rights and democracy do not necessarily share a symbiotic relationship as it is often believed. Moreover, the promotion of democracy has not necessarily concerned itself with human rights, social justice and human security. From the human rights perspective, many have adhered to the separatist theory, which argues that democracy is not immediately needed for the observation of human rights and for the maintenance of an essential link with human rights. Human rights and democracy may well have the effect of delaying the implementation of human rights norms in various states. A recent corollary to this kind of assumption is the view that regards democracy as neo-imperialism, criticising that democracy has mainly been reduced to a 'west-centric' approach to government and that it is not found indigenously in all societies and is not desirable for all people and culture as well (Normen, 2005). The charges against neo-imperialism of the western super powers are true and it is not at all desirable to impose their form of democracy to other societies, but it is also culturally insensitive to claim democracy as an option of the west which in incompatible with non-western cultures. Separation of human rights from democracy definitely undermines the opportunities of their implementation, as some human rights are intrinsically linked with the principles and institutions of democracy. Therefore, human rights amount to little more than charity if they are not functioning in a democratic set up (Anthony, 2003). The international actors have been invested substantially in promoting democratic developments around the globe by enhancing the resources, skills, techniques, capabilities and ideas of civil society associations, the mass media, the judiciary and electoral commissions in many of the incipient democratic regimes in the developing world. Knowledge about the long-term effects of democracy assistance remains limited.[26] The resulting knowledge of democracy promotion projects has the compiled very rarely into retrospective learning exercises. One reason for the dearth of accessible knowledge is the numerous challenges involved in evaluating democracy promotion. In particular, it is difficult to attribute success or failure to a particular democracy promotion effort, given that (i) the general impact of these programmes depends on a host of other internal and external influences, as well as wider democracy promotion and, more generally, good governance initiatives; (ii) the effects of democracy programmes may not be fully apparent for years; (iii) democratic processes are interlinked with other social, economic, political and historical processes and conditions; and (iv) quantitative indicators can only capture this reality to a limited extent. Nevertheless, though the 'menu' of democracy assistance has evolved and often adapted to new challenges and past mistakes, partial or sometimes minimal efforts are taken to share the knowledge of best practices and lessons. While it is challenging the impact of external donors in such a field, attempts to learn lessons have certainly remained 'below potential' thus far.

Since the end of the twentieth century and more precisely in the first decade of the twenty-first century, it has become an exigency to strike a proper chord between human rights and related movements, vis-à-vis, the issue of international terrorism. The greatest danger for human rights definitely comes from the state authority. When one's rights are violated, one is not merely denied of the goods to which one had a claim, but rather one's very status as someone with the authority to make and respond to moral claims is denied (Feinberg, 1980). The international terrorism, often in the name of preserving human rights, and right to self-determination and protection of identity, provides ample opportunities before different state authorities to curtail on and put strong vigilance on human rights activities. Thus, in the context of prevailing international terrorism, where regular security threat is being posed before the citizens a great paradox has developed regarding the relationship between democracy and human rights. Definitely now a newer approach is required to overcome this vicious circle. Democracy and protection of human rights do not necessarily share a 'symbiotic relationship' as is often assumed. There is a strong view that the third wave of democratisation has in its own way made 'rights' and 'democracy' part of a hegemonic narrative (Huntington, 1993). Whether the neo-liberals have co-opted the idea of human rights are as a basis for rationalising their agenda, the agenda reflects a view that the way to secure human rights are through the 'free market' and that 'civil' and 'political' rights are for those who go along with the economic goals of civilisation. They tend to argue that civil and political rights are qualitatively and significantly different from economic and social rights. Free markets and human rights are referred together. Today supporters of human rights also tend to be supporters of free trade, democracy, free market and open society.

Conclusion

Human rights are very much essential for a good and qualitative human survival. Human rights are something vital to the society for the economic well-being of a country. So we necessitate now to persuade that the human rights are tremendously imperative for the transition of a country. Rights are given to an individual but there might be certain conditions attached; social, economical, political or educational. But when we speak of human rights, we mean a certain type of universal phenomenon having no limitations in its applicative aspects. It gives a person a free space in order to shape his identity in the society. In the present context, there is an air of unreality about human rights, particularly in the third world. A large section of people are compelled to servitude. The more vulnerable among them are subjected to torture and inhuman treatment. Above mentioned theories or their descriptions may vary but the real intent of each of the political thinkers is the protection of human being. Even if a satisfactory basis for human rights can be constructed, further fundamental challenges emerge to both the 'human' and 'rights' dimensions of human rights. It is not self-evident what it is about humans that generates the moral entitlement to certain benefits, neither is the status clear of those humans who do not share these qualities. A particular problem is posed by the manner in which the benefits are asserted to be rights since this concept can operate in practical circumstances as a liberty, power, immunity, or claim-right. The focus of any corresponding duty for a claim-right is no less problematic. However, human rights must be examined more closely, because they are at once so important,yet so vulnerable to probing questions about their origin, foundation, substance and operation.

Notes

1. Divine Right of King is one of the best examples. Many kings considered this as their right to make his people obey. Moreover, they considered the rebels as persons who work against the will of God. Sometimes, it went to the extent that some of them claimed themselves as *god*. The Caesars in Rome claimed to be the descendants of Gods and urged for the worship of

people. Many Christians were persecuted for not worshipping them. BBC.2007. 10-11 accesssed on 2009-12-21.

2. Kant in his *Critique of Pure Reason* argued rights as an inalienable category of human beings. He, secularising the view in against the natural law of tradition which was held up by the Christians, paved the way among the philosophers and humanist thinkers for a general outlook of rights. As it was backed by thorough reasoning, it was well appreciated even among the political thinkers and among many atheists. So he tried to put these concept within the framework of religion in his second work *Critique of Practical Reason*, Many tend to follow the first book. Immanuel Kant (1991): *Kant: Political Writings*, ed. H. Reiss, Cambridge: Cambridge University Press.p.106

3. It took a long time to reach at the concepts of human rights. *Human right* is an ever-evoling phenomena, which is much discussed and debated theme in the international arena. New technologies provide new challenges and rules for the preservation of the rights of an individual. So we can claim that research on human rights a never ending endeavour. Donnelly, Jack (1989): *Universal Human Rights in Theory and Practice*, The argument is traced from Ithaca: Cornell University Press, p.23.

4. As explained earlier, one of the main tensions of developing rights were the age-old traditions of religious beliefs. With the renaissance, many started to question the beliefs that were said to be scientific and divine. It prompted the use of human reason, which shackled many such superstitions. Change of social structure in the industrial revolution further consolidated this arguments by overthrowing the age-old feudal system. Aravind Kumar,(1998): *Encyclopaedia of Human Rights, Violence and Non-violence*. Vol. I. Institute for Sustainable Development, Lucknow. Anmol Publications Pvt. Ltd. New delhi, 1998.p.1.

5. Rights dominate most modern understandings of what actions are proper and which institutions are just. Rights structure the forms of four governments, the contents of our laws, and the shape of morality as we perceive it. To accept a set of rights is to approve a distribution of freedom and authority, and so to endorse a certain view of what may, must and must not be done. "Stanford Encyclopaedia of Philosophy." Stanford University. July 9, 2007. accessed on 2009-December-21.

6. Leviathan is a biblical term which Hobbes used to denote the political forces which stand against the social contract theory. For him, there were many who opposed the theory of Social Contract by which the rules in certain societies were formed. They were motivated by selfish intests which curtailed the common good of the community against which the community fought from time immemorial. Hobbes, Thomas, (1996): *Leviathan*, Cambridge: Cambridge University Press.

7. Locke, being liberal in his outlook, stood more as a humanist philosopher. For him, man and his innate thriving for freedom made him work for the

social relationships which were more comprehensively accepted by the liberal humanists. Human beings were the centre of attraction. As argued by many, he was trying to separate religious values from political values. The powers of state are more argued for than its religious aspirations. Clack, George, *Introduction to Human Rights*, (The American Library, American Consulate General Gemini Circle).

8. Cranston, Maurice (1968): (trans.), *The Social Contract*, Baltimore: Penguin, p.50. Jean-Jacques Rousseau, For Rousseau's views of the connection between religion and the state, see: Book IV, ch.8. one of the main notes to be given among the revolutionaries is their attitude towards the social order which was perpetuated by the Christian thinking. It was not the Christian ideals but the breach in those ideals provoked them to think that religion is something against the welfare of human beings. The arrogance, autocracy and manipulations of the clergy and their turning away from the poor caused them to think so. They believed the religion as something to be with the people to guide them in their growth to human perfection.
9. The political writings of Kant were more influenced by his *Critique of Pure Reason* where he places freedom as a basic human category. It can be framed and could be thought of in the human minds. Immanuel Kant (1971): *Political writings*, Cambridge: Cambridge University Press.p.121
10. Burke (1998): Discusses rights in his *Reflections on the French Revolution*, pp29-33No.2. December. (Source *Encyclopaedia Britannica* 1989 edition). Burke's attempt to connect it with the culture is noteworthy. It was because of the enlarged world views which the West acquired by encountering the Eastern traditions. Each culture and tradition has a value embedded with it. This is true with respect to rights also. By the theory of inheritance of rights, unknowingly, he was appreciating the good in other cultures which could also provide certain specifications in the growth of the concept of rights. Though the concept is well appreciated today, it was not so in his life time when the people of West considered their system as something superior to other traditions. Still now we could see certain remnants of it the attitude of certain so called 'democracies'.
11. Thomas Paine (1737-1809 American political theorist and writer), from *Rights of Man*, 1792. The rise of existentialism, along with its traits of humanism is evident in the works of Paine. (Cf. Clack, George, *Introduction to Human Rights*. (The American Library, American Consulate General Gemini Circle).
12. Internet Encyclopaedia of Philosophy A peer-Reviewed Academic Resources www.iep.utm.edu/bentham/sh. accessed on 7.2.2012. The tension between political thinkers and their explanation of juridical system is well known. As the one contains the other and they function as a whole, it was almost impossible. Moreover, the inter-relationship between these two is more complex and overlapping at many points of reference. Bentham's argument

against the common rights is basically against the preamble where the fundamental characteristics of the rights are qualified as being 'natural, unalienable and sacred'.

13. Karl, Marx,(1977): "On the Jewish Question" in *Karl Marx: Selected Writings*, David McLellan (ed), Oxford: Oxford University Press, p. 54 Marxian collectivism is a disputed and contested concept in many of its aspects. Many modern thinkers argue that it is a theory to be used in a selfless-state. He, formed is political ideologies from a background which was overburdened by religious manipulations. He wanted a just society for which he designed the laws. But what he forgot was the selfishness of human beings.
14. Prickett, Stephen (1989): *England and the French Revolution*, Macmillan, p.49. Inheritance theory is an extreme of humanism where the proponents want, somehow, to prove the inalienability of individual's rights. Though the modern critics outplay this, the attempt for rights through inheritance was a historical fact. But as we see in the history, it was not an attempt to gain common good for the people but to keep certain privileges by the individual. Such things still exist in the community in its new forms.
15. Rawls, John, (1999): *A Theory of Justice* (second edition), Oxford: Oxford University Press. Though laws or concept of rights, especially human rights were an integral part of ethics, it was less discussed in details. With the advent of new technologies, especially after the rapid growth in the medical research, the ethics started to point to certain human rights in detail as in the stem-cell research or, in a wider sense, in medical bio-ethics.
16. Territories of states not recognized by the United Nations are not excluded due to the United Nations' position that they are part of some United Nations member state. Available online at http://www.un.org/en/members/growth.html.
17. "Stanford Encyclopaedia of Philosophy." Stanford University. July 9, 2007. Accessed on 2009-12-21. *Right to welfare* as part of public rights in contrast to the private rights. Public rights are the ones which are supposed to be given by the governments to its citizens so that common good is preserved. It is the right of the individual as a part of a community and the duty of the government to provide it.
18. These rights are also often referred to as physical integrity or (personal) security rights.
19. *See, e.g.*, David Cingranelli and David Richards, *Measuring the Level, Pattern, and Sequence of Government Respect for Physical Integrity Rights*, 43 International Studies Quarterly 407 (1999); Welsley T. Milner, Steven C. Poe & David Leblang, *Security Rights, Subsistence Rights, and Liberties: A Theoretical Surevy of the Empirical Landscape*, 21 Human Rights Quarterly. 403 (1999).

20. *See* Robinson ,Fiona (2003): *NGOs and the Advancement of Economic and Social Rights: Philosophical and Practical Controversies*, It outlined that discrimination and violations of social and economic rights function as underlying causes of conflict, creating the deep grievances and group identities that may, under some circumstances, motivate collective violence. Abuse of personal integrity rights is associated with escalation, and intermediately repressive regimes appear to be most at risk. Denial of political participation rights is associated with internal conflict because full democracies experience less conflict. Genesis and Evolution of the U.N Declaration on the Rights of Indigenous Peoples, Charters and Stavenhagen, *Making the Declaration Work,* 49-51, 74.
21. United Nations Universal Declaration of Human Rights 1948- Watchlist watchlist.org/wordpress/wp.../Universal-declaration-of-human-rights.pdf claimed the Universal Declaration of Human Rights the full text of which appears in the following pages. Following this historic act the Assembly called upon all. Metadata SISU Metadata, Document Information. document manifest Available online at http://www.jus.uio.no/lm/un.universal.declaration.of.human.rights. 1948/sisu-manifest.html
22. Rights International Covenant on Civil and Political Rights (ICCPR) in the Domestic Law of State Parties: An Initial Global Survey through United Nations Human Rights Committee Documents. *Human Rights Quarterly*, 22(1), February, pp.187-260.
23. For a general overview of the positivist position, see M.P Golding, ed., the Nature of Law (New York: Random House, 1966), 1-6. For a more detailed and refined account, H. L. A. Hart. 'Legal Positivism' in Paul Edwards, ed., the Encyclopaedia of Philosophy (New York: The McMillan Co. and the Free Press, 1967, 4 (418-20).
24. Harland, Christopher (2000): The Status of the International Covenant on Civil and Political Rights (ICCPR) in the Domestic Law of State Parties: An Initial Global Survey Through United Nations Human Rights Committee Documents.
25. *Accountability in Development Cooperation*, 27 Human Rights Quarterly. 471 (2005). Under a human rights perspective, people and institutions are accountable. Beyond strengthened accountability, the next key added value of human rights. Furthermore,because development seeks to vindicate human dignity and freedoms.
26. Aeijaz, Tanvir Theoretical and Philosophical Foundations of Human Rights. Pdf. Journal of *Human Rights, Gender and Enviornment* Human Rights Theoretical and Philosophical. University of Delhi Available online at www.du.ac.in/ fileadmin/DU/Academics/course_material/hrge_01.pdf by T Aeijaz - Cited by 2 - Related articles.

2

Iraq: Socio-political Profile

Formerly part of the Ottoman Empire, Iraq was occupied by Britain during the course of World War I; in 1920, it was declared a League of Nations mandate under UK administration. In stages over the next dozen years, Iraq attained its independence as a kingdom in 1932. A "Republic" was proclaimed in 1958, but in actuality a series of strongmen ruled the country until 2003. The last was Saddam Hussein. Territorial disputes with Iran led to an inconclusive and costly eight-year war (1980-88). In August 1990, Iraq seized Kuwait but was expelled by US-led coalition forces during the Gulf War of January-February 1991. Following Kuwait's liberation, the UN Security Council (UNSC) required Iraq to scrap all weapons of mass destruction and long-range missiles and to allow UN verification inspections. In the aftermath of the September 11 incidents, the United States used the UNSC resolutions to start the US-led invasion of Iraq in March 2003 and the ouster of the Saddam Hussein regime.This chapter provides a brief outline of the socio-economic profile of Iraq.

Iraq: Socio-cultural Profile

The Republic of Iraq generally identified as a country in the Middle East across the north-eastern end of the Zagros mountain range, to the east of the Syrian Desert and to the north of the Arabian Desert. Modern Iraq covers almost the same area as ancient Mesopotamia. Iraq is blessed with two most imperative elegant rivers: the Tigris and the Euphrates that we know today as Iraq was a fount of civilisation (Simons, 2004). Iraq's well-off history dates back to ancient Mesopotamia. The expanse amid the Tigris and Euphrates rivers makes out the Fertile Crescent- the cradle of civilisation- and is also the birthplace of writing and saw the rise and fall of many cultures and settlements. They enrich Iraq with arable land in contrast to the wilderness that envelops a large amount of the Middle East.

In the medieval era, Iraq was the name of an Arab province that made up the southern half of the modern-day country. In today's Republic of Iraq, Islam the state religion claims the beliefs of 95 per cent of the population. Majority of them identify with the Arab culture. The second-largest cultural group is the Kurds, who are in the highlands and mountain valleys of the north in a politically autonomous settlement. The Kurds, who constitute fewer than 20 per cent of the country's population, are of a different ethnic stock to the rest of the Iraqis (Dawisha, 2009). The Kurds occupy the provinces of Sulaymaniyah, Dahuk and Irbil, the area which is commonly referred to as Kurdistan. Iraq shares its boundary with Kuwait and Saudi Arabia to the south, Jordan to the west, Syria to the northwest, and Turkey to the north, and Iran to the east. It has a shoreline settlement at Umma Qasr on the Persian Gulf. After the collapse of Ottoman Empire, successive attempts happened there by the French and British, by the Soviets and their communist allies, by the Americans, and also by the Arabs themselves but all had failed to produce constancy in the region in general, and especially in Iraq. From the very beginning of the state, there developed three undertakings in the state: First, the unification of the state and its governing institutions, second, the legalisation of the state through the framing of democratic structures, and finally, the creation of an overarching and thus unifying, national identity.[1] It traces every changes in the field of governance, Saddam Hussein administration, composition and conflicts of ethnic groups, war and its consequences and national identity, while at the same time, highlighting their mutual impact in shaping one aspect with the other. The secular and modernising intention of the pan-Arab dream, not at all supervised to conquer the distrusts of tribes, mosques, and national governments, failed to identify itself with the waiting counterforce of pan-Islamism. At the end of World War I the great schism between pan-Arabism and pan-Islamism had been implied while the bitter struggle between the Hashemites and the Saudis to control Mecca.

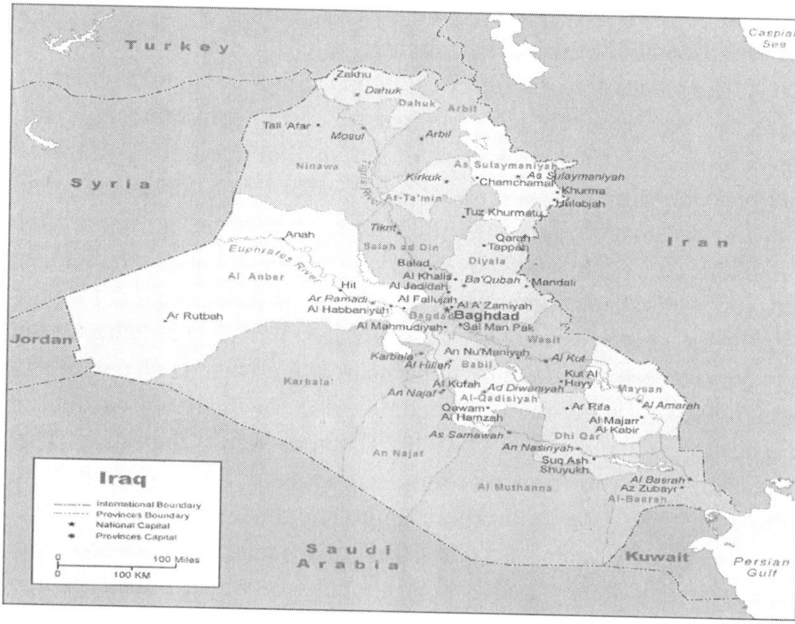

Source: Map Resources. Adapted by CRS.

Map of Iraq

The Hashemites in Jordan and Iraq believed in pan-Arabism as an ideal in itself, and as the mechanism that would enable the Arab world to modernise, develop and take its place in the great councils of the world. He was no great admirer of democracy, while his upholding committed to the dream of a Pan-Arab state, wanted to keep Iraq on the course of progress and modernisation begun by the Brititsh (Walker, 2003). Eighty years on, pan-Arabism has faltered, discredited by repeated failures and authoritarian rule, and by the rivalries between the various Arab nations. The British and French carved from the Ottoman corpse. Its most promising early exponent, King Faisal, initially saw pan-Arabism as a British gift rather than an Arab creation, and his monarchy was debilitated by its dependence on British support. By contrast, pan-Islam has found a generous sponsor in Saudi oil wealth and a ferocious new spearhead in Osama bin Laden and Al Qaeda. The final lesson of Iraq's complex career since independence was a secular and modernising pan-Arabism. In other parts, the British encouraged it along more genuinely. The British imposed a monarchy and a form of democracy but, even after the grant of formal independence in 1930, most Iraqis believed that the British really ruled the country (Hopwood, 2003). The succession of military coups and authoritarian rulers marked Iraq's course, especially to the aggressive and uncompromising pan-Islamic forces that now grip much of the Muslim world. Pan-Arabism was probably the only alternative vision that could have competed with the pan-Islamic fervour. And, in years to come, a secular and democratic pan-Arabism-if those terms are not inherently contradictory-may yet be able to play that role. Having taken a direct hand in forging a stable and democratic post-Saddam Iraq, Americans could do worse than consider two contrasting thoughts from Gertrude Bell, one of the foreigners who knew the Iraqi people best. The first was written in despair during the uprising of 1920: "The problem is the future. The tribes don't want to form part of a unified state; the towns can't do without it." The second, far more optimistic observation came at the end of her career a years later, when the British mandate was proceeding reasonably smoothly: "Iraq is the only country which pulls together with Great Britain and the reason is that we have honestly tried out here to do the task that we said we were going to do, i.e. create an independent Arab state" (Goodwin, 2003). She was always in things, before and after the birth of Iraq in 1921, with innumerable contacts, both among local people and the British administrators, who quarreled with each other and with London almost as much as the Iraqis themselves (Furst, 2005). She may have thought so, but few Iraqis truly believed it. For all their good intentions and achievements, the British, under the strains of war, recessions, and dependence on oil, were never quite able to surrender their remaining control over Iraq's independence until they were forced to do so. And by maintaining that control, the British excluded the development of a political system that might have produced a non-authoritarian regime capable of governing the unstable, improbable country they had created. But as an alternative to pan-Arabism or pan-Islamism, the hope of building an Iraqi nation based on a constitution and representative government appears to be the political goal of the American and British armies, just as it was eighty years ago.

Early History through British Influence (1920-1930)

The state of Iraq was formed by a number of elements which created the distinctive institutional environment in which Iraqi state policy was formed (Rogan, 2001). The World War I found England and France at war with Germany and the Ottoman Empire. The modern notion of colonial development was a highly conditional product of the expansion of the British empire in the Middle East-during the First World War (Satia, 2007). British forces occupied Iraq; they rechristened Mesopotamia, early in the war. British leaders had worked with Arab leaders in Ottoman Empire to launch a revolt against the sultan; in return they promised to help the Arabs form an independent Arab state once the Ottomans had been defeated. A number of prominent Iraqi officers who were serving in the Monotone Army then joined the British and helped them in the Iraqi campaign. The most the British would do was to organise protectorates, called mandates, over the Arab provinces, promising to help the population become self-governing within a specified period. Iraq and Trans-Jordan became the two main pillars of Britain's empire in the Middle East aftermath of World War I (Shlaim, 2001). The arrangement was approved by the new League of Nations in 1920. Iraq become a British mandate, with a government under British advisers, but headed by its own monarch, King Faisal I.

In 1921, the U.K. appointed Faisal Ibn Hussein, a Sunni, as a king of the newly created kingdom of Iraq, which was created by unifying the provinces of Mosul in the north, Baghdad in the centre, and Basra in the south, each a part of the Ottoman Empire that had collapsed at the end of the First World War. Under British influence, a parliamentary system was installed, but this system of government failed to prevent direct military interventions in the political process. The British kept their promises by their mandate. They worked out constitution for Iraq in 1925 that established a constitutional monarchy with an elected Legislature and a system of checks and balances. Political parties allowed, although most of them were groupings around prominent personalities and had no platform other than independence from the U.K. Britain obtained the permission to guide drafting of constitution from the League of Nations, the predecessor of the United Nations. Under the command of Arthur Harris, the British occupational forces used mustard gas and delayed action bombing to suppress Iraqi resistance to British rule, creating several civilian casualties. By 1926, an Iraqi parliament and administration were governing the country. The treaty of 1930 provided for a 25-year alliance with Britain.

The British mandate was terminated in 1932, and Iraq was admitted to the League of Nations.

"After the creation of Iraq as an independent kingdom in 1932, the monarchy sought to maintain the status quo of Sunni dominance, prompting conflict between the Arab Sunni establishment and several minorities (such as the Assyrians and the Kurds). But the monarchy also sought solutions, compromises, and certain forms of elections and democratic expression." Because the regime's legitimacy derived from its history in Arabia and its long experience in administration and ability to work with the British, it was able "to lead with less repression and coercion" (Ghabra, 2001).

In 1936, the first military coups in contemporary Arab history occurred in Iraq.[2] In 1958, another military coup led by Abd al-Karim Qasim overthrew the monarchical regime and replaced the parliamentary system with a single party, effectively a one-man dictatorship that continued through the rule of President Saddam Hussein (Bahgat, 2005). In 2003, 82 years after the British united Iraq, the U.S., another Western power, led an international coalition that toppled and arrested Saddam Hussein, another Sunni ruler. These eight decades of Arab- Sunni rule over a Shi'ite majority (about 60 per cent) and a Kurdish minority (approximately 20 per cent) were characterised by both severe internal violence and aggressive foreign policy. As one analyst argued regarding the internal situation, "the frequency of its political upheavals and the violence associated with them would seem to justify the opinion that Iraq is the least governable of the Arab countries."[3] Regionally, Iraq participated, albeit symbolically, in three wars against Israel (1948, 1967 and 1973), invaded Iran in 1980, and occupied Kuwait in 1990.

The Muslim population was divided into Sunni and Shi'a, as it is today. The Sunnis, though a minority, controlled the government and business by dominating urban life. The majority of Shi'as was mostly rural peasants they were migrants to the cities, where they formed a large underclass. In Iraq, the Shi'a did not participate in power while being the majority has not led to opposition and massive directions, as the Iranian Islamic government had hoped (Luciani, 1998). The Kurds, the largest non-Arab Muslim group, had incorporated arbitrarily in to the kingdom by the action of the League of Nations. The country also had a large Christian and Jewish communities, the latter tracing its origins back several thousand years to the exile of Jews from Palestine to Babylonia after the conquest of Jerusalem by Nebuchadnezzar. The Christians protected and favoured by the British, especially in the police and civil service because the British found them more cooperative than the Sunni Arabs. From the British, the Hashemite monarchy took over Iraq. Though imperfect in terms of human rights, they were better than other regimes in many ways. In 1932, Iraq got an independent kingdom, (Hunt, 2005) even when the monarchy sought to maintain the status quo of Sunni dominance. But the monarchy also sought compromises and certain forms of democratic elections and expression. Because of the regime's long experience in administration with the British and their ability to work in terms of legitimacy derived from its history in Arabia, it was able "to lead with less repression and coercion" (Ghabra, 2001).

The Iraqi economic depression of 1952,which had been worsened by a bad harvest and by the government's denial to hold direct elections, caused large-scale anti-regime protests; all the protests were violent, especially the one in Baghdad (Hunt and Cristina, 2004). During these situations, government prohibited all political parties, number of newspapers, declared martial law and imposed a curfew. The protests had showed the widespread dissatisfaction to the regime. The monarchies expanded education system which helped the middle class to grow considerably but they become increasingly alienated from the regime, because they were unable to earn an income appropriate to their status. Intolerance of disagreement and the heavy-handed treatment of the political opposition of Nuri as Said, an autocrat, had also alienated the middle class from the army. They were forced to flee because of which the opposition became more revolutionary.

A key characteristic of the Iraqi political system, both monarchical and Republican, has been the lack of institutionalisation. The oppressive nature of colonial occupation in addition to increased taxes and the British unwillingness to honour their commitment to end occupation soon led to the revolt of 1920 (Noorbaksh, 2008). The revolt brought together various tribes who valued the freedom that their lifestyle had offered them in these territories. The Shi'ite and Sunni tribesmen participated together in the war of liberation against the British occupation. The latter's tactic of blanket bombing of villages did not diminish the tenacity of resistance against the occupation. The British did not have any choice but to bring to power Faisal Ibn Hussein in 1921 in order to maintain control and influence. As a result, there have been frequent and violent changes of power. These include King Faisal I (1921-33), King Ghazi (1933-39), and Regent Abdullah bin Ali in the 1940s and early 1950s while King Faisal II (1939-58) was an infant. In 1936 and 1941, two military coups in Iraq heralded the first of such coups in Arab politics (Bahgat, 2005).

Finally, in 1958, Abd al-Karim Qasim carried out a successful coup and ruled the country until 1963, when another military coup, led by Abd al-Salam Arif, toppled his regime. Arif was killed in a helicopter accident in 1966, and his brother succeeded him until 1968, when the Ba'ath party took over the government in a military coup under the dual leadership of Ahmad Hassan al-Bakr and Saddam Hussein. This coup was supported by the U.S. because the Ba'athists were notorious for their brutality against communists in Iraq. The latter declared Saddam President in 1979 and ruled Iraq brutally until his regime was toppled by an American-led international coalition in March 2003.

V. The Role of Saddam Hussein and Socio-political Conditions

Saddam Hussein-era in Iraq was known for its severe violations of human rights. Secret police, torture, mass murder, rape, exiles, forced disappearances, assassinations and chemical warfare were some of the methods the country's Ba'athist government used to maintain control. The total number of deaths related to torture and murder during this period is unknown. Human Rights Watch and Amnesty International issued regular reports of widespread imprisonment and torture (Abdullah, 1989). Effectively a one-man dictatorship continued throughout the rule of President Saddam Hussein.

Saddam Hussein was born on April 28, 1937 and was elected Vice-Chairman of the Revolutionary Command Council in 1969 and President in 1979 (Balaghi, 2005). From 1979 until he was overthrown, Saddam Hussein established himself as the absolute ruler of Iraq. In fact, he ruled Iraq longer than any other leader in the country's modern history. His reign was more violent both internally and externally than those of all his predecessors and was arrested in December 2003.

Saddam Hussein Abd al-Majid al-Tikriti,[4] was the fifth President of Iraq, serving in this position from 16 July 1979 to 9 April 2003. His hold on Iraq was absolute up to that time, despite pressure from the international community since the Persian Gulf War (Shields, 2005). As a revolutionary leader of Arab Socialist Ba'ath Party, and the Bagdad based Ba'ath Party which espoused Ba'athism, a mixture of Arab Nationalism and Arab Socialism, Saddam played a key role in the 1968 coup (later referred to as the 17 July Revolution) that brought the party to power in Iraq. As Vice President under the ailing General Ahmed Hassan al-Bakr, and at a time when many groups were considered capable of overthrowing the government, Saddam created security forces through which he tightly controlled conflict between the government and the armed forces. In the early 1970s, Saddam nationalised oil and other industries (Simmang, 2013). The state-owned banks were put under his control, leaving the system eventually insolvent mostly due to the Iran-Iraq War, the Persian Gulf War, and U.N. sanctions of the 1970s, Saddam cemented his authority over the apparatuses of government because oil money helped Iraq's economy to grow at a rapid pace. Positions of power in the country were mostly filled with Sunnis, a minority that made up only one-fifth of the population. Saddam formally rose to power in 1979, though he had been the de facto head of Iraq for several years prior. He suppressed several movements, particularly Shi'a and Kurdish movements seeking to overthrow the government or gain independence, respectively and maintained power during the Iran-Iraq War of 1980 through 1988. In 1990, he ordered the invasion of Kuwait, leading to the Gulf War of 1991 (Finkelstein, 1992). Many venerated him for his opposition to Israel which included the use of military force but he was widely and equally condemned in the west for the brutality of his dictatorship.

In 2003 March, the U.S. and U.K. led coalition invaded Iraq to overthrow Saddam, after U.S. President, George W. Bush, and British Prime Minister, Tony Blair, accused Saddam Hussein possessing weapons of mass destruction and having ties to al-Qaeda, disbanded Saddam's Ba'ath party and attempted to make a changeover to a democratic system. Saddam was convicted on 5 November 2006, of charges related to the 1982 killing of 148 Iraqi Shi'ites and was sentenced to death by hanging and execution was carried out on 30 December 2006.

Social Situations

The complexity of Iraq's political, social, and economic development requires a sizeable range of historical cognition. Since then the rhetoric of Pan-Arab unity has been employed endlessly over any serious attention to social, economic, ethnic, and political events (Khakhar, 2013). Importantly, the ethno-sectarian divide had begun to slow. Deliberate negligence of municipal, social, and educational programmes in the north and the south had become the norm. Basrah, once perhaps the world's richest city, got thoroughly demolished. This is not only because of devastating wars, but pointedly owing to the appropriation of funds to security and military programmes with the unabated objective of pauperizing the populace in order to assure compliance, and their inability to climb up to meaningful places of government. This usage is far from over, and in light of the social ills donated by Saddam Hussein's rule, economic sanctions, and the current military occupation, the direction it could take is by no means settled. In Iraq, democracy and Islam are powerful global forces which shape not only many aspects of the lives of Muslims, but the lives of other citizens of the world as well (Paya, 2011). Democratisation in Iraq necessarily requires the reestablishment of civil institutions and social club. Iraq's entire educational, ethnic, political, and social structures need to be reconstituted. This is neither an exaggeration, nor a defeatist position.

Arabs, Kurds, and other cultural groups each have their own social stratospheres, and no one ethnicity dominates another. In terms of social class there is great disparity between rich and poor. Those who frame the high class in society of Iraq are essentially selected by the government, since there is no opportunity to commence a business or build a name for oneself without the sanction of the regime. The formerly dominant middle class of the 1970s has deteriorated in the facial expression of the economic crisis. These people, who are very well schooled, now perform unskilled labour, if they have chores at all, and have joined the ranks of the majority lower or poor category. Iraq faced, issues from a devastating sanctions regime, a suffocating reign of terror, and three unbearable wars in as many decades. Armed struggle is a troubled option for people's very existence since it can simply lead to further shock in an already shaken social structure (Isamel, 2004). Only a peaceful means, to retrieve a normal resemblance, through the careful reestablishment of society's civil institutions and the mending of ethno-socio-political bridges amongst city and village and within northern, central, and southern parts of the state can lead to a strong, countrywide social movement to drive the occupier and all its vestiges out and commence to restore the country's shattered ethno-socio-political mosaic. Iraq is a tattered country that needs relief from violence (Hamad, 2005). This constitutes the crux for people's aspiration for freedom and advancement. Differently, the land would be bogged down into a morass of retreat and despair, a position that will further confound people's suffering through immoral, tactically-ineffective killings of innocent civilians. A resistance that put down human life is not worthy of the name, and in effect becomes a formula not for release, but subjugation, regression, and indeed perpetuation of foreign business. This is what imperialist forces prayed for, and received. Such a resistance has to be condemned wholly and unreservedly.

Political Situations

Saddam Hussein, former President of The Republic of Iraq, with a brutal hand ruled Iraq and had been characterised as "the madman of the Middle East". This negative judgment was not only mistaken but was also dangerous. Transferring Saddam to the dominion of madness misled decision-makers into believing he was unpredictable when in fact he wasn't. Saddam Hussein's leadership of Iraq reveals him as a judicious politician, who by no means was irrational, but dangerous to the extreme. Kairallah was to become Saddam's father figure and his political mentor. In the Iraqi uprising of 1941 Kairallah had fought against Great Britain and had spent five years in prison for his nationalist agitation (Post, 1990). He filled the impressionable young boy's head with tales of his heroic relatives-his great grandfather and two great uncles who gave their lives for the cause of Iraqi nationalism while fighting foreign invaders. Gathering a strong desire for unlimited power, with absence of conscience, unlimited aggression, and a fearful outlook, made this political personality Saddam so dangerous. As a hateful pride, he had the destructive charismatic personality who unifies and rallies his downtrodden supporters by blaming outside enemies. Though Saddam was not charismatic, this psychological stance had the basis of Saddam's particular appeal to the Palestinians who considered him as a strong human. Who shares their intense anti-Zionism and would defend their cause. It was not by accident that Saddam Hussein lived for more than two decades as his nation's prominent leader in this chaotic region of the creation. While he was driven by aspirations of glory, and narrow political perspectives, he was a sharp diplomat who had a sense of forbearance. Able to justify the extremes of hostility along the foundation of radical needs, if the aggression was counterproductive, he would have established a pattern of turning his course when he miscalculated, waiting until a later day to achieve his revolutionary destiny. His campaign for power was not affected by these policy changes, but only turned the course.

Saddam Hussein was rather a ruthless political calculator who was ever ready to die to reach his ends. But his survival in power with his integral dignity was his highest priority. He could have been extremely life threatening and would holded back to zero if he was backed into a recess. If he believed his very survival as a world class political actor was threatened, Saddam could have responded with unrestrained aggression, using all the weapons and resources at his disposal; which would certainly be a tragic and bloody final act. International actors, ranging from states to non-governmental players, have an influence on what were once thought of as exclusively domestic processes of political change (Teixeira, 2011). The Republic of Iraq was divided into eighteen provinces, which were further subdivided into districts. Thither is a National Assembly elected every four years, and they gather twice annually and operate with the Revolutionary Command Council (RCC) to make legislative decisions. The RCC holds ultimate authority over legislative decisions, and the president of the RCC is also president of the state. The president exercises all executive decision-making powers, and he as well as the vice-president is elected by a two-thirds majority ballot of the RCC. Identification in Iraq has nearly always been along political lines. Sectarian or religious strife had scarcely taken place on any tangible scale, as any astute and objective scholar of history and sociology would attest to. Nearly every urban centre in Iraq comprises a mix of Muslims- Shi'ite and Sunni- Christians, and until the late sixties, and mostly in Baghdad Jews. Baghdad and Basrah, in particular, where the arch multicultural, multiethnic cosmopolitan cities on a par with many a current Western metropolises. Those Iraqis have coexisted happily, socialised together, intermarried, lived inside the same neighbourhoods, studied at the same schools and universities and worked in the same positions. Schisms, when they lived, were along political and ideological lines: one family had atheists and devout believers in a deity, and all in between. This peacefully coexisting and richly successful multi-cultural, multiethnic, and multi-religious mosaic was peculiar to Iraq amidst most of the Middle East.

Economic Conditions

During the Arab Socialist Ba'ath Party rule, this period began with high economic growth and soaring prosperity, but ended with Iraq facing social, political, and economic stagnation. The average annual income decreased because of several external factors, and several internal policies of the regime. During Al-Bakr's de jure rule, the country's economy grew, and Iraq's standing within the Arab world increased. However, several internal and external factors were threatening the country's stability. Since it did not have an economic policy of its own, the Ba'ath Party, when it took power in 1968, allowed the Five-Year Plan set up by the previous regime in 1965 to continue until its end date in 1969 (Alnasrawi, 1994). Following the 1979 Iranian Revolution, Iraq's economy deteriorated during the war, and the war lasted for eight years. When the war ended, Iraq found itself in the midst of an economic depression, owed millions of dollars to foreign countries, and was unable to repay its creditors. The Iraq Petroleum Company (IPC), the largest oil company in Iraq, was a private company. In March 1970, the IPC was forced to concede 20 per cent of the company's share to the government (Tripp, 2010). The full nationalisation of the IPC occurred when the company cut its oil production by half in March 1971; the decision would hamper Iraq's economic growth. The company was nationalised in June 1971. The nationalisation removed the last remaining element of foreign control over Iraq, and was popular among the Iraqi people. The government anticipated a loss of revenue, and therefore sent Saddam Hussein to the Soviet Union to negotiate a treaty. The visit was a success, and ended with the signing of the Iraqi-Soviet Treaty of Friendship and Co-operation and the establishment of a trade agreement. The trade agreement stated that the Soviet Union would buy some of Iraq's oil to soften the anticipated blow it would have on Iraq's oil exports. The Iran-Iraq war would halt Iraq's economic development and lead to the economic stagnation seen during Saddam's later rule. When Iraq implemented its plans to bomb Iran, Iran retaliated by bombing Iraq's oil facilities. By the end of the year, Iraq's oil exports had decreased by 72 per cent because of Iran's bombing strategy (Alnasrawi, 1994). Beginning in October 1982, Iraq's foreign assets began to dwindle as the government failed to repay its loans. At the end of the war, Iraq's monetary reserve had been depleted and international oil prices were not as stable (high) as they had been during the 1970s (Azhary, 1984). The economy was still healthy in late 1982, due to government expenditure on large development programmes. Before the war, Iraq's workforce stood at five million. During the war, one million were mobilised in the war against Iran.

Iraq's failure to achieve internal harmony has directly to its failure to establish peaceable relations with the outside world (Ghabra, 2001). As one analyst argued regarding the domestic situation, "the frequency of its political upheavals and the violence associated with them would seem to justify the opinion that Iraq is the least governable of the Arab countries." Unlike many other developing countries, Baghdad had the necessary ingredients to manufacture and develop strong non-conventional capabilities. These included massive financial resources due to skyrocketing oil prices and revenues, a progressive technical infrastructure managed by thousands of competent engineers and scientists, and relatively good relations with the major global powers at least until the invasion of Kuwait. These relationships enabled Baghdad to receive technical assistance from France and other European countries in the 1970s and permitted some degree of tolerance by the U.S. for its stockpiling and use of chemical weapons in the 1980s (Bahgat, 2005).

Iraq is a country in which ethnicity plays a crucial role in politics. The modern-day Iraq was part of the Ottoman Empire for centuries. Ethnic conflicts of Iraq are less in a permanent state of affairs and more in a temporary pattern of forces occasioned by war, state collapse, and foreign occupation. Scholars and policy-makers should pay less attention to supposedly stubborn cleavages and more to the internal dynamics of violent conflict (Kalyvas, 2007). Iraq was first created by the British as a nation-state in 1921, comprising several ethnic and religious communities (i.e., Arabs, Kurds, Turkoman, Assyrian, Sunni Muslims, Shi'ite Muslims, Christians, and Jews). Since the state's formation, transforming these multiethnic and multi-sectarian communities into an Iraqi national identity has been a major challenge. This ethno-religious fragmentation of Iraq has been further complicated and reinforced by considerations of geography.

The three major groups are concentrated in specific regions: Kurds in the north, Arab Sunnis in the central and western areas, and Arab Shi'ites in the south. Each of these communities has also had its own political aspirations. The two predominant sects of Islam, the Shi'ite and the Sunni, and the two major ethnic groups, the Arabs and the Kurds, have always been part of Iraq's national composition. Iraqi Sunnis dominated the politics of Iraq from the 1920s to the American invasion in 2003. Kurds, who are also found in Turkey, Iran and Syria, have succeeded for the first time in the modern history of the Middle East in playing a decisive role in the politics of Iraq and in their own self-rule (Noorbaksh, 2008).

The Arab Sunnis, who have dominated the political system in Baghdad since the state was created until the collapse of Hussein's regime, have always promoted Pan-Arabist sentiments and have attempted, unsuccessfully, to unite Iraq with other Arab states at different times (Fraser, 2009). From the Shi'ite majority, the response to Iraq's projection of its identity primarily as an Arab state has been mixed. When few of the Shi'ite population embraced Pan-Arabism, believing that it would put them on an equal footing with their Arab-Sunni compatriots; the others, remained closer to the spiritual leadership of the community mistrusted the Arab Sunnis' scheme and maintained some connection and loyalty to their co-sectarians in Iran.[5]

Iraq's two largest cultural groups are Arabs and Kurds. Arabs, who settled the region, intermarried with the local population producing the present Arab-Iraqi population (Spencer, 1994). Additional distinctive groups are Turkomans, Chaldeans, Assyrians, Iranians, Lurs, and Armenians. Arabic is the largest and regularly spoken language; Kurdish spoken in the north, and English is the most normally spoken Western language. About 75 per cent of Iraq's population is in the flat, alluvial plain stretching southeast toward Baghdad and Basrah to the Persian Gulf between the Tigris and the Euphrates (Diller, 1990). This area is interlaced with irrigation canals and small lakes and much of the land is fertile. Iraq is the real place where the Mesopotamian civilisation grew and went on to persuade the European and Asian evolutions. Therefore, in culture apprehension, Iraq has a well-off inheritance. The country, acknowledged for its writers, visual artists and sculptors, is excellent or unsurpassed in the Arab world in literary and architectural fields. In addition to this, Iraq is also known for producing very fine handiworks, together with carpets and rugs. The architecture of Iraq is best seen in the sprawling conurbation of Baghdad, where the edifice was wholly innovative, with a quantity of islands of delicate and multifaceted old constructions. The flag of Iraq has three come to straight posses-red at the top, white in the centre and black at the underside. Three green five-pointed stars in a horizontal line stretch out in the centre of the white band. The phrase Allahu Akbar (God is Great) in green Arabic lettering - Allahu to the right of the focal point celebrity and Akbar to the left of the middle celebrity-was put in January 1991 all through the Persian Gulf emergency. In the past, Iraq has been the middle of the Akkadian, Assyrian, Babylonian, and Abbasid empires, and part of the Achaemnid, Macedonian, Parthian, Umayyad, Sassnid, Ottomon and British empires. In the ninth Century, the Abbasids had developed the practice of importing foreign mercenaries to secure their rule (Simons, 2004). In Iraq, the human rights violations happened frequently by the different rulers and distinct ethnic communities, mainly the Kurds and Shi'ite Arabs (Ghabra, 2001).

Every ethnic group, especially the Arabs and the Kurds had their own social spheres; in such a system no single ethnicity can dominate the other. However, there is a large inconsistency among rich and poor in social class. The government is chosen only by the high rich class of the society. Others have no opportunity to start a business or make a name for oneself without governmental approval. In 1970s, the domination of well-educated middle class had deteriorated due to the economic crisis. Now, they are unskilled labours, having no jobs, and they have joined the ranking of the majority lower class (Kiely, 2009).

According to Ghabra, after 1958, the treatment against Shi'a was one of the worst political mistakes of that regime. Shi'a's had lost their majority and rights, alienating them despite their commitment to Iraq. In 1958, the Iraqi monarchy had been overthrown; even then human rights violations against Kurds occurred frequently. It also caused violence to break out when political negotiations broke down.[6] In each of the regimes, different negotiations developed but failed to satisfy Kurdish demands for autonomy which propelled violent reactions. Villages were bombed and burned and Kurdish fighters hunted down continuously. For their existence, they called themselves peshmerga that means "those who face death".

In 1920s, the Shi'ites were involved in the revolt against the British occupation. But the religious leaders of the Shi'ite and Sunni created an alliance against British colonialism and the occupation of Iraq (Bataru, 1978). Both national and religious sentiments were developed by the Shi'ite religious leadership against the colonial occupation (Momen, 1985). The Shi'ites were discriminated against in the politics of Iraq, after the war of resistance against British occupation. The Shi'ite community had faced inhibition and viciousness by rulers because the rulers were not willing to accommodate the discontent of this minority. In governmental level, their participation was not encouraged by the Sunni regimes whether it was monarchical or republican. In the socio-political and economic life of Iraq, the Shi'ite community had faced suppression and brutality by rulers.

From 1921 to 1958 both monarchical and republican regimes also shared the same attitude toward tribes. Though, during 1980s that attitude had been changed under the Ba'ath and Saddam regime because the tribes help was needed to mobilise for the war against Iran. It was an alternative to conventional tribal values, for example, communal honour and gallantry to encourage support of the war; they were represented as symbols of patriotism and courageousness. Those who backed the regime benefited from the Ba'ath ruling elite for roads, electricity networks, water systems, healthcare and educational capabilities in their communities. Immediately after the second Gulf War, country's different regions were allocated to different tribes for security in exchange of autonomy and financial reward (Noorbaksh, 2008). Shammar, Dulaym, Jubbur, al-Tikrit, Muntafiq, Anaza, Bani Lam, Al-bu Mohammad, al-Khazail, Anizah, Hushaim al-Agrah, Zubaydi, Ukaydat, Mulla, Saidat and Ubayd are the major tribes of Iraq today; most of them benefited from this new relationship with Saddam's government. For example, Shammar, is the biggest tribal confederation, with close to 1.5 million people and it includes a huge territory from south of Baghdad to the Syrian border and they were one of the most vital allies for Saddam's regime. Another tribal group, which was also one of the beneficiaries of this new relationship, was Al-Tikriti, the tribe of Ahmad Hassan al-Bakr and Saddam Hussein and affiliated with the Abu Nasir tribe, it covers 350,000 members.

In 1979, Saddam became the new president of Iraq; he became more hesitant to the Shi'ite clergy because of their organisations and activities within Iraq. The leadership of Ayatollah Khomeini and the Iranian revolution had contributed extremely to Saddam's awareness of a threat against his own regime (Woods, 2011a). Through the assassination and execution of Shi'ite activists, he had eliminated the threat, including Sayyid Muhammad Baqir al-Sadr and his sister, Bint al-Huda. Baqir Sadr, who is the spiritual founder of al-Dawa, was a well-known Shi'ite scholar, well-respected in the seminaries inside and outside Iraq for his contribution to political jurisprudence and encouragement of the political engagement of the religious establishment. Ali Sistani, a clergy, who participated less actively in politics, escaped Saddam's persecution for the most part, but he too did not totally escape from his restrictions and observation. In 1994, Sistani's mosque, Khadra was shut down, and he had placed under house arrest.[7]

Until 1979, the Ba'ath and its government were under the control of Ahmad Hassan al-Baker and Saddam Hussein, the party through a bloodless coup when Saddam took over the government. The Shi'ites and the Kurds were excluded from government and periodically were victims of the government's atrocious oppression during all these years. After the second Gulf War, the Shi'ites paid a more severe price; the U.S. promised but then failed to support their uprising. The Kurds benefited from the no-fly zone policy, while the Shi'ites were in depiction to Saddam's policy of containment and abolition. Many Iraqis had escaped to Iran, where thousands of Iraqis had used their resources, with the goal of toppling Saddam's government (Ryan, 2009). The Iranian government also offered them help to organise militant opposition groups. Nuri al-Maliki, Ibrahim Jafari's the Dawa party and the Supreme Council for Islamic Revolution in Iraq (SCIRI) of the al-Hakim family was among them.

Iraq is a home to about 2,000 clans, which constitute the foundation of 150 tribes; no less than three quarters of Iraq's population belong to its tribal structure. But the role of the tribes in building a new political structure and processes had been dismissed when the Ba'ath party took over the country with its political ideology (Hassan, 2007). Tribes were traditional institutions in the new Ba'ath regime that did not have any role to play in building a modern country dictated by the one-party system and Arab nationalism defined by the founders of the Ba'ath including Michal Aflaq, as its core ideology.

In the late 1980s and 1990s, the Iraqi government became more of a family enterprise with the support of the Sunni tribes. The National Security Council, headed by Saddam himself, controlled the whole security system. In the absence of Saddam, his son-in-law, Ali Hassan Majid, took over this function, later, Saddam's son, Qusay, was appointed. For the security of the regime and control of society, strengthening of tribal power was part of a new initiative and it restructured the relationship of clans and tribes with the central government (Cleveland, 2000). But unfortunately, Saddam's financial resources had been decreased severely by the two wars and also increased both the Shi'ite and the Kurds opposition to his government. The government had given an upper hand to control the citizen and attaining the allegiance of a considerable part of the Iraqi population; it kept the regime whole and maintained a sense of security for the Ba'ath government in Baghdad.[8]

III. Consequences of Iran-Iraq War (1980-1988)

During the recent decades people have witnessed several wars. The war between Iran and Iraq was one of the great human tragedies of the recent history of Middle East. Scholars do debates on the topic of Iraq's wars that began in 1980. Some choose to view the wars as discrete events: the 1980-1988 Iran-Iraq War (Karsh, 2002), the 1991 Gulf War, and the 2003 Iraq War. Others may argue that the period should be seen as one continuous war of Saddam Hussein. Iran-Iraq War, also known as the First Persian Gulf War, was an armed conflict between the Islamic Republic of Iran and the Republic of Iraq lasting from September 1980 to August 1988, making it the twentieth century's longest conventional war. It was initially referred to in English as the 'Gulf War' prior to the Persian Gulf War of the early 1990s. Saddam went to war with Iran in 1980, and the outcome of that war, particularly Iraq's indebtedness to its Arab neighbours, helped to set the conditions that led Saddam to invade Kuwait in 1990. That action, in turn, led to the establishment of a broad-based coalition to oppose Iraq, which ended in war (Takeyh, 2010).

Open warfare began on September 22, 1980, Iraqi army attacked western Iran along the countries' joint border, though Iraq claimed that the war had begun earlier that month, on September 4, when Iran shelled a number of border posts. The roots of the Iran-Iraq War, war lay in a number of territorial and political disputes between Iraq and Iran. It followed a long history of border disputes, and was motivated by fears that the Iranian Revolution in 1979 would inspire insurgency among Iraq's long-suppressed Shi'a majority as well as Iraq's desire to replace Iran as the dominant Persian Gulf state (Woods, *et.al.*, 2011b). Although Iraq hoped to take advantage of Iran's revolutionary chaos and attacked without formal warning, they made only limited progress into Iran and were quickly repelled; Iran regained virtually all the lost territory by June 1982. For the next six years, Iran was on the offensive position (Brands, 2011). A number of proxy forces participated in the war, most notably the Iranian Mujahedin-e-Khalq siding with Ba'athist Iraq and Iraqi Kurdish militias of Kurdish Democratic Party and Patriotic Union of Kurdistan siding with Iran-all suffering a major blow by the end of the conflict. Iraq wanted to seize control of the rich oil-producing Iranian border region of Khuzestan, a territory inhabited largely by ethnic Arabs over which Iraq sought to extend some form of suzerainty. Iraqi president Saddam Hussein wanted to reassert his country's sovereignty over both banks of the Shatt al-Arab, a river formed by the confluence of the Tigris and Euphrates rivers that was historically the border between the two countries (Woods, *et.al.*, 2011a). Iraq's economic involvement in the world market, largely dependent on oil exports, during the regime of Saddam Hussein it varied dramatically. Trading patterns have seemed to reflect the domestic situation in the country, from the Iran-Iraq war in the 1980s and ending in 1988, and to the invasion of Kuwait and the subsequent imposition of international economic sanctions. Iraq's economic future is dependent on its ability to draw on its vast oil resources (Jones, 2004).

The U.S. had received the information before hand that the Iraqi President Saddam Hussein was planning to invade Iran (Gibson, 2010). The 1991 Gulf War was a decisive battlefield victory for the U.S. led coalition but, at the end, the allied nations failed to compel Saddam to acknowledge his mistake; indeed, he had a conviction that he had won the conflict. As a result of Saddam's unwillingness to comply with a series of United Nations resolutions, the U.S. led coalition implemented a containment strategy against Iraq between 1991 and 2003. Saddam's continuing intransigence, combined with the widely held perception that containment had failed to halt Saddam's quest for nuclear, chemical, and biological weapons, led the U.S. and several allies to invade Iraq and overthrow Saddam in 2003 (Perlmutter, *et.al.*, 2003). Prior to this date there had been subversions by each country inside the other and also major border clashes. Iraq hoped for a lightning victory against an internationally isolated neighbour in the chaos of revolutionary upheaval. But despite Iraq's initial successes, the Iranians rallied and, using their much larger population, were able by mid-1982 to push the invaders out. In June 1982, the Iranians went over to the offensive, but Iraq, with a significant advantage in heavy weaponry, was able to prevent a decisive Iranian breakthrough. The guns finally fell silent on August 20, 1988 (Shalom, 2014).

Primary responsibility for the eight long years of bloodletting rests with the governments of the two countries- the ruthless military regime of Saddam Hussein in Iraq and the ruthless clerical regime of the Ayatollah Khomeini in Iran. Khomeini was said by some of having a "martyr complex", though, as U.S. Secretary of State Cyrus Vance wryly observed, people with martyr complexes rarely live to be as old as Khomeini. Whatever his complexes, Khomeini had no qualms about sending his followers; including young boys, off to their deaths for his greater glory. This callous disregard for human life was no less characteristic of Saddam Hussein. And, for that matter, it was also no less characteristic of much of the world community, which not only couldn't be bothered by a few hundred thousand Third World corpses, but tried to profit from the conflict (Shalom, 2014).

The Iraq-Iraq war, from 1980 to 1988, had a major effect on the society, and particularly on its social and economic status. Iraq's imposed war against the Islamic Republic of Iran which started with a large-scale invasion by the Iraqi forces on 1980, and lasted eight years had important legal and international dimensions. The support accorded to Iraq by Western and Eastern power during its war with Iran covered all political, diplomatic, economic, financial, military, and propaganda areas. A major reason behind that support was the West's concern about the victory of the Islamic Revolution in Iran and its regional and international repercussions. In fact, the supporting countries were concerned that the Islamic Revolution would sweep through all regional countries replacing political and revolutionary version of Islam for corrupt and mostly subservient regimes. On the other hand, it made the main pillars of the Western hegemonic system in the region quite shaky. In other words, Western European and American supporters of Iraq were above all concerned about their material and political interests in the region (Khalouzadeh, 2011).

Iraq's bloody war with Iran was prolonged by many reasons. It featured not only trench warfare and human-wave attacks, but also ballistic missile campaigns against the capital cities of both belligerents and the use of chemical weapons by both sides. Even though Iraq eventually prevailed, it paid a high price for its victory. Moreover, the experience of the war shaped its perceptions both of its neighbours. Chemical weapons were used by both belligerents against both combatants and civilians during the Iran-Iraq War (Gibson, 2010). The role of U.S. in the conflict also remains a topic of interest among scholars. U.S. was a de facto ally of Iraq in the conflict. In contrast, Iraqi state records may explore Saddam's suspicion on United States during this conflict. Cold War International History Project (CWIHP) 2004 contains oral histories of former American policymakers together with a collection of declassified American documents on the war. This invasion was one of the longest conflicts in the twentieth century, resulting in deaths and injuries of many military and non-military people. Iraq extensively used chemical weapons during the war. Mine-laid deaths and causalities have been occurring in the frontier localities yet. Despite of passing 24 years after the ceasefire, the injured people are one of the main health challenges in both countries (Payman, 2013). The war was ended by a 1988 cease-fire, though the resumption of normal diplomatic relations and the withdrawal of troops did not take place until the signing of a formal peace agreement on August 16, 1990. Saddam was also concerned over attempts by Iran's Islamic revolutionary government to incite rebellion among Iraq's Shi'ite majority. By attacking when it did, Iraq took advantage of the apparent disorder and isolation of Iran's new government- then at loggerheads with the U.S. over the seizure of the U.S. embassy in Tehran by Iranian militants- and of the demoralisation and dissolution of Iran's regular armed forces. Perhaps as many as a million people died, many more were wounded, and millions were made refugees. The resources wasted on the war exceeded what the entire Third World spent on public health in a decade (Parast, 2008).

The war cost both sides in lives and economic damages: half a million Iraqi and Iranian soldiers, with an equivalent number of civilians, are believed to have died, with many more injured; however, the war brought neither reparations nor changes in borders. The conflict has been compared to World War I in terms of the tactics used, including large-scale trench warfare with barbed wire stretched across trenches, manned machine-gun posts, bayonet charges, human wave attacks across a no-man's land, and extensive use of chemical weapons such as mustard gas by the Iraqi government against Iranian troops, civilians, and Iraqi Kurds. At the time of the conflict, the U.N Security Council issued statements that "chemical weapons had been used in the war." U.N. statements never clarified that only Iraq was using chemical weapons, and according to retrospective authors "the international community remained silent as Iraq used weapons of mass destruction against Iranian as well as Iraqi Kurds." In this period of time, the population growth increased to 3.9 per cent. In addition to the war, other factors triggered significant changes in the demographics of the Iranian population: the government's push to have more children, the allocation of subsidies, improvements in the health sector due to various health plans (i.e. regular and systematic immunisation and higher level in control of infectious diseases (Farhud, 1998). The birth rate increased more than 40 per cent whereas the mortality rate declined to less than 7 per cent. However, this regression was more gradual than the previous downward trend in the 1970s (Kiani, 2010). In addition, immigration from Afghanistan and Iraq to Iran contributed to the population growth during this period (Malekafzali, 2004).

Iraq had social, economic, ethnic, religious, and ideological conflicts, all of which delayed the process of state formation. However, in 1932, it became a sovereign state, by the inclusion in the League of Nations. For the new entity, the declaration of statehood and for fixed boundaries generated intense competition. In the emerging state structure, all groups fought energetically for their places- Sunnis and Shi'as, cities and tribes, shaykhs and tribesmen, Assyrians and Kurds, pan-Arabists and Iraqi nationalists. These conflicting demands had been overcome by the British imposed political system. The Iraqi constitution, adopted in 1990 under Saddam Hussein, was among the most secular in the Arab world (International Crisis Group, 2005). It made no mention of Sharia Islamic religious law, although Islam was named the official state religion. This prohibited all forms of discrimination, and guaranteed freedom of expression as part of the revolutionary, national and progressive trend. Algeria, Jordan, Lebanon, Libya, Morocco and Tunisia: They do not mention Sharia in their constitutions. The constitution of Lebanon, a mixed Muslim and Christian country, is the only Arab state not to name Islam as the national religion.

With the growth of the oil industry by the early 1950s, government revenues began to improve (Morton, 2011). New pipelines had been built to Tripoli, Lebanon, in 1949 and to Baniyas, Syria, in 1952. In 1952, a new oil agreement promised the government a 50 per cent of oil company profits before taxes. The result was that government oil revenues increased four-fold, from US $ 32 million in 1951 to US $ 112 million in 1952. The raised oil payments helped the masses hardly. As a result of the ineffective agreement, the government officials were grately corrupted. Oil companies employed relatively few Iraqis. In the economic level, the oil boom also had a severe inflationary effect. This inflation could damage especially in number of urban poor and the middle class salaried. The state increased economic power further isolated Nuri as Said and the regent from Iraqi society and difficult to understand from their view the weak nature of the monarchy's hold on power (Brown, 1979). In the foreign policy level, especially in the mid-1950s the monarchy did a serious blunder that ultimately lead to its overthrow. With the 1949 military coup in Syria that made Adib Shishakli to power, there was a confusion between Abd al Ilah who had called for a Syrian-Iraqi union, and Nuri as Said, who opposed the union plan. However, in 1954 with the help of Iraqi, Shishakli was overthrown and thus the union plan never came to be considered. However, the schism between Nuri as Said and the regent continued. Sensing the regime's weakness, the resistance made its anti-regime activity stronger. In 1955, major foreign policy mistake occurred by the monarchy, while Nuri as Said announced that Iraq was joining a British-supported mutual defense pact with Iran, Pakistan, and Turkey.

The Baghdad Pact had represented a direct challenge to Egyptian president Gamal Abdul Nasser. As a result, Nasser challenged the legality of the Iraqi monarchy and called on the officer corps to overthrow it (Anderson, 2011). The monarchy found itself completely isolated because of many reasons. In 1956, British-French-Israeli attack on Sinai further alienated Nuri as Said's regime from the growing ranks of the opposition. King Hussein of Jordan and Abd al Ilah proposed a union of Hashimite monarchies to counter the recently formed Egyptian-Syrian union in 1958. Nuri as Said was able to enclose the rising discontent only by resorting to even greater domination and to tighter control over the political process.

In the rise of Islamic civilisation, Iraq played a significant role and from A.D. 750, under Abbasid rule, it was the golden age of Islam. Baghdad became a bridge between ancient and modern worlds and became the centre of a civilisation that developed a new tradition in scientific and philosophical scholarship. In Baghdad in 1984, there were 30 independent schools, an engineering school and three medical schools. Private and public libraries were established and contained tens of thousands of books and manuscripts. From this fountain blossomed the multicultural, multiethnic mosaic of Islamic civilisation that fostered academic assortment and cross-cultural synergy (Ismael, 2005). In Mesopotamia, Muslims had created both civilisation and harmonious society with functioning institutions and a civil communications. In the thirteenth century, the Mongols destroyed Baghdad and it was the end of Abbasid period's monumental achievements. When it became part of the Ottoman Empire, the sense of permanence and continuity was not regained. Following World War I, with the empire's collapse, Mesopotamia was occupied by the British. Iraq consisted of three territories, Mosul, Baghdad and Basra. On the eve of this occupation, each administered and controlled independently. Even though all these territories had been part of the Ottoman Empire, politics and economy were localised in these territories (Fattah, 2009). Various tribes and ethnic groups had built typical social structures. Ottoman control was not strong and leading to a loose confederation of tribes. With the deficiency of a central authority, the tribes had established a construction for conflict declaration and resource management. Economy had developed based on a mode of subsistence. The camel-breeding tribes were at the top of the hierarchy, the sheepbreeders, peasants and Arab marsh dwellers followed this social structure. By imposing settlement policies and land-reform measures, in the mid-nineteenth century, the Ottomans tightened their control over the tribes in this region. But these naturally lead to a weakening of the tribes as a traditional source of power. However, the tribes had played a crucial role in the socio-political and economic structures of these societies.

On the constitutional role for Islam, Iraqis are entering a long-standing regional debate. All Arab states make explicit provision for Islam in their constitutions except Lebanon. Earlier, Arab constitutional documents tended to give fleeting nods to more extensive provisions on Islam but had growingly decided to incorporate. In almost all Arab states Islam is proclaimed as the official religion. However, in Arab politics, the first place prevents dis-establishmentarian tendencies that have been nearly absent. Religious instruction is normally ingredient of the officially mandated curriculum (Rubin, 2007). Many practices and traditions predate the constitution for instance a state mufti, accountable for advising political officials on substances of religious law and are unaffected by it. Islam as the official religion has been proclaimed by the Iraq's earlier constitutions. Some Arab constitutions require that the head of state is to be a Muslim. In 1964, in the interim constitution, Iraq only briefly adopted such a provision, even though all Iraqi heads of states have been Muslim. Some Arab constitutions offer that matters of personal status law governed in accordance with religious law (Ghabra, 2001). In 1925, Iraqi constitution did contain such a stipulation, but most following constitutions dropped the issue but the practical meaning of such a stipulation is not wide. It usually does no more than distinguish a surviving situation. Enshrining religious law for personal status does put off civil marriage, which is virtually unknown in the region anyway. Such language has not avoided far-reaching alterations on personal status law, so long as such reforms can be cast as falling inside lawful elucidations of Islamic law. The debate over personal status law has already begun Iraqi case, but it is likely to be fought on the territory of the normal legislative procedure rather than of the constitutional text. Islamic law, as a source of legislation especially in Arab constitutions, had seemingly engraved out increasingly determined roles for the Islamic Sharia. In 1950, the Syrian constitution introduced the idea that Islamic law should be a source for legislation, in 1962 and in 1971 Kuwait and Egypt followed the procedure. The Egyptian constitution was amended in 1980 so that "the source of legislation is by the principles of the Islamic Sharia (Brown, 2005).

Saddam's government rested on the support of the 20 per cent minority of Sunnis. Iraqi society is divided along lines of language, religion and ethnicity; The Ba'ath Party was increasingly concerned about potential Shi'a Islamist influence following the Iranian Revolution in 1979. The Kurds of northern Iraq who are Sunni, but not Arabs, were also permanently hostile to the Ba'athist party's pan-Arabism (Bengio, 2003). For controlling his power, Saddam tended either to provide them with benefits so as to co-opt them into the regime, or to take repressive measures against them.[9] The major instruments for accomplishing this control were the paramilitary and police organisations. Beginning in 1974, Taha Yassin Ramadan (himself a Kurdish Ba'athist), a close associate of Saddam, commanded the People's Army, which was responsible for internal security. As the Ba'ath Party's paramilitary, the People's Army acted as a counterweight against any coup attempts by the regular armed forces. As well to the People's Army, the Department of General Intelligence or Mukhabarat was the most notorious arm of the state security system, feared for its use of torture and assassination. It was commanded by Barzan Ibrahim al-Tikriti, Saddam's younger half-brother. Since 1982, foreign observers believed that this department operated both at home and abroad in their mission to seek out and eliminate Saddam's perceived opponents. For his own people, Saddam was a notable terror. Eye hollowing was one of the methods of torture; Amnesty International reported the case of a Kurdish business person in Baghdad who was executed in 1997. When his family got his body back, his eyes were scratched out and the unfilled eye openings stuffed with paper. It was a common way of torture for political prisoner (Aprim, 2003). Amnesty International reported one injured party who then had acid poured into his open injuries deferment from the ceiling. Victims blindfolded, exposed and suspended for hours by their wrists, frequently with their hands attached at the rear backs. This causes displacement and tearing of joints and ligaments.

During the late 1960s and early 1970s, formally the al-Bakr's second-in-command, as Vice Chairman of the Revolutionary Command

Council, Saddam built a status as a progressive, effective politician. Meanwhile, Saddam tried to strengthen and merge the Ba'ath party and new government and addressing the country's major domestic problems. In 1968, after the Ba'athists took power, Saddam's aim was attaining constancy in a nation puzzled with thoughtful tensions. Prior to Saddam, Iraq had been split in many levels- social, ethnic, religious, and economic fault lines; Sunni and Shi'ite, Arab and Kurd, tribal chief and urban merchant, nomad and peasant (Perlmutter, 2003). For the stable rule for the country, Saddam had to follow both massive repression and the development standards of living. So he changed in economic level, by adopting the reconstruction of the Iraqi economy together with making of a strong security to prevent coups within the power structure and insurrections separately from it, along with mass support closely followed the administration of state welfare and development programmes. Iraq's oil was centre of this strategy. In 1972, Saddam oversee of international oil interests' abduction. In 1973, with the energy crisis, world oil prices rose dramatically and skyrocketing revenues enabled Saddam to expand his agenda.

Within a few years among Middle Eastern countries, Iraq was providing social services that were unprecedented. Under the control of Saddam, he founded the "National Campaign for the Eradication of Illiteracy" and the campaign for "Compulsory Free Education in Iraq". Upto the highest education levels, the government established universal free schooling. Following the initiation of the programme, hundreds of thousands learned to read. The government also supported soldiers' family, granted free hospitalisation to everyone, and gave subsidies to farmers. Saddam earned an award from United Nations Educational Scientific and Cultural Organisation (UNESCO) for the modernisation of public-health systems in the Middle East (Pearson, 2000). Saddam implemented campaigns in Iraq, which helped the development of national infrastructure such as great progress in building roads, promoting mining, Iraq's energy industries, and developing other industries. Electricity was brought to nearly every city in Iraq, and many outlying areas. Saddam expanded largely oil-based Iraqi economy. Most of Iraq's people lived in the countryside and roughly two-thirds were peasants, before the 1970s but this number would decrease quickly during the 1970s as global oil prices helped revenues and the country invested into industrial expansion.

Saddam politically benefitted by the oil revenue, for his deeds Saddam earned admiration from abroad (MacKey, 2003). Following the decline in Egyptian leadership brought about by the disturbance of Israel's six-day victory in the 1967 war, He had a good intuition for what the Arab street demanded and the death of the pan-Arabist leader, Gamal Abdul Nasser, in 1970, and the "traitorous" drive by his successor Anwar Sadat, to sue for peace with the Jewish state. Saddam, posing himself as the protector of Arabism against Jewish or Persian interlopers, was heavy-handed, except dependable as a drumbeat. It helped, that his mukhabarat (secret police) put dozens of Arab news editors, writers and artists on the payroll. In the rural areas Saddam focused on fostering loyalty to the Ba'athists. Foreign oil interests had been nationalised, after that Saddam supervised the transformation of the countryside, mechanizing agriculture on a large scale, and allocating land to peasant farmers. In 1974-1975, the Ba'athists established farm cooperatives and the government also doubled expenditures for agricultural development. The state-owned banks were put under his thumb. Development went forward at such a fevered field that two million people from other Arab countries and even Yugoslavia worked in Iraq to meet the growing demand for labour.

In 1976, in the Iraqi armed forces Saddam rose to the position of general and he became the strongman of the government (Makiya, 1998). Al-Bakr became unable to execute his duties, both internally and externally Saddam took on an increasingly prominent role as the face of the government and also he became the draftsman of Iraq's foreign policy and stand for the nation in all diplomatic circumstances. Years before his formal enthronement to power, he was the de facto leader of Iraq and slowly began to merge his power over Iraq's government and the Ba'ath party. He soon built up a powerful circle of support within the party. Under Ba'athist leadership, in 1979, al-Bakr started to make treaties with Syria that would lead to unification between the two countries. Syrian President Hafez al-Assad would become deputy leader in a union, and this would drive Saddam to dimness. Saddam acted to secure his grip on power. On 16 July 1979, he forced the ailing al-Bakr to resign, and formally assumed the Presidency. On 22 July 1979, he convened an assembly of Ba'ath party leaders, throughout the assembly, which he ordered videotaped. Saddam claimed to have found a fifth column inside the Ba'ath Party and directed Muhyi Abdel-Hussein to read out an acknowledgment and the names of 68 alleged co-conspirators. These members had been labeled disloyal and were detached from the room one by one and taken into custody. Around sixty eight people arrested at the meeting were consequently tried together and found guilty of treason. Nearly twenty two were sentenced to execution. Other high-ranking members of the party formed the firing squad. By 1 August 1979, hundreds of high-ranking Ba'ath party members had been executed.[10]

Human rights groups have documented government-supported executions, take actions of afflict, and rape for decades-especially the Saddam Regime. In 2002, a declaration sponsored by the European Union adopted by the Commission for Human Rights, stated that there had been no enhancement in the human rights catastrophe in Iraq (Wilshire, 2008). The announcement denounced President Saddam Hussein's government for its "orderly, prevalent and tremendously severe infringements of human rights and worldwide humanitarian law." The resolution insisted that Iraq straight away put an end to its "summing up and subjective implementations, the make use of rape as a political instrument and all implemented and spontaneous vanishings" (BBC News, 2000). Complete political involvement at the nationwide stage was limited only to members of the Arab Ba'ath Party, which make up only 8 per cent of the populace. As a result, it was impracticable for Iraqi citizens to alter their government. Iraqi citizens were not allowed assembling lawfully unless articulated by the government. The Iraqi government prohibited the concern of political parties, regulated their inside affairs and supervised their activities (Glass, 2004). Police checkpoints on Iraq's roads and public roads put off commonplace citizens from travelling out of the country lacking government authorisation and luxurious way out visas.

Iraqi women could not journey outside of the country without the escort of a male family member. The activities of citizens living surrounded by Iraq who obtained money from relatives out of the country were closely monitoring (Jordan, 2003). Following the 2003 assault of Iraq, a number of accumulation graves were originate in Iraq enclosing a number of thousand bodies whole. Also following the attack, numerous torture centres found insecurity offices and police stations throughout Iraq. The aims of these centres included: fasteners for hanging public for striking, equipments for electric shock, with extra apparatus frequently establish in homelands through cruel safety repairs.

Qusay Hussein (1966-2003), son of the President, beginning of the influential Republican Guard, considered to be chosen by Saddam as his descendant. Uday Hussein (1964-2003), son of the President, had a confidential torment chamber and of the rapes and killings of countless women. In addition to this, he was leader of the paramilitary forces. "Saddam executed as numerous as a million of his citizens, lots of with poisonous gas (Spagat, 2010). He afflicted, maimed and jailed countless more. His unprovoked assault of Iran is approximation to have left one more million populace dead. His capture of Kuwait threw the Middle East into disaster. Extra dangerous, debatably, was the emotional injure he inflicted on his own ground. Hussein generated a nation of informants- companions, spheres contained by circles- making the whole inhabitants complicit in his rule." (Filkins, 2007) Estimations for the number of deceased in the Iran-Iraq war diverge from 500,00 to 1.5 million (John, 2002 and Hitchens, 2005).

Conditions for political prisoners in Iraq were brutal and degrading. The subsequent portrayal of prison situations are based on British Government's description (World Report 2013). The "Mahjar" prison, situated on the Police Training College site in innermost Baghdad, was previously the house of the Police Dog Training Centre. The regular tenancy of the "Mahjar" is 600-700 populaces. Thirty of the cells are subversive and thirty other cells utilised to be trouble kennels. Prisoners were beaten twice a day and the women frequently raped by their guards. They obtain no medical dealing, except a few prisoners stay alive of a year in the "Mahjar". Two huge oil storage tanks every by way of a competence of 36,000 litres have been built secure to the "Mahjar". The tanks occupied of petrol and connected by pipes to the prison constructions in the "Mahjar". The prison authorities had teachings to place light to the petrol and wipe out the "Mahjar" in an urgent situation. The "Sijn Al-Tarbut" (the chest prison) is located on the third subversive level of the innovative Directorate of General Security (DGS) structure in Baghdad. The hostages were kept in line-ups of rectangular steel boxes, as originate in mortuaries, awaiting they confess either to their offenses or die. There were around 100-150 boxes which were unlocked for half an hour a day to permit the prisoners a few light and air.

The "Qurtiyya" (the can) prison is positioned in a DGS compound in the Talbiyyah area of the Saddam City district of Baghdad. This consists of 50-60 metal boxes the dimension of old tea chests in which detainees were locked up under the equivalent conditions as the "Sijn Al-Tarbut". All boxes had a tap for water and a floor made of web to permit the detainees to defecate.

Between 1993 and 1998, about 3,000 prisoners from the "Mahjar" prison executed in a carrying out region called the "Hadiqa" (garden) next to the prison. The "Hadiqa" consisted of an open area and sand bank that covered by a steel awning. Prisoners from the "Mahjar" executed in the "Hadiqa" by machine gun. A Special Oversight Committee at the prison decided on the executions- Persecution of the Kurds- under Saddam's rule, Iraq's Kurdish communities have practiced dreadful distress. They took into custody and executed in 1983 of 8,000 Kurdish males aged 13 and upwards. Amnesty International, in 1985, drew awareness to reports of hundreds additional dead and missing, as well as the disappearance of 300 Kurdish kids arrested in Sulaimaniya, of whom some were afflicted and three died in custody. In 1988, Iraqi government thoroughly demolished Kurdish rural communities and killed inhabitants. According to Amnesty International's approximations, over 100,000 Kurds were killed or departed. The list used by the Bush Administration to help out quarrels that the 2003 Iraq war was next to Saddam Hussein and the Ba'ath Party control, somewhat than aligned with the Iraqi people (Amnesty International, 2014).

In middle-2000, the RCC supported taking away of the tongue as an innovative punishment for insult or rude comments concerning the President or his family. These sentences put into practiced mostly on political dissenters. Iraqi TV has transmitted depictions of these penalties as a caution to additional. In October 2001, 23 political prisoners, mainly Shi'a Muslims, executed at Abu Ghraib. According to an Amnesty International account published in August 2001, 'torment is making use of thoroughly alongside political detainees.' The balance and strictness of afflict in Iraq can only consequence from the getting off its utilise at the highest level.' Amnesty and other human rights organisations get thousands of reports of persecution and interviewed many torment wounded (Rubin, 2001). Even though Iraqi law prohibits the put into practice of agony, the British Government law is not conscious of a solitary container of an Iraqi administrator believed to be carrying out torment brought to impartiality. According to bureaucrats of the U.S. States Department, loads of human rights mistreatment were occurred in Saddam Hussein's Iraq, mainly carried out in being or through the arranges of Saddam Hussein and eleven extra citizens. The expression "Saddam's Dirty Dozen created in October 2002 and made use of U.S. bureaucrats to portray this group. The majority associates of the group detained far above the ground locations in the Iraqi government and association went all the way from Saddam's private protector to Saddam's sons".

The techniques of torment reported to international human rights groups, for instance Amnesty International and Human Rights Watch, by the fatalities of the persecute or their families. Victims, essentially women, were raped and sexually exploited, as well as there were reports of broken bottles being forced into the victim's anus. Victims were forced to lie face down and then hit on the soles of their feet through a cable, frequently losing consciousness. Extinguishing cigarettes on a mixture of parts of the body, removal of fingernails and toenails and thrashings with bamboos, beats, hose pipes and metal rods were common (World Report, 2012). Victims were told that they were to be executed by firing squadron and conducted a mock execution. Victims hooded and brought before a firing squad, which then flames empty rounds. David Scheffer, U.S. Ambassador-at-Large for War Crimes, reported that photographic evidence showed that Iraq had used acid baths during the invasion of Kuwait. Victims hung by their wrists and regularly lowered into the acid. Now human rights abuses in Iraq are as bad as they were under Saddam Hussein and are even in danger of eclipsing his record, according to the country's first Prime Minister after the fall of Saddam's regime.[11] Upsets applied to a variety of parts of the body, including the genitals, ears, tongue and fingers

Summary

Today, the political system of Iraq is going all the way through a process of renovation and empowerment of the Shi'ites and the Kurds standing for an independent state. It is vital to ensure that all Iraqi ethnic and religious groups, including the Sunni-Arabs, have a stake in Iraq's future and are enfranchised by the political system. This will require a reinvention of an Iraqi identity and a reordering of state power and institutions. The regional security issues that affect Iraq are further worsening. This scale up Iraqi security concerns as well as challenges the security environment in the region. The fall of Sunnis' from power may eliminate the penchant for adventurism and the hold of an Arabist image, but a future rise in Iraqi militancy will only be headed off by a broader approach in regional security. In the monarchical period the governance was instilled with an adequate amount of civility and self-discipline to consent to abide oppositional views and activities, eventhough not for the whole time of the monarchy, but at least for some considerable periods within it. The emergence of a stable regime in post-Saddam Iraq will have to adopt a constructive approach in both domestic and foreign policy and will depend on the successful pursuit of these two strategies. It will be a long process and it will undoubtedly include many setbacks, but will bring about a successful reconstruction of Iraq's domestic political system, addressing the roots of regional insecurity. The world's obligation is to stop this beating on human rights. As Iraqi people were waiting for a new period of democratic system, a signal of pressure by radical groups took place to compress their anticipation and an aggressive repression of civilians extended all over Iraq.The continuous war atmosphere and its consequences together with the fall of government severely deteriorated the economic situations in Iraq.The social setup of Iraq was seriously disturbed, along with increasing the insecurities faced by women and children,adding to its misery.

Notes

1. Seymour M. Hersh U.S. Soldiers brutalized Iraqis. How far up does the responsibility go? http://www. newyorker.com/fact/content/?040510fa-gact. The 372nd's abuse of prisoners seemed almost routine—a *fact* of Army life ."The purpose of an Article 32 hearing is for us to engage witnesses and discover *facts*," Gary Myers, network, go to Strongbox at *http://* tnysbtbxsf356hiy http://www. newyorker.com/fact/content/?040510fa-gact.
2. For a thorough analysis of military coups in contemporary Arab politics see Eliezer Be'eri, Army Officers in Arab Politics and Society (New York: Praeger, 1970).
3. Michael Hudson, Arab Politics: The Search for Legitimacy (New Haven: Yale University Press, 1977), 267. An impressive work of scholarship on the political culture and changing society of the entire Arab world. The author gives us a good picture of each country as he pursues his general themes of legitimacy, nationalism, Arabism, and the inevitable 'modernization.'

4. Saddam, is his personal name, meanings the stubborn one or he who confronts in Arabic (in Iraq also a term for a car's bumper). Hussein (Sometimes also transliterated as Hussein or Hussein) is not a surname in the Western sense, but a patronymic, his father's given personal name; Abid al-Majid his grandfather's; al-Tikriti means he was born and raised in (or near) Tikrit. He was commonly referred to as Saddam Hussein, or Saddam for short. The observation that referring to the deposed Iraqi president as only Saddam is derogatory or inappropriate may be based on the assumption that Hussein is a family name: thus, the New York Times refers to him as "Mr. Hussein", while Encyclopaedia Britannica uses just Saddam. A full discussion can be found (Blair Shewchuk, CBC News Online.
5. Iraq has its Kurds, Sunni Arabs and Shi'ites and its modern history has been a struggle over monarchy, republicanism and the one-party state. Charles Tripp, "The Foreign Policy of Iraq," in Raymond Hinnebusch and Anoushiravan Ehteshami, The Foreign Policies of Middle East States (Boulder, CO: Lynne Rienner, 2002), 169.
6. Winning the Peace Conference Report, p. 5.Genocide in Iraq/The Anfal Campaign Against the Kurds/A Middle east Watch Report/Human Rights Watch dated 1993, report at Human Rights Watch Web site, accessed on 21.03.2007.
7. For Sistani's life and views consult Reidar Visser, Sistani, the U.S. and Politics in Iraq: From Quietism to Machiavellism (2006), Available online at http://www.mafhoum.com/press9/274P4.pdf; Ali A. Allawi, The Occupation of Iraq: Winning the War, Losing the Peace (Yale University Press, 2007); Ayatollah Sistani's website: www.Sistani.org.
8. See Moron Mike (Sun Aug 21st, 2005 at 11:57:11 PDT). Saddam's Constitution Outshines All in Middle East (& New One). Conservatives are always quick to point out how any government would be better than Saddam's. Maybe not. From the Lexington Herald-Leader: Article nr. 14721 sent on 17-aug-2005 01:19 ECT www.uruknet.info?p=14721.
9. Helen Chapin Metz (ed.) Iraq: A Country Study:"Internal Security in the 1980s", Saddam Hussein information. Saddam justified nationalism. Library of Congress Country Studies, 1988. Available online at http://info.olsonb.com/index.php?p=Saddam%20Hussein.
10. See A Documentary on Saddam Hussein 5, Bay Fang. "When Saddam ruled the day." U.S. News & World Report. 11 July 2004. Jan 7, 2011 - On 30 June 2004, Saddam Hussein, held in custody by U.S. forces at the U.S. On 5 November 2006, Saddam Hussein was found guilty of crimes. Available online at http://www.usatoday.com/news/world/iraq /2003-08-01 accessed on 01.08.2003.
11. Peter Beamount (2005) foreign affairs The Observer Sunday November The Guardian www.theguardian.com. News Abuse worse than under Saddam.

3

U.S. Interventions and Humanitarian Crisis in Iraq

Introduction

U.S. invasion and occupation of Iraq, assisted and abetted by the British, was seen around the world as a war without any basis in international law. During most of the last decade, the Bush administration's activities justified the war in Iraq. It also created, by building, rebuilding, and deconstructing, problems and issues in Iraq. It was an intrusion of a sovereign country. This chapter considers the two wars, its impact, humanitarian crisis and human rights violations etc. Subsequent to the first Gulf war, consecutive U.S. Administrations used a policy of repression toward Saddam Hussein's Iraq. It involved the hold up for U.N. inspectors searching for weapons of mass destruction and sanctions against Saddam, which had disastrous impact on the Iraqi people. It would have sufficed to make sure that Iraq be made incapable of delivering weapons of mass destruction. In the short term, it means a willingness to undertake military action as diplomacy was clearly failing. In the longer term, it means removing Saddam Hussein and his regime from power. That now needs to become the aim of U.S. foreign policy (Cameron, 2002). In the attempt to make the world safe for the U.S., the U.S. army has committed unpardonable crimes in Iraq, which are against human rights. U.S. cannot sit in judgement over the rest of the world. According to rules of international law and international human rights law, U.S. must gets away from interfering in the affairs of sovereign self-governing countries such as

Iraq. It is one of the biggest intrusions onto a sovereign country in recent times and apart from those in power, the civilians of the U.S. are equally guilty of having supported the evil schemes of the administration by electing junior Bush for a second term in spite of having waged a monstrous war.

Gulf War (1991) and its Consequences

The First Persian Gulf War, also known as the Gulf War 1991. This conflict involving Iraq and U.S. led coalitions in the late twentieth and early twenty-first century. It was an armed conflict between Iraq and a coalition of 39 nations including the United States, Britain, Egypt, France, and Saudi Arabia; 28 nations contributed troops. It was a result of Iraq's invasion of Kuwait on August 2, 1990. Iraqi president Saddam Hussein declared that the invasion was a response to overproduction of oil in Kuwait. Iraq peaked in relative power prior to the Gulf War and was in acute relative decline at the time it invaded Kuwait, explaining Saddam Hussein's war decision as a failure of strategic adjustment to changes in his strategic environment. These results show the relevance of relative power analysis to the study of war in developing regions and elsewhere. Moreover, given the greater instability of structural change shorter periodicity of the cycles at the regional level, the greater frequency of critical points (rapid inversion of expectations) may helps to explain why politics within some regions is more unstable and full of conflicts than at the central system level (Parasiliti, 2003). On August 6, 1990, the U.N. Security Council imposed comprehensive economic sanctions on Iraq in response to its invasion of Kuwait and a military build-up began which eventually resulted in the six week Gulf War in early 1991. The air campaign against Iraq was launched January 16, 1991, with a ground force invasion of Kuwait a month later on the February 24, 1991.

The extraordinary legal measures taken by the Coalition against Iraq seemed to justify faith in the power of law even in time of war (Burnham *et.al.*, 2006). President Bush received congressional approval to commit U.S. military forces; and the Coalition prosecuted its war under the legal authority of U.N. Security Council Resolutions. More significantly, Coalition political and military leaders repeatedly referred to the laws of war to justify their actions and to condemn Iraq's conduct, both leading up to and during actual combat. It was often stressed that by respecting the law, Coalition forces were sparing Iraqi civilians from the hardship of war to the greatest extent possible (Kinsella, 2008).

One of the few things that proponents and opponents of a new campaign against Iraq seems to agree that the first Bush administration should have solved the problem of Saddam when it had the chance. Certainly, everyone would be better off today if the U.S. military had marched into Baghdad. But the Bush administration's decision to stand down in February 1991 made excellent sense at the time. All those arm-chair generals who declare they would have taken out Saddam forget that the Gulf War coalition included Arab countries, such as Saudi Arabia, who never would have openly joined a U.S.-led invasion to topple an Arab regime. Witness the growing Saudi reservations about hosting a U.S. military presence even in peacetime. And since Western intelligence analysts believed that Saddam's humiliating defeat would shortly prompt a coup among unsatisfied military officers, sitting back and waiting for matters to take care of themselves seemed like the smart thing to do. Military forces from a coalition of 34 countries were involved in the war against Iraq. The number of coalition military personnel that were killed is well documented.[1] However, the number of people in Iraq directly killed by the war is much harder to set up and many of the estimates appear to be little more than exercises in propaganda. The most widely quoted numbers were those made by the U.S. Defence Intelligence Agency (DIA) who estimated that 1,00,000 Iraqis were killed (plus or minus 50,000) this is a huge overestimate and that the Iraqi dead were only around 1,500. Both these ideas are established on a figure of dubious assumptions and seem to be little more than conjectures (Heidenrich, 1993).

A more 'scientific' analysis by Daponte (1993) based on epidemiological and demographic techniques concluded that 56,000 soldiers (plus or minus 7,000) and 3,500 civilians were killed directly by the war.[2] The War illness is not linked with psychological stresses (Knights, 2005). The heavy bombing of Iraq resulted in serious harm to infrastructure- bridges, roads, water, sewer and electrical power systems. Most of the deaths of 'innocent' people in Iraq were a result of the collateral effects of the bombing of these infrastructure facilities and an inability to restore these facilities due to the economic sanctions. These infrastructure facilities were categorised as 'dual use targets' and deliberately targeted, often with precision weapons systems.

An article in the U.S. Air Force journal *Air and Space Power Chronicles* explains the legal and moral, basis for these bombing targets; a key exemplar of such double-use targeting was the devastation of Iraqi electrical power facilities in Desert Storm. While crippling Iraq's military command and control capability, destruction of these facilities shut down water purification and sewage treatment plants. As a result, epidemics of gastroenteritis, cholera, and typhoid broke out, many as 1,00,000 civilian deaths and a doubling of the infant mortality rate, the U.S. Air Force has a vested interest in attacking dual-use targets so long as dual-use target destruction serves the dual purpose of destroying legitimate military capabilities and indirectly targeting civilian morale (Rizer, 2001). It is estimated that, as a consequence of the warfare and sanctions, Iraq's GDP fell by about two-thirds in 1991, due to an 85 per cent fall in petroleum output.[3] Per capita income fell from $3,416 to $1,500 in 1991 and has since fallen to less than $1,036 (and has been estimated to be as low as $450 in 1995). Meanwhile, average shop prices for essential commodities stood at 850 times the July 1990 level (SCID, 2000).

The U.N. Development Programme (UNDP) field office in Iraq, summarised the situation simply, "the nation has seen a shift from relative affluence to massive poverty" (U.N. Security Council 1999). It is easily proven that mass poverty causes increased ill health and an increased danger of death. The Gulf War and economic sanctions that have had the greatest sum of destruction and suffering amongst the ordinary masses of Iraq. Tony Blair and the U.K. government blame Saddam Hussein for the effects of the economic sanctions which are planned to ensure Iraq's compliance with U.N. resolutions. The economic authorities have not followed in gaining this compliance, but they have resulted in the untimely deaths of many young Iraqi children and considerable suffering. The number of innocent people killed indirectly by the war (Conetta, 2004). The demolition of the electricity and water distribution infrastructure had resulted epidemics of cholera, typhoid, fever, and gastroenteritis, particularly among youngsters. Mortality rates doubled or tripled among children admitted to hospitals in Baghdad and Basra (Harvard Study Team, 1991). In autumn 1991, the U.N. Children's Fund (UNICEF) carried out a more comprehensive survey, which found that the child mortality rate was more than three times higher than that of 1986. They calculated that there were about 46,900 excess deaths among children less than five years of historic period during the first eight months of 1991. The deaths resulted from infectious diseases, the lessened quality and accessibility of food and water and an impoverished healthcare system which lacked drugs and supplies (Ascherio *et.al.*, 1992 and Eisenberg 1997). In 1995, the U.N. Food and Agricultural Organisation conducted a community study of the nutritional status and mortality among children below the age of five in Baghdad, which found that the death rate among children under five years in Baghdad had increased five-fold since the warfare ended in 1991. That report concluded that "The moral, fiscal, and political standing of an international community intent on maintaining economic sanctions is challenged by the estimate that since August 1990, 5,67,000 children in Iraq have failed as a result" (Zaidi and Fawzi, 1995; Court, 1995). The most reliable appraisals of the numbers of small fries who have passed away as an indirect result of warfare and economic sanctions comes from the 1999 Iraq Child and Maternal Mortality Surveys, carried out under the auspices of UNICEF (Ali and Shah, 2000).

Different experts may point out the different substances to 'Bush Doctrine'. The Bush Doctrine is a phrase applied to describe various related foreign policy of the President George W. Bush. In fact, the Bush Doctrine does "represent an abrupt and unprecedented shift in U.S. foreign policy". The U.S. had been the most influential country in the intact universe with its immense military power and dominates the economic position, but with this doctrine came a wave of unexpected anti-U.S.=ism. The architects of the Bush administration strategy had long recommended a strategy of hegemony based on the role of U.S. exceptional military capabilities (Jervis, 2003). Reshaping the Middle East is pivotal to the winner of this project for various causes. The policy of preventive warfare, which held that the U.S. should depose foreign regimes that represented a potential threat to the security of the U.S., still if that threat was not prompt; a policy of spreading democracy around the globe, particularly in the Middle East, as a scheme for combating terrorism; and a willingness to unilaterally pursue U.S. military interests (Schmidt, 2007).

After the Gulf War the Bush administration did real mistakes. Foremost, as percentage of the cease-fire agreement negotiated by General Norman Schwarzkopf, U.S. agreed to let the Iraqi regime use its own helicopters to fly its leaders around the state. This agreement instead allowed the Iraqi military to use gunships to suppress subsequent Shiite and Kurdish rebellions. Second, the White House neglected to support those uprisings because it feared that the dissolution of Iraq could destabilise the entire region (Strauss, 2002). The main resistance to U.S. hegemony is also concentrated in the Muslim Middle East, for two inter-linked reasons: U.S. support for Israel and recurring Western intervention in the Middle East to control oil supplies. Indeed, securing U.S. hegemony in the Middle East, at least if it is not to rest on continual coercive intervention, requires that U.S. support for Israel be balanced by alliances with Arab clients. Specifically, since support for Israel antagonizes Arabs, balancing requires U.S. leadership in the Arab-Israeli peace process aimed at a compromise land for peace solution to the conflict. However, this balancing act has been found-Israel's colonisation of the much occupied land that had to be the basis of a compromise peace settlement. Nevertheless, all U.S. presidents sustained this balancing policy until Bush Jr: as he abandoned or deviated historic balancing for an overtly pro-Israeli policy, the invasion of Iraq was seen as an alternative to balancing and a key to a military version of hegemony in the Middle East that would dispense with one based on accommodation of Arab interests (Schwenninger, 2003).

The international environment and methods of attaining power had changed including the means and justification for warfare (Ehrenbery *et.al.*, 2010). In the process, millions of children are forced to lead impoverished life in Iraq. It raises the conscience of human rights advocates in the U.S. administration (Azam, 2001). Following the attacks of 11 September 2001, George W. Bush administration resolved to embark on regime change in Iraq. The administration used the weapons of mass destruction issue to justify and secure support for war on Iraq, but war was never necessary to disarm Iraq. Hussein Kamil, Saddam Hussein's son-in-law, told Western intelligence agencies after his defection from the regime in 1995 that Iraq's weapons of mass destruction had been secretly destroyed following the earlier war (Kristof, 2003). The U.S. insisted that enforcing regime change in Iraq was about toppling a ruthless dictator intent on wrecking the order and stability created in the post-war by acquiring weapons' of mass destruction. Opponents to the war saw the invasion as the pursuit of narrow U.S. objectives, not the wider human rights objectives the administration claimed they were so sensitive to U.S. implementation of Bush Doctrine in Iraq created dangerous situation and the precedence may have been set for future conflicts. It is clear that the Security Council neither advocated the use of force nor did it find Iraq to be in a breach of peace (Singh, 2004). One of the main pillars of U.S. global hegemony is its protectorate over the "world" oil reserves concentrated in the Persian Gulf; oil is a strategic commodity that everybody needs and is crucial to military power while assuring its flow to the world economy makes U.S. power globally indispensable (Bromley, 1991).The debate on Iraq is fundamentally a debate about how far the U.S. can push the private gains dimension of its military power without the public good properties of America security provision dropping out, and without perturbing the order such provision purports to create (Norrlof, 2010). The U.S. government's policies have had a profound effect on Iraq, from its insistence on the maintenance of a punishing sanctions regime to its invasion and occupation of the country (Fawn and Raymund, 2006).

The U.S.-led occupation, however, moved swiftly to implement its pre-determined concept of removing all traces of the Ba'athist regime in order to have a clean slate on which to start building the new 'free and democratic' Iraq. Instead of identifying and strengthening capable and legitimate elements of the existing state, it moved to dismantle it by removing key institutional and human resources. The U.S. troops in particular, became 'obsessed with force protection and tracking down the insurgents who are attacking them', leaving the Iraqi public and their property largely unprotected (Pollack, 2004). This has led to the emergence of a gun culture, hitherto unknown in Iraq. Private security guards, many recruited from the ranks of the unemployed Iraqi military, as well as foreign mercenaries contracted from around the world, contest the streets with insurgents, also both national and foreign, as well as criminal gangs. It is important to recognise that legitimacy cannot be based solely on re-establishing security and authority, but should be earned through advocating reconstruction policies that are inclusive and accountable. Rather than demilitarising Iraqi society and promoting civil governance, the disbanding of the army promoted the rule of the gun, thereby restricting not enhancing the participation of civilians in public life.

The chaos of war often destroys or discredits traditional social structures and authorities, while new political structures may remain fragile, having yet to build their profile with the public-they too lack legitimacy and credibility and their reputation is frequently tarnished by perceived links to partisan interests. In Iraq, having dismantled the regular army and police without making arrangements for an international police force, the CPA began to rely on militia groups, as Saddam had done, and even to recruit intelligence and security agents who had previously served the regime, allowing themselves to be discredited by association (Dodge, 2003). Thus, the violence in Iraq is not solely an issue of security but also one of governance and credibility (Barakat, 2005). Building the capacity of government to deliver and account for reconstruction policies at the national and sub-national levels, while providing a conducive environment for recovery, is a difficult but very important aspect of successful reconstruction.

Understandably a post-conflict situation brings with it high expectations from the people, in direct contrast to the low capacity of the state to deliver. If the body politic is not sustained, the likelihood is disillusionment, with a corresponding diminution in the credibility and therefore the legitimacy of the land, making the peace dividend hard to understand as far as the soul is concerned (Collier *et.al.*, 2003). The second major error of judgment by the CPA was its 'debaathification' policy. A blanket policy of purging the top four ranks of the civil service of Ba'ath party members was excessive and denuded public institutions of experienced managerial personnel and frontline staff, either because of the actual purges or because many disillusioned civil servants remained at home (Dodge, 2003; Pollack, 2004). Some were even re-engaged by the CPA. The policy disabled rather than built the capacity of the state administration, without necessarily succeeding in removing the influence of key associates of the regime. Another important dimension of collaborative governance is for the state to develop the ability to invite civil society groups and local communities to participate effectively in the identification and development of reconstruction programmes. This is critical not only to ensure the ownership and relevance of the programmes but, more importantly, to create spaces for political dialogue. This is particularly important in the case of emerging social groups which have become politically sensitised and aware, such as ex-combatants and their leaders, returning refugees,

Diasporas returnees etc, who tend to exercise a politicising impact on the local scene.

Leading the U.S. occupation, were mainly concerned to establish a new Iraqi government that would promote the U.S. interests in the region. A 'reconstruction from on high' approach, reminiscent of that adopted in the early 1990s by Saddam Hussein, was adopted in the public sector (Stansfield, 2003). All ministries were under the control of U.S. administrators, most of whom spoke no Arabic and therefore relied heavily on the unpopular 'Michigan bunch' of exiles as translators and interpreters of a reality on the ground of which neither had any current knowledge (Dodge, 2003). As a result, instead of identifying and promoting Iraqi best practice to find solutions to reconstruction problems, attempts were made to reproduce U.S. administrative norms (Pollack, 2004). These strategies did nothing to arrest the deterioration in the security and employment situation. The proposal was vehemently denounced by the leading Shia cleric Sistani and by the majority of Iraqis and had to be abandoned. The principle objection was not so much that it would be unelected (although a short time frame to a fully elected government was demanded) but that it would be selected by caucus along ethnic quota lines and accorded powers inconsistent with a caretaker government (Brahimi, 2004a). When the CPA at this point called in the U.N. to broker a solution, the U-turn in U.S. policy appeared to be complete. However, the eventual composition of the Interim Government installed in June 2004 ignored Brahimi's advice, based on Iraqi public opinion, that a technocratic caretaker government, involving neither political aspirants nor sectarian interests, was needed in order to prepare for fully democratic elections (Brahimi, 2004b). Despite a tactical retreat, the U.S. ignored the evidence that its vision of Iraq was not shared by the majority of Iraqis and, far from collaborative governance, pursued its original plan of installing a government sympathetic to U.S. interests. The transparency of this intention inevitably undermined any legitimacy that the formal transfer of sovereignty to an Iraqi administration with U.N. endorsement might have achieved. The armed challenge to the occupation escalated and was met with a show of U.S. military strength. It was in this context of intense military operations, counter-violence and mistrust, but equally of hopes that a turning point had been reached, that a moment of opportunity might, with the right kind of international support, afford the chance of a better future, that elections were held in January 2005. A substantial number of Iraqis were able and also willing to vote. The number of Iraqis who couldn't and didn't vote belies this. Nevertheless, it has created an opportunity for Iraqis to begin to take the control of the reconstruction process and to negotiate their future (Barakat, 2005).

According to Iraq hawks like columnist Charles Krauthammer, "The Arab street has fallen silent… because the U.S. astonished the street with one of history's great show of arms. Message to the hawks: Just about every government in the Middle East had reason to oppose a U.S. attack on Iraq, Iran, Syria, and Libya all stood accused by the Bush administration of sponsoring terrorism (and in some cases, developing weapons of mass destruction), and they had no desire to support a precedent for toppling an Arab regime. Iran and Syria preferred to see Saddam Hussein contained and weak, rather than share a border with a U.S.-backed regime. Egypt didn't want to see Iraq re-emerge as a competitor to its leadership in the Arab world. And by the way, Egypt was concerned about $2 billion a year it earns in trade it conducts with Iraq through the U.N.-administered oil-for-food programme. Arguably, however, if the U.S. was determined to topple Saddam, it only needed the support of two Middle Eastern nations: Saudi Arabia and Turkey. In the event of a large-scale invasion of Iraq, those countries' military bases, port facilities, and logistics sites were considered vital. But convincing Riyadh and Ankara to participate was an uphill diplomatic battle. Saudi Arabia had a long list of concerns: the breakup of Iraq, retaliation with weapons of mass destruction by Saddam, popular unrest, isolation in the Arab world, and a backlash among Islamic extremists. Ankara's chief concern was that an independent Kurdish state in northern Iraq might encourage the secessionist aspirations of Turkey's own restive Kurdish population. But Turkey had worries about the economy too. The country was stuck in its worst recession since 1945, and that its tourist revenue and foreign direct investment have dried up post-September 11, it depends on exports for foreign currency-exports that were surely to be disrupted by a Middle Eastern war. Turkey was also no doubt wary of the inevitable influx of Kurdish refugees, who cost the government $1.5 million a day in 1991 (Strauss, 2002).

The death rate of U.S. military personnel in Iraq 20 March 2003, when the U.S. military began its invasion of Iraq, and 30 September

2006, a total of 2,706 deaths occurred to U.S. troops in Iraq. This number includes deaths from all causes, whether combat-related or not, as well as deaths that were directly related to in-theatre operations in Iraq even though they occurred in another country. The conventional denominator for a death rate consists of an estimate of person-years lived during the period in which deaths are recorded (Preston, *et.al.*, 2001). Estimate person-years lived on the basis of counts of troop strength in Iraq that were made every three months beginning on 31 March 2003 and extending to 30 September (Buzzell, 2007). The result is an estimated total of 673,783 person-years lived between 20 March 2003 and 30 September 2006. The ratio of deaths to person-years lived, 4.02 per thousand, is the death rate of military personnel in Iraq. Thus, the chance of death is approximately one in 250 per year. One obvious comparison is to the population of U.S. residents, a standard with which many are familiar. The death rate for residents of the U.S. in 2003 was 8.42 per thousand (National Centre for Health Statistics, 2006a). Thus, the annual risk of death for a member of the military in Iraq is less than half of that for a randomly chosen U.S. resident. The comparison is imperfect because a much higher fraction of the U.S. population is elderly and at high risk of death from age-related diseases. A more suitable comparison group is young men and women. The death rate for U.S. residents aged 20-34 in 2003, standardised on the basis of the distribution by sex of U.S. troops in Iraq, is 1.32 per thousand, about one-third of that of soldiers in Iraq (Gordon, 2003). But it is not difficult to find conditions equivalent to combat existing in U.S. cities. In Philadelphia, for example, the death rate for black males aged 20-34 in 2002 was 4.37 per thousand, 9 per cent higher than for troops in Iraq. A slight majority of the deaths were from homicide.

The level of violence has remained down from its 2006-2007 peak, dozens of bodies could be found on Baghdad's streets every morning-Iraq still endures a level of violence that in any other country would be considered a crisis. Still, the end of former Iraq President Saddam Hussein's brutal regime represents a considerable global good, and a nascent democratic Iraqi republic partnered with the United States could potentially yield benefits in the future. No U.S. government has ever advanced a justification for the use of force, and it has profound implications for the existing international legal framework regulating the recourse to violence (Wheeler, 2003). But when weighing those

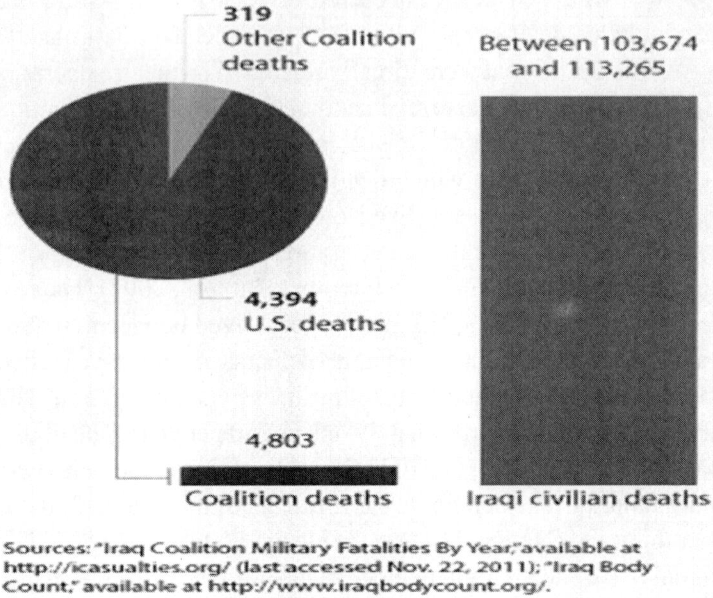

Fig. 1: Human Costs

possible benefits against the costs of the Iraq intervention, there is simply no conceivable calculus by which Operation Iraqi Freedom can be judged to have been a successful or worthwhile policy. The war was intended to show the extent of U.S. power. It succeeded only in showing its limits. The costs into three categories:

The Iraq invasion was sold to the U.S. public on the basis of Saddam Hussein's supposed possession of weapons of mass destruction and his alleged relationship with Al Qaeda. When both claims turned out to be false, the Bush administration justified the intervention on the idea that a democratic Iraq would be an ally in the "war on terror" and an inspiration for democratic reform in the Middle East. These arguments remain, at best, highly questionable (Morrissey, 2009).

The numbers for total deaths and Iraqi civilian deaths represent the lower end of estimated deaths caused by the Iraq war. Wartime casualties affect both soldiers and citizens (Kriner, 2010). Other studies shows that, such as those carried out by the Johns Hopkins Bloomberg School of Public Health and the Iraq Family Health Survey, estimate much higher civilian deaths as a result of the war.

- Total deaths: Between 110,663 and 119,380
- Coalition deaths: 4,803
- U.S. deaths: 4,484
- U.S. wounded: 32,200
- U.S. deaths as a percentage of coalition deaths: 93.37 per cent
- Iraqi Security Force, or ISF, deaths: At least 10,125
- Total coalition and ISF deaths: At least 14,926
- Iraqi civilian deaths: Between 103,674 and 113,265
- Non-Iraqi contractor deaths: At least 463
- Internally displaced persons: 1.24 million
- Refugees: More than 1.6 million

The financial costs-dealing the expense of the war and of the continued care for its veterans:

- Cost of Operation Iraqi Freedom: $806 billion.
- Projected total cost of veterans' healthcare and disability: $422 billion to $717 billion.
- The strategic costs dealing with the impact of the Iraq intervention on U.S. power and influence in the Middle East and on the global stage.

The foregoing costs could conceivably be justified if the Iraq intervention had improved the U.S.'s strategic position in the Middle East. But this is clearly not the case. The Iraq war has strengthened anti-U.S. elements and made the position of the United States and its allies more unstable (Sofer, 2013).

Neo-conservatism is a political movement emerged in the U.S. during the 1960s. Many of its supporters rose to political distinction during the Republican presidential administrations of the 1970s, 1980s, 1990s and 2000s. Neo-conservatives peaked in influence during the presidency of George W. Bush, when they played a major role in promoting and planning the Iraq invasion. The history of neo-conservative ideals, beginning with the inception of neo-conservatism during the Vietnam War, to demonstrate that these values have been consistently present in U.S. foreign policies (Langille, 2008). The neo-conservatism, sometimes call neo-Reagnites, the key concept is not perpetual war but "moral clarity backed by military strength".

Over the past decade, the neo-conservatism have argued that the U.S. should challenge evil regimes in the Middle East and Asia, spread freedom, democracy and capitalism, abandon Cold War thinking based on deterrence and containment, and de-emphasise old treaties and alliances that get in the way. Turning Iraq into a democracy that would create a wave of reform across the Middle East, as the neo-conservatism imagine, would be wonderful. Explosive hates between the major Iraqi population groups and other potential complications, that the neo-conservatism have accurately estimated the duration of the U.S. occupation, the cost to the U.S. treasury and the ultimate chances for success (Black, 2013).The development of the Bush Doctrine was influenced by neo-conservative ideology, and it was considered to be a step from the political realism of the Reagan Doctrine. The Reagan Doctrine was considered key to U.S. foreign policy until the end of the Cold War (Muravchik, 2006). The Reagan Doctrine was strongly criticised by the neo-conservatives, who also became disgruntled with the outcome of the Gulf War (Kwiatowski, 2007). Neo-conservatives are widely known to have supported the overthrow of Saddam Hussein in Iraq.

An influential group of foreign policy thinkers sees the possibly imminent overthrow of Saddam Hussein as just one early step in an ambitious blueprint to spread democracy throughout the world and eliminate threats to the U.S. Although they developed their thinking long before the September 11 attacks, the strategists, often called neo-conservatives or neo-conservatism have increased their influence over the Bush administration since September 11. Critics argue that the neo-conservatism ideas, including 'regime change', are a recipe for perpetual war, because they would steer the U.S. into many confrontations. Daalder and Lindsay say the Bush Doctrine represents a shift in U.S. foreign policy, but they reject the notion that this grand strategy was neo-conservative (Daalder and Lindsay, 2005). The Bush Administration applied the democratic peace theory to its foreign policy in hindsight as a strategy to minimise regional threats by spreading U.S. values abroad (Lynch and Singh, 2008).

But the neo-conservatism themselves and their supporters say that the U.S. has an unprecedented historical opportunity to reshape the world in ways that will make our country safer and the rest of the world freer. Neo-conservatism in the justification strategy of exceptionalism and argues that the shift in the Bush Doctrine is apparent in "the particular strength with which it adheres to a justification framework for democracy promotion" rather than the presence of ideological interests in U.S. foreign policy (Monten, 2005). After the declaration of the War on Terror and War on Iraq, the Bush Administration increasingly attempted to shape domestic governance abroad and elevated justification to a central role in U.S. foreign policy. Neo-conservative elements were present in the Bush Doctrine, this preference towards neo-conservatism was evident when weapons of mass destruction were not found and was not the primary justification for the invasion (Lynch and Singh, 2008).

All the intellectuals, politicians, and the informed public are belatedly searching with mounting costs and casualties for an explanation as to why the U.S. decided to venture down the road to regime change in Baghdad. There is uncertainty about President Bush's constant argue that in the global war on terror Iraq is the central front, it is worsened by the fact that almost all of his administration's official reasons for the war had proved to patently false, and by the even more worrying fact that the 'reordering' of the Middle East that was claimed would follow from deposing Saddam Hussein may well be coming true, but in ways often at odds with those advertised by the war's proponents and with perhaps dire costs (Schmidt and Michael, 2007). The focus of much of this re-examination has been neo-conservatism. If at the beginning of the Bush presidency there was a general failure in the academic community to appreciate the influence that neo-conservatism had on U.S. foreign policy, there is today a torrent of literature and documentaries illustrating how in the days after 9/11 neo-conservatives were able to steer U.S. response to the terrorist attacks in the direction of an invasion of Iraq. At the same time, as the situation in Iraq has worsened, this was most visible in a paid advertisement that appeared in the *New York Times* before the campaign to overthrow the Ba'athist regime began on 20 March 2003 in which many prominent realist scholars openly made the case against using military force against Iraq. They argued, quite simply, that war with Iraq was not in U.S. national interest.[4]

Here to understand of both the debate over the war in Iraq and its implications for the future of U.S. foreign policy by examining the relationship between neo-conservatism. It seeks to establish the connection that exists between the core tenets of neo-conservatism and the arguments for war against Iraq that were put forth by Bush Administration officials. These links are most apparent when we turn our attention to the neoconservative Bush Doctrine that served as the primary justification for the Iraq War. The neoconservative vision of U.S. foreign policy provided the theoretical and policy content of the Bush Doctrine, which in turn strengthened the verdict to invade Iraq in 2003 and depose the leadership of Saddam Hussein (Gordon, 2006). Even though, an observer, Charles Krauthammer's declaration that "the Bush doctrine is, for neoconservative foreign policy a synonym" is one that commands widespread assent across the political spectrum.[5] While there had been a good deal of analysis of the Bush Doctrine, particularly on the question of whether or not it represents an abrupt and unprecedented shift in U.S. foreign policy, it is revealing to extract its essential elements.[6] The Bush Doctrine begins by embracing the notion that the U.S. is now the sole superpower in the world and seeks to preserve its hegemonic position for the indefinite future. June 2002 in President Bush's graduation speech at West Point, he stated that "U.S. has, and intends to keep, military strengths beyond challenge- thereby making the destabilising arms races of other eras pointless, and limiting rivalries to trade and other pursuits of peace".[7] In his September 17, 2002 report on "The National Security Strategy of the United States of America," Bush declared that "the U.S. must build and maintain our defences beyond challenge." He continued "our forces will be strong enough to dissuade potential adversaries from pursuing a military build-up in hopes of surpassing, or equalling, the power of the U.S".[8] Neoconservatives view U.S. omnipotence and leadership as a requirement for an orderly and peaceful world. William Kristol and Robert Kagan declare that "U.S. hegemony is the only reliable defence against a breakdown of peace and international order".[9] Francis Fukuyama's article, entitled "The Neoconservative Moment," puts downs Charles Krauthammer's (democratic globalism theory's most ardent proponent), excessive idealism and zeal for the export of democracy to the Middle East: All of the different visions had now come to be related with neoconservatives.

The transformation of Iraq into a Western-style democracy and also to democratise the broader Middle East was the U.S.' declaration (Makiya, 1998). But it struck Fukuyama because these same neoconservatives had spent much of the past generation warning about the dangers of ambitious social engineering, and how social planners could never control behaviour or deal with unanticipated consequences. If the U.S. is not able to eliminate poverty or raise test scores in Washington, DC, how does it expect to bring democracy to a part of the world that has stubbornly resisted it and is virulently anti-U.S. to boot.[10] A prevalence of U.S. power is held to be beneficial to both the U.S. and the rest of the world and, as Robert Jervis argues, the commitment by the U.S. to establish U.S. hegemony, primacy, or empire is the element of the Bush Doctrine that ties all of the others together.[11] It is worth mentioning that the neoconservative's adherence to a grand strategy of primacy predates President Bush's 2002 National Security Strategy and West Point speech.[12]

In March 1992, a U.S. grand strategy of primacy that aimed to "prevent the emergence of a new rival" was outlined in a secret five-year Defence Planning Guidance paper that was leaked to the press. The primary author of the paper was Paul Wolfowitz, who was then serving as Under Secretary of Defence for Defence Secretary Richard Cheney during the George H.W. Bush administration (Mearsheimer, 2001). In their advocacy of U.S. hegemony, neoconservatives express their theoretical antipathy to traditional balance-of-power politics. A hegemonic order led by the U.S. is viewed as clearly superior to a balance-of-power order.[13] In this respect, Iraq was a threat to the U.S. and its interests. By keeping an important piece of the hegemonic puzzle from being put in place for the U.S., Hussein would have been able to challenge U.S. leadership. It is in this capacity that Iraq was a larger threat than Iran and North Korea. Iran, while militantly anti-U.S. and ardent supporters of terrorism abroad, particularly in Israel, had not invaded a surrounding country and has never acted upon a clearly enumerated regional ambition. Both countries also had a larger capacity to cause huge loss of life in a military conflict.[14] With North Korea able to level Seoul with massive artillery barrages within hours of conflict, and Iran proving it had the stomach for a war of attrition with human wave attacks and a much larger and better-equipped military than Iraq, Iraq was, of the three, an easier target. In addition, the U.S. had a pretext for a confrontation with Iraq - the 1991 Gulf War (Karsh, 2002). U.S. has, in a sense, been in an almost de facto state of war with Hussein's regime, enforcing U.N. sanctions and resolutions and punishing the regime for infractions. No such military pretext existed with either Iran or North Korea. Rather than a prescription for peace, as most realists maintain, neoconservatives view balance of power politics as both unnecessary and a hindrance to achieving U.S. national interests, while U.S. pre-eminent position in the world obviates the need for traditional balance of power diplomacy.

Seeing U.S. power as essentially benevolent, they argue that it is unnecessary for other countries to be concerned about the global imbalance of power, and conclude that a return to a multi-polar balance of power would be a direct threat to both U.S. security interests and international order (Roper, 2009). In rejecting balance of power politics, John Mearsheimer argues that neoconservatives instead "believe that international politics operate according to 'bandwagoning' logic".[15] According to this logic, rather than attempting to check the power of a more powerful state, weaker states actually join forces with it. As Mearsheimer explains, the underlying assumption of bandwagoning "is that if a state is badly outgunned by a rival, it makes no sense to resist its demands, because the adversary will take what it wants by force anyway and inflict considerable punishment in the process".[16] Thus, rather than challenging the U.S., neoconservatives believe that threatened states and smaller powers will join forces with, and jump on, the U.S. bandwagon (Croft, 2006). In advocating the war, for instance, Robert Kagan and William Kristol concluded that "once Iraq and Turkey- two of the three most important Middle Eastern powers- are both in the pro-western camp; there is a reasonable chance that smaller powers might decide to jump on the bandwagon".[17] As we will see, this view is supplemented by a specific vision of the nature of U.S. power as representing a force of democratisation that all people desire and will support if only they are given the opportunity to do so (for example, the removal of oppressive political regimes). Bandwagoning, in this sense, is seen as a moral-political process as well as a military-strategic calculation, and this outlook provided neoconservatives with yet another rationale for invading Iraq. The another element of the Bush Doctrine is the commitment, when the circumstances warrant, to the pre-emptive use of military force.[18] The policy of pre-emption is perhaps the most controversial element of the Bush Doctrine and because of the profound implications of the policy, it has received the lion's share of attention.[19]

In the light of the 9/11 terrorist attacks on the World Trade Centre and the Pentagon, the Bush administration depicted a threat environment radically different from that which existed during the Cold War. The most worrisome threats were deemed to be rogue states and terrorists armed with weapons of mass destruction (WMD). 9/11 had dramatically shown the willingness of terrorists to inflict large-scale destruction and death on U.S. soil (McCresken, 2009). In the climate of fear that existed after 9/11, and intentionally inflamed by neo-conservative analysts appearing on MSNBC and Fox News, scenarios of rogue states or terrorists armed with WMD were portrayed as major and even imminent threats by Bush administration officials.[20] Bush judged it necessary to eliminate such threats before they fully materialised in the form of a mushroom cloud over Los Angles or Manhattan. The 2002 National Security Strategy declares "they must be prepared to stop rogue states and their terrorist clients before they are able to threaten or use weapons of mass destruction against the U.S. and our allies and friend, they should deter and defend against the threat before it is unleashed".[21] The national security discourse constitutes, the construction of a privileged space where the states makes terrorism meaningful and terrifying at the same time (Campos, 2007).

In addition to justifying pre-emption on the basis of preventing the nightmare scenario of WMD being used on U.S. soil from becoming reality, there was the argument that the traditional methods of deterrence and containment were no longer credible when it came to rogue states and terrorists (Hershberg, 1993). According to the 2002 National Security Strategy, "traditional concepts of deterrence will not work against a terrorist enemy whose avowed tactics are wanton destruction and the targeting of innocents; whose so-called soldiers seek martyrdom in death and whose most potent protection is statelessness".[22] While the policy of pre-emption does indeed have radical implications for the prevailing rules and norms regarding the use of force, especially those embodied in the U.N. Charter, it is important to recall that during the Cold War many neo-conservatives never fully supported the policy of deterrence. Several of the neoconservatives in the Bush administration advocating pre-emption and preventive war were influenced by Albert Wohlstetter's critiques of the policy of nuclear deterrence and mutually assured destruction (MAD), and his promotion of a much more forceful policy toward the Soviet Union including plans to fight and win a nuclear war.

VI. The U.S. Invasion of Iraq and its Justification

The post-invasion period in Iraq, also known as occupation in Iraq followed the 2003 March 20 by a multinational coalition led by the U.S., this overthrew the Baath party government of Saddam Hussein. More than five years later, the U.S. was still mired in what some alternatively called an insurgency or a civil war, as large numbers of Iraqis resisted the occupation of their country. During this period, academics, politicians and journalists from around the world were trying to make sense of both the causes and the long-term consequences of the Iraq war on the domestic, regional and international level. Political leaders from France and Germany to Russia and Canada were opposed to the war and refused to participate in either the war or the post-war pacification and reconstruction of Iraq. Christian leaders also displayed an unusual degree of unanimity on this point (Northcott, 2004). The invasion of Iraq launched by George W. Bush appeared to combine all three motives. Saddam Hussein had defied U.N. sanctions for over decade, was falsely thought to be committed to building weapons of mass destructions, and was projected as a bloody dictator. The Bush Doctrine and the subsequent invasion of Iraq stand as a stark warning to future U.S. Presidents developing policy for the Middle East. The miscalculation at the heart of America's debacle in Iraq was driven by a potent mix of ideology and hubris, creating a catastrophic defeat for the U.S. when it should have been at the peak of its post-cold war power.

But U.S. failed to strongly present its own rationale for the war, especially in the months leading up to the war. As the primary mechanism of the global governance, international law rendered the Bush Administration's first attempts to justify the war primarily in legal nature. There are lots of justifications for the attack on Iraq in early 2003. First the administration claimed that Saddam Hussein possessed weapons of mass destruction, which posed a 'real and present danger' to his neighbours, to Israel, and to all democratic Western states. So far, no such weapons have been found (after more than 1,000 U.S. specialists have spent months looking for them) (Zizek, 2004). Then the administration argued that even if Saddam Hussein does not have any weapons of mass destruction, he was with Al Qaeda in the September 11 attacks and therefore should be punished and prevented from launching future assaults. But the U.S. President George W. Bush had to concede in September 2003 that the U.S. had no evidence that Saddam Hussein was involved with September the 11th. Finally there was the third level of justification, that even if there was no proof of a link with al Qaeda, Saddam's ruthless dictatorship was a threat to its neighbours and a catastrophe to its own people, and these facts were reason enough to topple it. Effectively there were three ideal reasons for the attack. First of all, a sincere ideological belief that the destiny of the U.S. is to bring democracy and prosperity to other nations; Secondly, the urge to brutally assert and signal unconditional U.S. hegemony and thirdly the need to control Iraqi oil reserves. Each of the three levels works on its own and deserves to be taken seriously; none of them, including the spread of democracy; should be dismissed as a simple manipulation and lie. Each has its own contradictions and consequences, for good and ill. But taken together, they are dangerously inconsistent and incompatible and all but predestine the U.S. effort in Iraq to failure. But when Bush said in his January 2003 State of the Union message, "The liberty we prize is not America's gift to the world, it is God's gift to humanity," (Zizek, 2004) this apparent burst of humility, in fact, concealed its totalitarian opposite. Every totalitarian claim that, in himself, he is nothing at all: His strength is only the strength of the people who stand behind him, whose deepest ruthless only he expresses. The catch is, those who oppose the leader by definition not only oppose him, but they also oppose the deepest and noblest aspirations of the people. But if freedom is God's gift to humanity, and the U.S. government sees itself as the chosen instrument for showering this gift on all the nations of the world, then those who oppose U.S. policies are rejecting the noblest gift of God to humanity.

Seeing that for the second reason, the urge to demonstrate unconditional U.S. hegemony, the Bush administration's National Security Strategy calls for translating America's position of unparalleled military strength and great economic and political influence', into, decades of peace, prosperity and liberty (Zizek, 2004). Concerning the third reason for launching an attack, it would be simplistic to assume that the U.S. intended to take over Iraq's oil industry lock, stock, and barrel. But in a country that, as Deputy Defence Secretary Paul

Wolfowitz put it 'floats on a sea of oil,' the installation of a U.S. blessed government that is committed to permitting foreign investment in its oil industry and that enjoys an influential perch at the Organisation of Petroleum Exporting Countries was surely an important consideration for U.S. policymakers. In reality, to ignore that consideration would have been a case of strategic malpractice on a grand scale (Zizek, 2004). In spite of everything, the post cold war world effectively begged for some global power to fill in the void. The problem with today's U.S. is not that it is a new global empire, but that it is not, i.e. that, while pretending to be an empire, it continue to act as a nation-state, ruthlessly pursuing its interests. Indeed in a perverse reversal of the old ecological slogan, the plentiful sticker for the Bush administration's foreign policy could well be 'act globally, think locally'. Seem to be, for example, at the U.S. decision to impose steel tariffs, ruled illegal by the World Trade Organisation and certainly in violation of its own sacrosanct advice to developing countries to open themselves to the global market.

U.S. is powerful country in the global level; it controls a quarter of the world's productive resources. U.S. is not nations where norms of real politick consciously respected among political elites, so the logic of power politics does not provide concrete explanations of how aggressive primacy rationalised in the policy-making process. U.S. could have showed its diplomacy in its efforts to influence Saddam to withdraw his aggression from Kuwait. However, the influence of power brought egotism to U.S. government when dealing with Iraq. Saddam Hussein in Iraq was regarded as a paper-pushing bureaucrat with a handy preference for brutality. He believed his army, which had fought off Iran for eight years, was capable of inflicting such losses on the U.S. military that its people would not tolerate. U.S. aggressively went to Kuwait and deconstructed the Iraqis air defence system within hours of invasion (Murray and Robert, 2003). The U.S. administration placed sanctions to prevent Iraq from rebuilding its military infrastructure and isolate the nation economically from the rest of the world. The Bush strategy was to attack perceived enemies first, and Saddam Hussein was marked as the number one enemy to U.S. government. In many ways, Iraq was the most secular country in the region, and was not involved in the September 11 attack on U.S. The attack on Iraq was to show the rest of the world that U.S. would not sit by and watch its currency decimated by Saddam's actions. The Bush Administration believed that Iraq was an eminent danger to the Middle East region because there had been disputes between them for several years.

The disappearance of Saddam's chemical and biological weapons, remain an issue of controversy to the rest of the world. Critics of the Bush Administration then claimed that Bush exaggerated the evidence for Iraqi ongoing chemical and biological weapon programme, and that the absence of the weapons demonstrated the Bush Administration's deception in the months leading to the war. The administration quickly defended its actions towards the war, although they admitted that a major intelligence failure occurred. They supported their views before the war by arguing the reason why Saddam continued his aggression tactics towards Iran, in the time leading up to the war, if he was not in possession of such Saddam and WMD (Pitt, 2002). Again, they pointed out that Saddam took pains to convince other nations of the world, that Iraq possessed a large arsenal of these destructive weapons. Now, we can see clearly that U.S. invasion of Iraq was a big mistake to their economy and security.

Thousands of soldiers returned from the war with severe mental illnesses and significant fractions which will be chronic afflictions (McCutcheon, 2006). U.S. government took a strategic move by setting-up a Central Bank to help rebuild the huge cost of the war. The lesson U.S. learnt in the war with Iraq was the failure of institutions such as U.N. and U.S. Congress to provide adequate checks and balances. The creation of U.N. after World War II was to prevent armed aggression but it failed in preventing the U.S. attack on Iraq. According to the U.N. Charter, U.S. are only entitled to take up arms in self-defence, or if the Security Council permits force. However, U.S. exercised their power on Iraq out of its own interests while ignoring U.N. and the great majority on the Security Council. It is clear that the Iraqi war was neither for self-defence, nor was authorised by the U.N. Security Council. The U.S. invasion amounted to an act of aggression and a violation of international law (Neff, 2005). U.S. did not respect international law and their action seems to promote that other countries may as well wage war on their enemies to fight for their interests, without U.S. authority. There is evidence that after the war with Iraq, the image of U.S. declined in Muslim countries.

Role on U.N. and the International Community

The progressive universalisation of the human rights norm carried out through a large number of legal conventions and promoted, however imperfectly, through substantial legal machinery and the central and irreplaceable role of the Security Council as the core of the international law enforcement system. Except in cases of self-defence, only the Security Council can decide whether or not it is lawful to go to war. The U.S.victory in Iraq has come at the price of re-legitimising wars of choice as an instrument of unilateral state policy and will usher in more determined efforts by many countries to acquire weapons of mass destruction, since nothing else is capable of deterring external attack posed a challenge of heroic proportions to the U.N. Since 9/11 the USA, with its unrivalled military power, has reasserted its dominant function in international protection by increasing attention to protracted crises and failed states considered bastions of terrorism (Roth, 2004).

U.S. developed a common strategy against Saddam Hussein's regime in Iraq that called for action based on a worst-case scenario involving threats of weapons of mass destruction (WMD), and a best-case scenario if rapid intervention would occur. U.S. along with coalition partners, disapproved of the political position and apparent lack of support from the U.N. Security Council. The USA based its intervention on a country's right to self-defence, and not its right, or obligation, to intervene elsewhere to protect people others than their own. In addition, the intervention was first considered a war to remove a hostile regime. A major humanitarian component to the war was considered unlikely (Allawi, 2007). This unilateral action began a world-wide unilateralism versus multilateralism policy debate that exists to this day. The U.S. since 9/11 has gone down the route of unilateral intervention on the basis of 'self-defence' and in the case of Iraq has extended this concept by placing humanitarian as well as military operations under the single command of the Defence Department. As the world community entered the twenty-first century it faced the reality that more people were being killed by their own countrymen than by outside forces.

The outmoded language of the 1945 U.N. Charter primarily addresses cross-border wars, but is clearly ineffectual in dealing with the complicated politically driven internal conflicts and genocide that now dominate the list of human-induced disasters. At the core of debate and dispute is the U.N. Charter's Article 2, which does not authorise the U.N. to intervene in matters which are essentially within the domestic jurisdiction of any nation-state (Ahram, 2002). Demands by the international community to 'do something' to protect a vulnerable population from serious harm from internal state-state war and engagement have led to divisiveness among U.N. member states. The office of Secretary General offers considerable prestige and has provided several incumbents, including Kofi Annan, with genuine influence over international relations. Annan's early leadership on human rights, and developing the framework for enhanced world security and global economic growth was extremely important. But the U.N.'s involvement in Iraq has brought Annan much grief, through the death of fellow workers in Baghdad, bitter divisions among member countries on how best to contain former President Saddam Hussein and the findings of Volcker Inquiry on the Oil for Food Programme that were extremely critical of U.N. management. For many, the crisis over Iraq in 2002 and 2003, then the deadlock in the Security Council, and the outcomes that followed, were a profound letdown, precipitating the U.N.'s broader crisis of trust. James Cockayne, an Australian scholar very familiar with the dramatic play, says: The crisis in Iraq is, by many reckonings, evidence of a transformative disintegration of an existing U.N.- centred world order. A Hobbesian race for security replaces a growing global interdependence. Maybe the central transformation in the Council since its participation in Iraq has been a increase in ambition without an equivalent growth in capacity to execute decisions (Malone, 2006).

The Security Council repeatedly faced toughened calls from the U.S., U.K. and some others to enforce its own previous resolutions or become irrelevant to the fast moving sequence of military action. Yet in the meantime, polls consistently showed worldwide anti-war opinion to be deep, broad and strengthening. Indeed the gap between opinion around the world and the voting equation in the Security Council in New York recalled the cynicism captured in Soviet dissident Alexander Solzhenitsyn's remark that at the U.N., the people of the world are served up to the designs of governments. Time was when those threatening to go to war had to prove their case beyond reasonable doubt. And compliance with Security Council resolutions was demanded of Iraq, those impatient to wage war insisted on freedom of action from the very same front of international authority. Democrats and Republicans updated their factual beliefs as conditions changed, but translated the same factual beliefs quite differently. Democrats consistently interpreted a given level of troop casualties as higher than Republicans did. Whereas almost all Democrats interpreted the failure to find WMD in Iraq as evidence that they never existed, many Republicans inferred that Iraq had moved, demolished, or hidden the weapons (Suzanne, 2008). Because most of the emerging evidence changed in a way that reinforced existing opinions for Democrats and challenged them for Republicans, Democrats used interpretations to facilitate, and Republicans to resist, opinion updating. Both the circumstances of the warfare and the panel data serve our research goals well. The invasion produced increasing intense partisan acrimony, with potential to induce partisan responses to new data. At the same time, two developments- the rise in troop casualties and the bankruptcy to find WMD- received wide news coverage throughout the period under survey. The media presented massive amounts of information and comment on both subjects, ensuring their salience to most U.Ss. With regard to the data, and unlike cross-sectional national survey data gathered up during this period, the panels track opinion change and constancy. They offer a singular chance to compare the mental operations of different partisan groups as they observed the same events unfold. More generally, citizens' responses to this highly partisan issue provide a window into the mental processes of polarised politics (Gaines, 2007).

On August 6, 1990, the U.N. Security Council passed Resolution 661, immediately implementing economic sanctions as a means of countering Iraq's invasion of Kuwait just four days prior. While it would eventually take a U.S.'s-led military effort to remove Hussein's army from Kuwait, the end of the First Gulf War. But the military defeat of Iraq did not end the sanctions programme that was targeted at the country (O'Driscoll, 2008). The chaos created by the invasion and the instability of Iraq suffers today calls for the need to defend arguments regarding the illegality and immorality of the invasion. Extending beyond Resolution 661, the Security Council passed resolutions 687 and 688 in early April of 1991, which outlined additional U.N. demands upon Hussein's government regarding weapons inspections, reparations to Kuwait, and the leader's repression of Iraqi citizens during the post-war period. Though the sanctions programme would be further modified over the years, these key 1991 resolutions inaugurated a 13-year period of sanctions that would last until the fall of Hussein's government during a second U.S. led invasion in 2003. Fulfilling the requirements of the April 1991 resolutions, especially those which dealt with WMDs and weapons inspections, became the official focus of the UNSC. But while Hussein played games with U.N. weapons inspectors over the years, U.S. administrations continued to express what they interpreted as the broader issue: the need for regime change in Iraq. To be sure, every U.S. presidential administration since 1990 expressed this goal as justification for their wilful support of the Iraq sanctions programme. U.S. leaders made clear to the international community their justification for the continuation of the sanctions programme. For example, on May 20, 1991, shortly after the end of the First Gulf War, George H.W. Bush outlined his administrations policy toward the sanctions program in Iraq. "At this crossroads, his position does not desire to lift these sanctions as long as Saddam Hussein is in power." Under Bill Clinton, the U.S. government emphasised the same insurance, although Clinton occasionally tried to draw the distinction that U.S. support for the sanctions programme was more due to Hussein's failure to comply with U.N. demands. However, on March 26, 1997, Madeleine Albright put Clinton's policy in line with that of his forerunner. In her first major foreign policy address as Secretary of State, she said: "We do not concur with the nations who argue that if Iraq complies with its obligations concerning weapons of mass destruction, sanctions should be lifted" (Dobbs, 2000). During George W. Bush's first administration and nearly a year prior to the second U.S. led invasion, Secretary of State Colin Powell highlighted the U.S.' commitment to the long-term goal of applying sanctions to remove Hussein from power: "Sanctions and the force per unit area of sanctions are part of a strategy of government change, backing for the opponent, and reviewing additional options that might be available of a unilateral or multilateral nature."

With the removal of the sanctions programme in 2003, it is now important to begin assessing the plan in the luminosity of this primary goal that was continually shown by U.S. presidential administrations since 1990. But as uncontroversial as this suggestion may seem, many have refrained from evaluating the sanctions programme in terms of this goal because it was never an official, U.N. endorsed requirement for the removal of sanctions (Al-Araji, 2001). However, with the second invasion of Iraq and subsequent removal of Hussein now in the past, an assessment of the sanctions programme in terms of all the consistently highlighted goals is essential for two principal reasons: first, in order to craft an objective evaluation of the Iraq sanctions programme as a whole; and second, for the purpose of engendering a fuller and more nuanced understanding of economic sanctions as a puppet of foreign policy.

Because of the sanctions, the economic cycle is halted, paralysing vital services. Inflation has raised an unprecedented thousand-fold. The fabric of society has been torn apart. Things that never used to happen-or were unusual-have become common. The suicide rate, especially among middle-aged men and women has become alarming. In the southern city of Basra, a father recently committed suicide by poisoning himself and his wife and all his children because he could not feed them. Organised crime such as daylight robbery and kidnapping for ransom is another new phenomenon. Prostitution is endemic. In Baghdad a man was stabbed to death and his belongings stolen from him, even his finger rings, while people watched (Roth, 2005). Throughout Baghdad and other places, people believe that organised crime is carried out largely by the security forces themselves. The sanctions and associated hardship have had an alarming effect on crime-suicide, prostitution, robbery and kidnapping. People are now finding themselves in such a difficult situation that they have no choice but to sell parts of their bodies too. There is money to be made by international racketeers, these issues came out in Sweden recently. The education system is collapsing. Schools lack basic requirements- books, blackboards, tables. Pencils were banned along with a hundred other items from the list of proposed educational purchases because they were thought to be for (military) 'dual use'. Children are leaving school on a large scale and joining the workforce. Many schools have become places for military training or weapon storage (Salman, 2000).

The economic sanctions have brought real misery and death to the people of Iraq. Children under five are dying at the rate of one child every ten minutes. The discrimination policy of the regime has also worsened the situation. For Saddam Hussein, Baghdad or even just part of Baghdad is his concern. He has no interest in the population living in the towns and cities south of Baghdad and of course the Kurdish areas. Saddam hates them for the position they took against him during the uprising in March 1991. In fact, almost all the factories there were dismantled and either moved north or used for spare parts. The U.S. led occupation of Iraq and a plan for a long-term military presence in the country is expected to cost the U.S. more than a trillion dollars. Iraq experienced years of turmoil under Saddam Hussein resulting in economic mismanagement, a war with Iran and U.N., imposed sanctions. After four years of U.S. occupation, Iraq suffers from extreme unemployment and poverty, with over four million internally and externally displaced refugees. The country's infrastructure is in ruins and U.S. reconstruction plans have been mired in fraud, mismanagement and incompetence. Regarding chemical weapons, UNSCOM discovered that Iraqi nerve agents had lost most of their lethality as early as 1991. Operations Desert Storm and Desert Fox, and U.N. inspections and sanctions effectively destroyed Iraq's large scale chemical weapon production capabilities. For both reasons, it appears that thereafter Iraq focused on preserving a latent, dual-use capability, rather than on weapons production. And surveillance evidence reveal that the regime is rebuilding facilities that it had used to produce chemical and biological weapons. U.S. policy after the Gulf War supported the United Nations led weapons inspection regime and the economic sanctions imposed to encourage Iraq's compliance with that regime (Dale, 2008). Every chemical and biological weapon that Iraq has or makes is a direct violation of the truce that ended the Persian Gulf War in 1991. Yet, Saddam Hussein has chosen to build and keep these weapons despite international sanctions, U.N. demands, and isolation from the civilised world. The world has also tried economic sanctions and watched Iraq use billions of dollars in illegal oil revenues to fund more weapons purchases, rather than providing for the needs of the Iraqi people. The world has tried limited military strikes to destroy Iraq's weapons of mass destruction capabilities only to see them openly rebuilt, while the regime again denies they even exist (Cirincione, 2004).

Under the economic collapse caused by the sanctions regime, young adults freshly trained and graduated find it extremely difficult to find employment. Thousands of young people who should be actively employed were idle. Unemployment among men in particular has become nothing short of critical. Increased levels of frustration, impatience, anger, and boredom are apparent, as is a widespread despair concerning the future (Briggs, 2013). The economic hardships place concomitant strains on maintaining social relationships: in a situation where the basic cost of living has increased many fold and where even a modest standard of living has become impossible to attain or sustain, it becomes difficult or even impossible to marry or remain within existing marriages. In the case of unemployment, thousands of professionals find themselves doing jobs that pay more than teaching, the civil service, or some other appropriate intellectual activity. Civil servants and university professors took another jobs. Medical doctors and engineers guarded the U.N. premises in Baghdad. Often underreported are the consequences of the sanctions for the social structure. Children were perhaps the most conspicuously hit by sanctions. U.N. sanctions were imposed in Iraq and the result was the tragic dealth of half a million children. Bombing in Iraq was a daily affair (Pilger, 2000). Many were forced to become breadwinners, with a corresponding school drop-out rate of some 20-30 per cent and this in a country long recognised throughout the Arab and wider world as having very high educational standards through the university level. Not only were many children expected to put food on the table and contribute to the well-being of the family, some were even forced into street crime previously unknown in Baghdad and other Iraqi cities. Child begging became commonplace. The long-term damage of this will become apparent in the years to come, as street children, plus many rural children, grow up without the benefits of a basic education or a strong family and extended family environment. Unchecked, illiteracy rates and other educational deficiencies increased, thereby having a negative impact both on family well-being and the country's productivity.

The various changes ultimately threaten the social order throughout much of Iraq and have weakened the prime importance normally accorded to the well-being of children. Sanctions have bitten deeply into the fabric of Iraqi society and norms, greatly straining traditional Iraqi and Islamic family values (Halliday, 1999). Divorce rates soared up. Many single-parent homes-mothers struggled alone, men unable to cope simply walked away from their responsibilities, others forced to flee overseas for employment. The sale of homes, furniture, personal belongings, and books for survival became common. Among the very poor, even prostitution is resorted to in order to put food on the table. The devaluation of the dinar has wiped out the savings and earnings of professionals and wage earners alike. In 1990, one dinar purchased three U.S. dollars. Within a couple of years after sanctions came into power, it took 1,500 dinars to purchase one dollar. This destroyed the buying power of the average family and has put normal consumer goods beyond reach of most Iraqis. It also excluded fresh meat, vegetables, and fruit from the family table. One tragic spinoff of this situation was the growth of corruption, previously uncommon. Precise figures were never known, especially since significant numbers have exited illegally, but it was estimated that over two million Iraqi professionals were working abroad. These men and women were the driving force behind intellectual endeavour, technological growth and change, and an educational system that for many years was of extraordinarily high calibre. They were also relatively high income earners in a middle and professional class now vastly reduced. Again, the negative implications may be most acutely felt in the long term with Iraq's diminishing ability to compete in regional and world technology change, in world markets, and in scientific pursuits and advancement. Not only did the loss of expertise impede Iraq's ability to recover economically and technologically, but their departure ripped families apart, leaving single-parent inadequacies that have contributed further to the social damage sanctions have created. Another negative, though less recognised, impact of the sanctions regime had been a reduction in the increasingly prominent role that women were beginning to play in the conservative, society. Their participation in the economy levels was significantly boosted during the Iran-Iraq war when new professional opportunities, including teaching, civil service functions, policing, and bus drives, became available for women.Women have always suffered from the chaos, lawlessness and lack of security and have been subject to harassment and abductions, as well as sexual abuse and rape (Al-Ali, 2005).

Women's capacity to continue to work as middle- and senior-level civil servants is undermined by monthly income levels equal to perhaps one-tenth of the price of a pair of shoes. In other words, for many women it became too expensive to go out to work, and many have been obliged to give up their suddenly low-paying civil service jobs in order to work at menial but better paid occupations (Enloe, 2004). Some were able to continue as civil servants because their families are able to subsidize their transportation and work-related expenditures. They did this in order to stay in touch with the relative sophistication of civil service functions and for the possibility of access to ideas and up-to-date reading material. Other less fortunate professional women were obliged to work in sweatshops as part of a family effort to put food on the table. Young professional women were obliged to abandon hopes of marriage and a family of their own in order to support existing family members. Thus, many advances that women in Iraq had made in previous decades were set back and opportunities were lost, in many cases forever. The education system of Iraq had taken a beating as well.

The lack of basic child healthcare, lack of school transportation, and the often pitiful state of classrooms, not to mention the lack of books and other supplies, contribute to low attendance rates among students (Susskind, 2007). The state of disrepair of some 8,000 schools and the sad state into which the learning environment in general had fallen served only to exacerbate the situation. Even more crucial was the effect on the teaching profession. It had been estimated that thousands of registered teachers have left the profession due to the intolerable conditions teachers or lecturers face daily in addition to the need to earn more. The result of all this had been the sharp increase in drop-out rates at the primary and secondary levels. It is not surprising that illiteracy rates grew accordingly. Iraq is the only instance of a sustained increase in mortality outside or war, famine or genocide in a population of more than two million in the past two hundred years. An environmental and medical catastrophe with a four billion year half-life-one for which Iraq, its hospitals and infrastructure eviscerated by sanctions, is now completely unprepared (Salman, 2000). Hundreds of thousands of elderly people have died as well. The number of cases of diseases related to cancer has risen sharply- which no one has mentioned so far today- as a result of depleted uranium bombshells used by the U.S. during the Gulf War. Malaria and typhoid have reappeared in a large part of the country. Hospitals lack basic medicine and electricity -which is needed to refrigerate the vaccine against deadly polio and diphtheria. Much of the infrastructure has still not been repaired since its devastation in 1991, including many of the water treatment facilities contaminated by the sewage system. Electricity cut-off time can be more than sixteen hours a day. In Baghdad, it is officially six hours and in other cities fourteen hours a day but the reality is different. So imagine those sixteen hours each day, in the summer time when the temperature rises above 48°C. They receive a smaller share in the distribution of food and medicine; and sometimes the ration coupon is used as a weapon of punishment, either reduced or even withheld from those not 'with' the government. Few may now believe that sanctions effectively 'contain' Saddam Hussein's weapons development programme with minimal human suffering.

Iraqi and Mesopotamian culture also suffered under the sanctions regime. The destruction of antiquities during the Gulf War and the neglect of sites since have led to looting and sale of invaluable items overseas. Iraq is a delicate political entity generated in the aftermath of World War I throughout the involuntary union of ethnically and religiously various portions of the previous Ottoman Empire (Terrill, 2003).Within the school system, many national projects aimed at assisting in the development of cultural maturity were cancelled due to the lack of funds or facilities for their implementation, such as the major National Faith Campaign for the development of Islamic education. This placed great impediments on Iraq's ability to develop its appreciation for foreign cultures as well as its ability to nurture its own.

VII. Human Rights Violations due to the 2003 War

Drawing inferences from casualty data is a risky exercise. In wars, especially those involving powerful armed forces and long durations, large numbers of people may be killed or wounded, including civilians. The belief that U.S. forces regularly violate the norm of non-combatant immunity- the notion that civilians should not be targeted or disproportionately harmed during the war- has been widely held since the outset of the Iraq conflict. The well-documented abuse of Iraqi detainees by U.S. troops at Abu Ghraib and the failure of U.S. authorities to live up their international legal obligations to provide basic security during formal occupation period. Indeed, a growing chorus of commentators contends that the U.S. military has engaged in systematic civilian victimisation in Iraq (Kahl, 2007). There are numerous estimates of civilian casualties in Iraq, all of which are problematic. Iraq Body Council (IBC), a non-profit organisation that derives estimates from English- language and translated media sources, suggests that as many as 7,393 civilians may have been killed during major combat. Other estimate by the Project on Defence Alternatives, which corroborated media reports with hospitals and burial records and filtered out likely combatant fatalities, suggests that 3,230-4,327 Iraqi civilians were killed. Even if, by the end of 2006, the actual number of Iraqi civilian deaths was probably closer to 70,000 than 600,000, no one should trivialize the horrific carnage in Iraq. The overall scale of civilian deaths is an indictment of the U.S. government's failure to adequately plan for post-invasion contingencies, which allowed chaos to emerge in the wake of regime change. The number of deaths attributed to U.S. forces and crossfire also provides evidence that troops have sometimes engaged in activities that put Iraqi civilians at high risk of death and injury (Kahl, 2007).

Although some might argue that improvements in precision-guided munitions account for the majority of this historical differences, many of the non-combatants at destroying enemy morale, not incidental by products of crude targeting and guidance technologies. Given the nature of the conflict, the number of civilians killed in Iraq, however awful, is not sufficient to suggest systematic U.S. noncompliance with the norm of non-combatant immunity. On the contrary, compared with conflicts where civilians were directly targeted (Kahl, 2007). The abrupt crash of the U.S. invasion of Iraq's economic and social life was relatively limited. Civilian casualties were fewer than most humanitarian agencies had expected, and the nightmare predictions of millions of refugees fleeing the tide of war did not come true. The worst damage came later, inflicted by the application of a blinkered ideological approach. Supporters of the U.S. invasion that Paul Bremer, a conservative career diplomat who had earlier served as a ambassador at large for counterterrorism, was appointed as the head of the occupation administration, dubbed the Coalition Provisional Authority (CPA), and a team of twenty-five Iraqi political leaders who were prepared to cooperate with it were appointed to a body dubbed the Iraqi Governing Council. His solution about the Iraqi army- making some 400,000 armed and trained men unemployed- was a serious mistake. The move was justified at the time as part of a process of de-Ba'athification- the removal of all remnants of the regime of Saddam Hussein from Iraqi life (Fawn and Raymund, 2006).

The U.S. created police and armed forces lack credibility as Iraqi institutions: they are widely regarded as mere tools of the occupier. It is unemployment and poverty that drive men to join them, not belief, although this wins them no sympathy from the resistance groups, which attack recruits pitilessly. Their primary goal is to survive from one day to the next. As a result, people complain of a law-and-order situation that is much worse than it was under Saddam's regime. Even though Saddam Hussein was a brutal dictator, but he was contained and his regional and global influence was weakening. It is good that he is no longer in power, but the sad truth is that the living situation and human rights conditions for most Iraqis is not much better and for some groups like Christians and women conditions have deteriorated (Repetto, 2010). Theft and burglary are common; the kidnapping of individuals by criminal gangs for ransom by their families, practically unknown before the U.S. invasion, is now a common occurrence; all middle class families have either experienced it for themselves or have friend who have. The streets have become no-go-areas at night for women in Baghdad and the other central Iraqi cities.

A bench mark was made recently when the World Health Organisation (WHO) identified violence as a worldwide health problem. They define violence as the "intentional use of physical force or power, threatened or actual, against oneself, another individual, or against a group or community, that either results in or has a high likelihood of resulting in wound, death, psychological harm, mall development or deprivation" (Krug, 2002). This functions as a solid base definition. Both of these descriptions as initial reference points for our survey, i.e., they are not "theoretical models"; but rather, definitions with which to function as we move towards explanatory models. Placing these two definitions side-by-side in the same paragraph serves to highlight the core problem of the kinship between war and violence the connection between these two concepts, both of which prove to capture field realities. It matters theoretically that all war is violent, but not all violence is war.While the trend in anthropology to focus on violence as an overarching concept is appropriate (Aijmer and Abbink, 2000; Schmidt and Schroder, 2001; Stewart and Strathern 2002), it is significant that an equally clear focus on warfare as a concept that reflects a special slice of human lifespan is not sacrificed. There are two main reasons for this concern. Foremost, as omnipresent as violence is in both North America and globally, as a word or concept or symbol, it carries significantly different (not worse or better) emotive connotations of the word or concept or symbol war. Elizabeth Colson correctly identifies 'war'as a key symbol in North U.S. culture (Colson, 1992). Second, in the experience of those who have lived with it on a daily base in Iraq, the word 'war' resonates with interlocutors in ways different from 'violence'. To inquire how they are different and interconnected moves us to a more nuanced and global understanding of wildness and a more particular and meaningful understanding of warfare. The following section outlines an expanded concept of violence consisting of three conceptual constellations. Conceptual constellations are clusters of sufficiently similar juxtaposed ideas that when brought together create what anthropologist Richard Preston calls a 'feeling quality' that greatly enhances our perception without sacrificing too much precision of definition. The cluster of thoughts that are juxtaposed in this department add up from Pierre Bourdieu and Johan Galtung (Bourdieu, 1994 and Galtung, 1996). The three constellations include: direct or physical violence, structural or economic violence and cultural or symbolic violence. When Bourdieu and Galtung developed their ideas it appears that they did not mean to apply them as lenses to understand war. Bourdieu tends to emphasise processes of domination and hegemonic power and Galtung places greater stress on social organisations and their purpose in keeping order. For Bourdieu, a significant component of the point is to explain the inadequate distribution of cap; while Galtung is intent on realising the mysterious structure of public security. To interpret the war against Iraq, both of their violence models are applicable. Together they comprise a constellation of ideas that embody significant explanatory power. There are two reasons to expand the definition of violence. Foremost, people who experience suffering at the workforce of "invisible forces" understand that invisible force to be violence and identify it as such (Nordstrom, 2004). In this concur with Martin and Nordstrom's observation that expanded definitions of violence "have been useful in passing on a voice to systems of violence, no less powerful by virtue of their intangibility" (Nordstrom and Martin, 1992). Secondly, a minute understanding of violence often supports politically motivated decisions that try to mask harm inflicted upon civilian populations. By bracketing any violence that is not strictly an overt kind of physical force that injures and kills specific people, government policies that do great damage by cutting across a broad swath of social reality can be masked to such a degree that aspects of war can be made to look like pears.

In this portion of the analysis shall introduce each conceptual constellation and then utilise it to examine an aspect of the war against Iraq. Although begin with direct or physical violence, move to structural or economic violence, and finally examine examples of cultural or symbolic violence, the decree is not significant. It would be best to conceive of these three kinds of violence as mutually reinforcing and reciprocating processes. In concert, wherever we choose to commence the analysis, these three conceptual constellations constitute a common chord of violence (McCutcheon, 2006). As use them in what succeeds, each constellation serves as a "violence lens" through which we can examine a different proportion of warfare. Here postulate that to wage war requires the act of all three violence constellations. In other words, together they serve to determine the process and substance of war.

This constellation is primarily concerned with conveying the idea of violence mediated directly through force that is applied to persons in the singular or collective. It is the form of violence most narrow in scope but immediate in effect. Bourdieu understands this to be an aspect of overt violence: there is nothing hidden about it. And it is physical in the sense that it impacts directly (and sometimes via the destruction of property) on our corporeal bodies. This is true whether it is actualised through a knife blade entering a rib cage or a stealth bomber dropping a cluster bomb on a village. In either case the harm that is done to persons is immediate and visible. Its effects are generally seen and felt for decades in both scarred bodies and scorched earth (Webster, 1996). There is nothing euphemistic about it. And soldiers, who in war are responsible for deploying this form of violence, must go through extensive training to perpetrate it (Grossman, 1995) and many pay dearly for it both during and after the fact (Shay, 1994).

In the case of war against Iraq the direct or physical violence was evident throughout the war against Iraq. While many will recall the technologically enhanced displays of so-called "shock and awe" at the beginning and end of the war in 1991 and 2003, what was masked for the duration of the war was the constant nature of the direct or physical violence. A constant bombing campaign and a consequent effort by the Iraqis to target the airplanes doing the bombing were a permanent feature of the war. In between these high tides of direct or physical violence, there was a constant engagement of military force. The U.S. economy significantly larger than when it compared to the previous wars in Iraq, its consequences was also high. U.S. and British aircrafts dropped more than 1800 bombs and hit 450 targets. The cost to British tax-payers is more than 800 million. There is bombing almost every day: it is the largest Anglo-U.S. aerial campaign since the Second World War; yet it is mostly ignored by the U.S. and British media (Pilger, 2002) Aid workers recounted personal stories about the direct engagement of physical force. Carmen Pauls, who worked and lived in Baghdad for a non-governmental organisation at the time, recorded one such incident. "a plane dropped a bomb on the main road between Najaf, a city 170 kilometres south of Baghdad, and Monathera city. This highway is lined with homes and mechanics' shops. A second bomb fell near a grain storage silo. Fourteen civilians were killed and 18 wounded, including women and children and labourers on their way home from work" (Pauls, 1999). Later in her biweekly report she says that since her earlier report, "an additional 18 persons have been killed and 54 wounded in similar attacks". In one incident, air strikes hit shepherds in their pastures near Mosul, leaving 14 persons dead and 22 wounded. There is no dearth of direct empirical evidence that the bombing was taking place and that the Iraqi army was setting about to answer. U.N. officials consistently filed reports about their experience of being in the vicinity of the bombing. It is perhaps worth mentioning that the weapons being used were not so-called precision guided weapons systems. In February 2001, well before the invasion of Iraq started, they were cluster bombs. As William Arkin notes, commenting on this particular attempt, these are weapons "that possess no real aim point and that kill and wound innocent civilians for years to get" (Arkin, 2001).

Generally speaking, persons using the phrase "structural violence" are attempting to describe a situation wherein, to use Galtung's definition, "their actual somatic and mental realisations are below their potential realisations" (Galtung, 1969). Unlike direct or physical violence this conceptual constellation operates at arm's length. As global processes come to the fore, structural or economic violence is often mediated by economic mechanisms like trade policies and sanctions, promoting forceful, often unwanted, change in human collectives. The violence of these economic engines is often resisted and even transformed (Ferguson, 1990), but still, those who experience it, often in the so-called developing world, recognise it as violence. Social structures work hand-in-hand with economic processes to wreak havoc on civilian populations in war-zones. A narrow focus on "structural" violence is insufficient for capturing the contours of this form of violence. There is clear evidence that economic processes now dominate the global system of exchange, whether it is an exchange of material or information. By including explicitly the economic dimension in this constellation, a form of violence not all that new when thought of in terms of the ancient art of the siege, the central role these processes play in contemporary warfare in a global environment. In the case of Iraq, the combination of structures supporting economic processes led to very tangible impacts on the civilian population.

Since 2003, the basic infrastructure of the country has been destroyed by military operations. Several Iraqi cities have been severely destroyed; under the pretext of attacking "terrorists", while the result is massive killing of innocent civilians. In order to hide the size of these crimes, the occupation forces prevent humanitarian aid and journalists from entering these cities (Fisk, 2006). More than two-thirds of the population has no access to clean drinking water, and just 19 per cent have a functioning sewage system. The occupation forces have used, and are using, weapons that are banned by international law or widely considered unacceptable and inhumane, including cluster bombs, white phosphor, DU and napalm. International Humanitarian Law standards prohibit the use of weapons that do not distinguish between military targets and civilians, and inflict indiscriminate harm or unnecessary suffering. A thorough investigation is urgently needed to assess the full impact of these weapons on life in Iraq.

The Iraqi medical service was amongst the most developed in the region, according to the WHO report of March 2003. Since the occupation, a severe deterioration has occurred in this sector so that it cannot meet the needs of the population. The general effect of the health deterioration on the Iraqi population amounts to a serious violation of international humanitarian law (Mason, 2007). The Fourth Geneva Convention demands that an occupying power "ensures the effective operation of medical services, including hospitals and public health programmes, with special focus on preventing the spread of contagious diseases and epidemics, and allowing medical personnel to carry out their duties." The Iraqi Medical Association reports that 90 per cent of the hospitals in Iraq lack basic medical supplies, including equipment and drugs (Belder, 2007). In addition to the repeated attacks of the occupation forces, militias have been given free rein in the medical facilities, often dragging away patients for execution.

Meanwhile, a medical crisis stemming from continuing violence festers, despite efforts to rebuild the nation's healthcare system, reports the Canadian Medical Association Journal. "Under-five mortality rates (46 per 1000) and maternal mortality rates (84 per 1,00,000) are far higher than in neighbouring countries, and higher than they were before the invasion (WHO, 2000). One in eight deaths is violence-related. Roughly 38 per cent of pregnant women are anaemic. Diarrhoea and acute respiratory infections - further compounded by malnutrition - account for about two-thirds of deaths amongst the under-five population," says the report (Brunham *et.al.,* 2003). Two thousand physicians have been murdered since 2003, and 18,000 have fled—about half the pre-war total. The Iraqi Human Rights Ministry said October 13th "that at least 85,000 people had been killed by bombs, murders and fighting in 2004-08," numbers collected via death certificates issued by the Ministry of Health. Another 10,000 people are missing from that period, the most violent of the war. Death certificates could be issued by other local agencies, and the Ministry of Health was under the control of the followers of Moktada al Sadr, the Shia militant, until late 2007, so the numbers are partial at best. The ministry noted, moreover, that 15,000 unidentified bodies were found in those four years, and that "thousands of Iraqis killed since 2003 without being identified by their relatives were buried in special cemeteries called unidentified body cemeteries." Even before the war, only one-third of all deaths were reported to or by the Ministry of Health. Under the stress of war and sectarian politics, the portion of reported deaths would likely be considerably lower. Despite the fact that the U.N. did not countenance the war, especially those with active programmes in Iraq. Unofficially began internal planning for pre-conflict evacuation of expatriate staff and post-conflict recovery of services. There was concern that, given the already poor health situation in Iraq before the war, a major relief effort would be needed, requiring a coordinated effort of Iraqi nationals and to correct basic public health deficiencies, yet without significant combat-related civilian casualties (Burkle *et.al.*, 2005).

One of the greatest losses due to the invasion is Iraq's heritage. The U.S. and its allies have left Iraq's archaeological treasures without protection, exposing them to looters and art thieves, in a flagrant violation of their responsibilities under international law. The Iraqi Museum, one of the world's richest in artefacts, and the very rich Iraqi National Library, were looted as well as 14 other provincial museums and several libraries. The occupations forces have used archaeological sites as military bases as is the case of the city of Babylon, and have destroyed historic cities during military operations.

In its "Iraq Fact Sheet" of (28 March 2003) UNESCO wrote that, except for the 1991 sanction period, the education system in Iraq was one of the best in the region, with over 100 per cent Gross Enrolment Rate for primary schooling and high levels of literacy, both of men and women (Al-Khateeb *et.al.*, 2014). The higher education, especially the scientific and technological institutions, was of an international standard, staffed by high quality personnel. Due to the consequences of the invasion and occupation, the entire higher educational system is in a state of collapse. Attacks on universities, by the occupation troops or others, have driven away students from continuing their studies (Miller, 2013). On 27 July, 2007, UNICEF and the UNHCR issued a joint appeal warning that a generation of Iraqis could grow up uneducated and alienated. So far there is no sign of any improvement in this sector.

Economic reconstruction has been disastrously mishandled. Iraq's infrastructure had decayed since the late 1980s as a consequence of war and sanctions. During the U.S. led invasion and its aftermath, bombing and the movement of heavy tanks along streets fractured water and sewage pipes, already in state of poor maintenance; water supplies remain in a unreliable in many areas. Electricity is often available for twelve hours or less a day in Baghdad, and most of the country receives a supply of less than three hours (O'Hanlon *et.al.*, 2007). Insurgent attacks and the deterioration under Saddam of the supply system, which now necessitates large-scale repair programmes, were blamed, but this is no consolation to most Iraqis. They contrast the present state of the repair effort unfavourably with in 1991, when the old regime restored electricity supplies to pre-Gulf War levels in a matter of weeks. In the ten months before the invasion, Baghdad has electricity almost round the clock. The unreliability of the electricity supply has worsened the problem of fuel distribution. Power outages stop pumps from working, leading to lengthening queues of frustrated motorists at gas stations. In the country with the second largest oil reserves in the world, they may wait five hours to fill up their cars unless they can afford to go to a hawker, who will sell them gasoline for up to fifty times its official pump price. Those who can afford to have bought private generators that they can use whenever the electricity supply fails, but this has increased demand for gasoline, which would be better used earning export revenues.

The U.S. economy significantly larger than during any previous war or conflict and can more easily absorbs the costs today. Moreover, the resources in Iraq are not just being invested in bullets and bombs. They have to rebuild the schools, courts houses and other infrastructure as well as security forces so the country can thrive long after U.S. forces depart (Repetto, 2010). More than 4000 families have lost loved one serving in the army in Iraq. All too, often forgotten particularly in Bush administrations mishandling of veteran's affairs- are the tens of thousands, scared both physically and mentally by the war. Beyond the human costs, U.S. taxpayers are now spending about $12 billion a month for the war- all for a policy that still has no clear and realistic end. The Iraq war has resulted in broader strategic failures. When historians look back on 2003 to 2008 they will see a period when U.S. ability to shape and influence events around the world became severely constrained. Pbebe Marr is a senior fellow at the U.S. Institute of Peace; he says that the Bush administration wanted to believe that the insurgency in Iraq would be limited and that Washington could rapidly turn over the country's management to pro-U.S. Iraqi exiles. And also he emphasises that, occupation did bring some benefits- new political parties, a strong civil society, and a less dogmatic educational system- but these benefits did not. In Larry Diamond's view, he is a disillusioned participant in the reconstruction effort, have written books analysing what went wrong. As the book's titles indicate, both assign much perhaps too much, of the blame to U.S. policy. In his view be more important than the negatives. The collapse of public order in the immediate aftermath of the war devastated Iraq's infrastructure and opened the door to terrorists, feeding the insurgency and the chronic disorder that have stunted progress. For Diamond, the administration's worst sin was not going to war, but going so unprepared. Although he opposed the war, he believed in achieving the peace and signed on to serve as an advisor to the CPA (Marr, 2005). The infant mortality rate is nearly twice its pre-invasion level (Fawn and Raymund, 2006). The U.S. did not realise, moreover, the depth of the fault lines in Iraqi society- between Kurds and Arabs, Sunnis and Shiites, and the members' of different tribes and locals religious groups. Now because of the destruction of the old Iraqi society, for the first time in centuries, power is in the hands of the Iraqi Shiites'. The Bush administration has set out to spread democracy in Iraq and Middle East more generally. In the long run, democracy can prevail, but the process will not be easy. A free and fair election, moreover, is not the best first step toward democracy in a country that has no history or tradition of self-government. Without adequate preparations, elections simply allow people to vent their frustrations against the corruption and inadequacies of the incumbents and vote in the opposition, regardless of its characteristics. A better start would be concentrate on education, the emancipation of women, and the creation of economic opportunity. Next should come to a focus on implementing the rule of law, strengthening the independence of the courts, and building up the civil-society institutions necessary for democracy. Only then will free elections lead to a more democratic order. In this struggle today, the U.S. should remember the principles and policies that guided its responses to Cold War threat and accept that no single power, religion or ideology can conquer the world or remake it in its own image. The world is too diverse. Different races, cultures, religions, languages and histories require different paths to democracy and the free market. Societies in a globalised world will influence and affect one another (Yew, 2007).

Summary

There is no way in which the war in Iraq can be justified as ethical or even essential. Informed people across the world including scholars have been subjecting the Iraq war to scrutiny on several counts and their opinions are sharply divided. It was with the slogan "war on terror" that Bush ordered his armies into Iraq. Is it not ironic that since the war Iraq has turned into a safe haven and breeding ground for terrorists from all over the world? Resistance to U.S. troops have galvanised terrorists the world over to come together; a situation that would not have happened had it not been for the U.S. occupation of Iraq (Azarva 2009). In a region that is not used to or is even averse to representative governments there is the dilemma of having to establish a strong government at the centre to hold divisive groups together and that of 'making the world safe for democracy' by promoting representative institutions that would legitimise political power. Equally divided is the opinion on the legality of invading a sovereign nation with a stable government of its own.

Notes

1. Seymour M. Hersh U.S. Soldiers brutalized Iraqis. How far up does the responsibility go? http://www. newyorker.com/fact/content/?040510fa-gact. The 372nd's abuse of prisoners seemed almost routine—a *fact* of Army life ."The purpose of an Article 32 hearing is for us to engage witnesses and discover *facts*," Gary Myers, network, go to Strongbox at *http://* tnysbtbxsf356hiy http://www. newyorker.com/fact/content/?040510fa-gact.
2. The RAC (Research Advisory Committee on Gulf War) report updates *scientific* research published since the Committee's, a substantial impact on *scientific* and clinical thinking about *Gulf War* illness, on other health *problems* and mortality among *Gulf War* veterans. Available online at http://www.bu.edu/sph/2014/04/28/gulf-war-illness-new-report-lauds- treatment-research-confirms-toxic-causes/ accessed on 28.04.2014.
3. An article in *Iraq* Today on *22 September* 2003, Iraq Country Report April 2005 Country Information Policy and Unit, Immigration and Nationality Directorate Home Office, United Kingdom. Apr 1, 2005-Website north-east of the country, formed what after the 1991 *Gulf War*, economy, and the *government's access* to foreign exchange. 2003 estimated that *Iraq's* key reconstruction needs through *2007.* Available online at http://www.cpa-iraq.org/government/TAL.html accessed on 22.09.2007.
4. See Peter Liberman "War with Iraq is Not in America's National Interest," *New York Times* paid advertisement, Available online at *www.academia.edu.* Accessed on 26.09.2002.
5. Charles Krauthammer, "The Neoconservative Convergence," *Commentary* (July-August 2005), The Post-Cold-War era has seen a remarkable ideologi-

cal experiment. Available online at http://www.commentarymagazine.com/ article/ the-neoconservative-convergence/. Accessed on 07.08.2005.

6. For various interpretations of the Bush Doctrine, see John Lewis Gaddis, "Bush's Security Strategy," *Foreign Policy*, 133 (November/December 2002) 50-57; Andrew J. Bacevich, "Bush's Grand Strategy," U.S. Conservative accessed on 04.11.2002.
7. Melvyn P. Leffler, "Bush's Foreign Policy," *Foreign Policy* 144 (September/ October 2004); 22-28: John G. Ikenberry, "America's Imperial Ambition," *Foreign Affairs*, 81 September/October 2002); 44-60; Ivo H. Daalder and James M. Lindsay, *America Unbound: The Bush Revolution in Foreign Policy* (Washington, D.C.: Brookings Institution Press, 2003) and Stanely A. Renshon and Peter Suedfeld eds., *Understanding the Bush Doctrine: Psychology and Strategy in an Age of Terror* (New York: Routledge, 2007).
8. See George W. Bush, "Remarks at the 2002 Graduation Exercise of the U.S.Military Academy," West Point, New York, June 1, 2002 (www.whitehouse.gov/news/releases/2002/06/20020601-3.html).See *The National Security Strategy of the U.S.*, Washington, D.C., September 2002, Available online at www.whitehouse.gov/nsc/nss.html.
9. See more by *William Kristol* and *Robert Kagan*. speak vaguely of replacing Clinton's vacillation with a steady, adult *foreign* policy under Robert Dole. William Kristol and Robert Kagan, "Toward a Neo-Reaganite Foreign Policy," *Foreign Affairs* 75 (July/August 1996). Available online at *http://www.foreignaffairs.com/articles/52239/william-kristol-and-robert-kagan/toward-a-neo-reaganite-foreign-policy.* For additional information about the 1992 Defense Planning Guidance paper, see David Callahan, *Between Two Worlds: Realism, Idealism, and U.S. Foreign Policy After the Cold War* (New York: Harper Collins, 1994), pp. 90-94; Halper and Clarke, *America Alone*, pp. 145-146; and Patrick E. Tyler, "U.S. Strategy Plan Calls for Insuring No Rivals Develop, " *New York Times* (March 8, 1992).
10. On the differences between a hegemonic and balance-of-power order, see G. John Ikenberry ed., *America Unrivaled: The Future of the Balance of Power* ,Ithaca, New York: Cornell University Press, 2002).
11. During the Iran -Iraq War, Iran did in fact Iraq in a counteroffensive, but only after Iraq first invaded and occupied Iranian territory.
12. John J. Mearsheimer, "Hans Morgenthau and the Iraq War: Realism versus Neo- Conservatism," Available online at www.openDemocracy.net, accessed on 19.05.2005, p. 2.
13. Robert Kagan and William Kristol, "What to do about Iraq," in *The Iraq War Reader*, eds. Micah L. Sifry and Christopher Cerf (New York: Simon and Schuster, 2003), 247.
14. While the Bush administration has articulated a doctrine of pre-emption and attempted to cast the invasion of Iraq in terms of a preemptive war, perhaps in the vain attempt to acquire legal legitimacy as some international

lawyers argue that the right to self-defence allows states to strike first if they are facing an imminent threat, in actuality the U.S.launched a preventive war as the threat that Iraq posed was a distant one at best. For a good general discussion of the differences between preventive and pre-emptive war, see Dale C. Copeland, *The Origins of Major War* (Ithaca: Cornell University Press, 2000).

15. Richard Falk, "The New Bush Doctrine," *The Nation* (July 15, 2002). For an interesting account of how the neo-conservatives used the media to help create a general climate of fear and inflame public opinion.
16. See Halper and Clarke, *America Alone*, pp. 182-200, and Douglas Kellner, *From 9/11 to Terror War: The Dangers of the Bush Legacy* (Lanham, Md.: Rowman and Littlefield, 2003); and, more broadly, Stuart Croft, *Culture, Crisis, and America's War on Terror* (Cambridge: Cambridge University Press, 2006.
17. On the role that threat inflation played in selling the war to the U.S. people, see Chaim Kaufmann, "Threat Inflation and the Failure of the Marketplace of Ideas: The Selling of the Iraq War," *International Security* 29, no. 1 (Summer 2004):5-48.
18. Additionally, see Jon Western, "The War over Iraq: Selling War to the U.S. Public," *Security Studies* 14 (2004/2005) and A. Trevor Thrall, "A Bear in the Woods? Threat Framing and the Marketplace of Values," *Security Studies* 16 (2007).
19. See. Overview of America's National Security Strategy. The White House. USA Freedom Corps. Faith-Based and Community Initiatives Office of Management and Budget.georgebush-whitehouse.archives.gov.
20. *The National Security Strategy of the U.S.*, Washington, D.C., September 2002. Available online at www.whitehouse.gov/nsc/nss.html accessed on 14.7.2013.
21. See Prevent our enemies from Threatening Us, Our Allies and Our Friends with Weapons of mass Destruction, georgebush-whitehouse.archives.gov. *The National Security Strategy of the U.S.*, Washington, D.C., September 2002. Available online at www.whitehouse.gov/nsc/nss.html accessed on 4.8.2014.
22. Nipunika Lecamwasam (2013) June 6. 2003 Iraq Invasion: A Just War or Just War. An Evaluation of US Conduct within the framework on Just War Theory. E-international Relations Students. The world's leading website for students and scholars of international students. Available online at http:/ /www.e-ir.info/2013/06/06/iraq-invasion-a-just-war-or-just-a-war/ accessed on 03.08.2014.

4

Human Rights Issues in Post-Saddam Era

Introduction

The earlier periods of Iraqi history, had constituted a marked and vital removal especially in the political and social landscape of the Iraqi state under the Ba'athist rule, particularly Saddam's rule. The traces of earlier tendencies and policies can be observed in the Saddam's era. Although to argue that these traces in some way are to be held responsible for the development of Saddam's political order is at best a gross generalisation. The country, Iraq, was the exclusive creation of the man who had efficiently ruled for almost thirty-five years. He builds up ultimately, refines an unyielding police state that was defined almost exclusively by its persistent and barbaric agencies of intimidation. Such oppression was not physical, but intellectual. Ever since the birth of the monarchical state of Iraq in 1921, the elementary values, rights and beliefs were not entirely vanquished to the dictates of a long-winded hero-president. Unlike earlier authoritarian periods in Iraq, and much like the Soviet Union under Stalin, Saddam's Iraq was a country which was held hostage to the whim's and fancies of one all-pervading oppressor. The fledging political order would come under a concerted two-pronged assault that in the summer and fall of 2004 would create the worst conditions of instability since the fall of Saddam (Dawisha, 2009). That stability with the transfer of sovereignty to the people of Iraq was the blissful hope of the long suffering population and they had their hopes cruelly dashed almost immediately.

IV. Post-Saddam Iraq and Governmental Mechanism

Human rights in post-invasion Iraq have been the subject of concerns and controversies since the 2003 invasion. The power transition from Saddam to his successor was expected to be almost certainly hectic, but there was confusion as to whether the transition would ensue from a coup, assassination, insurrection, lucky bomb, or natural causes.[1] At the same time Iraq had no tradition of peaceful regime change, and civil society to be shattered. The substitution could have come either from inside Saddam's current power base or outside it (Davis, 2005). For ending Hussein's regime many Iraqis had welcomed U.S. troops as liberators and as the price, were willing to accept some hardship from the devastation of the invasion, to start a new era of freedom. Iraqis believed that that the U.S. would go quickly to fix the spoiled infrastructure, to re-establish basic services, and to capture Hussein.[2] They also anticipated that Bush would stand by his pre-war assurance to turn the country over to the Iraqis.

After the overthrow of Saddam Hussein's regime by the invasion, the U.S. administrators were handicapped by their lack of a post-war plan for occupation and stabilisation. There was no talk about democracy or a quick transfer of power to Iraqis during the early months of the occupation, in its place, the U.S. occupying authorities used non-democratic means to rule Iraq (Karsh, 2002). Saddam's removal deferred at least two benefits for the region and for the U.S. First, any successor to Saddam would very likely be far more cautious. In the aftermath of the Islamic revolution of 1979, considering Ayatollah Khomeini a potential threat, Saddam made a pre-emptive attack on Iran rather than go to the negotiating table. In 1990, to avoid economic hardship Saddam attacked Kuwait rather than to focus on economic development. Nor have the repeated crises in Baghdad since then given any sign that Saddam had learned his lesson: he persists to bully, threaten and provoke. Although a successor to Saddam would possibly be a risk-taker, in Iraq's foreign policy, any alternate even one who shared Saddam's aims would most likely be far more cautious than Saddam is. The second focal point is that relation between Iraq and its neighbours and between Iraq and the U.S. Saddam was a revengeful man and he preserved his honour, which in turn entailed dominating any argument. He was willing to wait for years to take revenge on his distinguished enemies, killing and torturing those he considered to have slighted him or his family. With a similar motive in mind, Saddam tried to assassinate former President George Bush, the designer of the military coalition that defeated him. His sense of honour demanded that those who were ashamed or defeated him be punished, a view that made better relations with Kuwait, Saudi Arabia, or the U.S. unlikely. Saddam also played up domestic hostility to the U.S. and its regional allies, blaming them for the impoverishment and isolation of Iraq. Improving relations at that point undermined what little credibility he possessed amidst the Iraqi public. Saddam's replacement would have neither affected the personal nor political baggage that has arisen from 10 years of confrontation, making moving beyond the past and working with Iraq's former opponents easier. The U.S. and its allies shouldn't have continued to seek Saddam's removal, but should have prepared for trouble down the road, especially in the event that they succeeded incompletely as a leader from the same power base emerged.

Saddam's power base consists of military and paramilitary organisations, mainly, the Republican Guard, the Special Republican Guard, and the Popular Army-intelligence services, several key Sunni tribes and a smaller number of Shi'a tribes, non-tribal elements from or near Saddam's hometown of Tikrit, and Ba'th party hacks (Hamza and Jeff, 2001). This individual could have been one of Saddam's sons, a close family member, or an uneasy junta that represented various key elements of the regime. At any cost, Iraq's security and elite military forces were likely to be important actors (Sada, 2006). In 1995, CIA study contended that like Saddam, his successor would come from the same "political culture", sharing a commitment to Iraq's hegemony and hostility to the West (Baram, 2000). In March 2000 Assistant Secretary of State David Welch testified, "they have doubt that Iraq will take the sensible steps necessary to get hold of the lifting, or the deferral, of sanctions as long as Saddam Hussein stays in power."[3] Iraq under Saddam was always aggressive and dangerous; Washington increased its support for the Iraqi opposition (Byman, 1999 and Byman, *et.al.*, 1999). Fear, distressed about the Saddam regime's use of chemical weapons on its own people and against Iran, suggested the possible future use of other weapons of mass destruction (WMD) (Okawa, 2013). Like other possible leaders of Iraq, Saddam took risks to invade his neighbours, use WMD, repress communities at home, and destabilised his region.[4]

The removal of Saddam Hussein from power in Iraq, correctly, was one of the primary goals of the U.S. government for the Persian Gulf region. Saddam was a cunning and manipulative man: like the communist leader Josef Stalin, on whom Saddam modelled himself, and was truly a genius at doing evil. He was a man without a conscience. He was ruthless and brutal, and there was nothing he wouldn't do to achieve his own ends. He killed many times and ordered the brutal murders of hundreds of thousands of their own people. In Arabic, Saddam's name actually means 'The Crasher'. It is a word to use whenever there's an auto accident-when two cars crash into each other (Sada, 2006). Since the invasion of Kuwait in August 1990, the U.S. had viewed Saddam as a second Hitler: aggressive, adventurous, and peace in the region cannot be assured until he was gone. President George W. Bush, former President Bill Clinton, senior U.S. government officials from both parties, and leading congressional and media voices all called for Saddam's removal. Outside experts share this general opposition to Saddam. The true motives for the Bush administration's determination to overthrow Saddam Hussein remain mantled in obscurity. It was possible to speculate what these motives were, but impossible to identify them with certainty, because they were never discussed (Soros, 2004). Rend Rahim Francke, argues, "The problems that exist in Iraq are inherent in the regime of Saddam Hussein and will not go away as long as he is there. Moreover, the longer he is there, the more they will fester, and the more intractable they will become" (Puram, 2002). This focus on Saddam drove many aspects of U.S. policy toward Iraq, including sanctions, arms inspections, and support for the Iraqi opposition. A few years into the post-2003 era, it would have become that, while this formulation was most appropriate for the development of a stable and democratic Iraq, it actually had little chance of being implemented, given the reality of the country's historical experiences and its socio-political condition (Dawisha, 2009). Washington tied its support for lifting sanctions to Saddam's removal.

A post-Saddam regime which was less willing to embrace risks and less aggressive in its intentions was also less likely to seek biological and nuclear weapons. Most leaders would probably recognize the tremendous political and economic price that Iraq would have paid and has already paid for pursuing biological and nuclear weapons (Layne, 1991). A new regime, therefore, was expected to be willing to abandon the quest for these weapons if international pressure was high. If not, a key distinction is the possession of WMD particularly biological and nuclear weapons- as opposed to the use of WMD. A successor regime led by a more cautious individual than Saddam was also more likely to be satisfied with the defensive possession of WMD. Even possession, however, will lead to proliferation in the region and increase the chance of accidental use. Any future Iraqi regime would also face tough choices in its quest for balance between Iraqi unity, domestic peace, and human rights. Iraq's sense of national unity was never strong. Years of misrule, particularly the brutality of Saddam, has only worsened communal relations.

Removing Saddam, however, was not an answer for Iraq's miseries. The focus on Saddam overlooked the potential dangers that his successor could have posed and understated some fundamental problems that are inherent in Iraq's strategic position, which were to make the relationship between Iraq and its neighbours tense for years to come, regardless of its leader (Duelfer, 2004). Saddam's continuation in power also has some surprising benefits. First, Saddam's aggressiveness and absolute evil have created a strong and broad consensus that Iraq must be contained to some degree. Any successor to Saddam, even if cast from the same mould, would probably receive control over Iraq's purse strings from the U.N. warm welcome in most regional capitals, and the benefit of the doubt most generally. Second, Saddam's incompetence as a general matched only by his ineptitude as a diplomat. The U.S. and its allies were to continue to seek Saddam's removal, but prepared for trouble down the road, especially in the event that they succeed incompletely and a leader from the same power base emerges.

In addition to the slaughter of the Kurds and the Shi'a, Saddam also pitted tribe against tribe and decimated Iraqi civil society. Even though Saddam and his henchmen are removed from power, their bitter legacy will remain strong. Kurds in particular are highly suspicious of any regime in Baghdad that seeks more than nominal control over their activities. Irredentism has a long history in Iraq. Iraq's leadership before the 1958 revolution sought to persuade the British to include Kuwait in a confederation with Jordan and Iraq (Elsheshtawy, 2002). After Kuwait's independence in 1961, 'Abd al- Karim Qasim claimed Kuwait as part of Iraq- even though this declaration isolated Iraq in the Arab world- foreshadowing the claims Saddam would make almost 30 years later. Although a successor regime would not have Saddam's personal honour entangled in Iraq's claim on Kuwait, it would have possibly used this claim to shore up its flagging popularity or otherwise distract Iraqis from domestic struggle.

U.S. goals were for a unified, democratic, and federal Iraq that can sustain, govern, and defend itself and is an ally in the global war on Islamic militancy. Political disputes in Iraq played a significant role (Katzman, 2009). The formal political transition from the Saddam regime to representative government is largely completed, but tensions remain among the dominant Shiite Arabs, Sunni Arabs that have been displaced from their former perch in Iraqi politics, and the Kurds who fear renewed oppression of all of Iraq's Arabs. There are also substantial schisms within these communities.

After the fall of the regime, also known as Coalition Provisional Authority (CPA) or Occupation Period, the U.S. set up an occupation structure, believing that immediate sovereignty would favour established anti-Saddam factions and not necessarily produce democracy. The occupations with which most Iraqis were familiar were the British control of their country of the World War I and Israeli occupation of the West Bank and Gaza, then in its fourth decade (Dobbins, 2009). The Administration initially tasked Lt. Gen. Jay Garner (Rtd.) to direct reconstruction with a staff of U.S. government personnel to administer Iraq's ministries; they deployed in April 2003. He headed the Office of Reconstruction and Humanitarian Assistance (ORHA), under the Department of Defence (DOD), created by a January 20, 2003, Executive Order. Garner and aides began trying to establish a representative, successor regime by organising a meeting in Nassiriyah (April 15, 2003) of about 100 Iraqis of varying views and ethnicities. A subsequent meeting of over 250 notables, held in Baghdad April 26, 2003, agreed to hold a broader meeting one month later to name an interim administration. In May 2003, President Bush, reportedly seeking strong leadership in Iraq, named Ambassador L. Paul Bremer to replace Garner by heading a "Coalition Provisional Authority" (CPA). Bremer discontinued Garner's transition process and instead appointed (July 13, 2003) a non-sovereign Iraqi advisory body: the 25-member "Iraq Governing Council" (IGC) (Katzman, 2014). In September 2003, the IGC selected a 25-member "cabinet" to run the ministries, with roughly the same factional and ethnic balance of the IGC (a slight majority of Shiite Muslims). Although there were some Sunni figures in the CPA-led administration, many Sunnis resented the new power structure as overturning their prior dominance. Bremer and others maintain that recalling the former regime's military would have caused Shiites and Kurds to question the prospects for democracy.

Transitional Administrative Law

The Bush Administration initially made the end of U.S. occupation contingent on the completion of a new constitution and the holding of national elections for a new government, tasks expected to completed by late 2005. However, Grand Ayatollah Sistani and others agitated for early Iraqi sovereignty, contributing to the November 2003 U.S. announcement that sovereignty would returned to Iraq by June 30, 2004, and national elections were to be held by the end of 2005 (Katzman, 2004). That decision was incorporated into an interim constitution-the Transitional Administrative Law (TAL), drafted by the major factions and signed on March 8, 2004.[5] The TAL provided a roadmap for political transition, including (1) elections by January 31, 2005, for a 275-seat transitional National Assembly; (2) drafting of a permanent constitution by August 15, 2005, and put to a national referendum by October 15, 2005; and (3) national elections for a full-term government, by December 15, 2005. Any three provinces could veto the constitution by a two-thirds majority, which would trigger a redrafting and re-vote by October 15, 2006. The Kurds maintained their autonomy and militia force.

Interim Government or Allawi government as of the handover, the state of occupation ceased, and a U.S. Ambassador (John Negroponte) established U.S.-Iraq diplomatic relations for the first time since January 1991. A U.S. embassy opened on June 30, 2004; it is staffed with about 1,100 U.S. personnel.[6] The Ambassador is Christopher Hill, previously U.S. negotiator on North Korea nuclear issues, replacing Ryan Crocker, who took over from Zalmay Khalilzad (July 2005-April 2007). Reconstruction management and advising of Iraq's ministries were taken over by a State Department component called the "Iraq Reconstruction and Management Office" (IRMO) (Luft, 2005). With the expiration of that unit's authority in April 2007, it was renamed the "Iraq Transition Assistance Office" (ITAO). The ITAO's focus is promoting efficiency in Iraq's ministries and Iraq's management of the projects built with U.S. reconstruction funds. The authority has also expired for a separate DOD "Project Contracting Office (PCO)," under the Persian Gulf Division of the Army Corps of Engineers. It is training Iraqis to sustain its projects, which were mainly large infrastructure such as roads, power plants, and school renovations.

V. Post Invasion of Iraq and Humanitarian Issues

The removal of the regime of Saddam Hussein has presented the U.S. with a historic opportunity as large as anything that has happened in the Middle East since the fall of the Ottoman Empire and the entry of British troops into Iraq in 1917. Iraq is rich enough, developed enough, and has the human resources to become as great a force for democracy and economic reconstruction in the Arab and Muslim worlds as it has been a force for autocracy and destruction (Makiya, 2003). Unfortunately, much of the pre-war debate over Iraq that took place in Europe, in the Arab world, and even in the U.S., was a selfish one, centred on the threats to the West and its friends on the one hand and on the moral issues arising from U.S. hegemony on the other. The change that has occurred in U.S. policy toward Iraq is driven of course by strategic U.S. considerations since September 11, 2001. This change has been heartily welcomed in Iraqi opposition circles, even as it is feared and criticized in the rest of the Arab world. It is not the time to pay attention to these fears. They have and will come to nothing in the end, as they came to nothing during the Gulf War and the war in Afghanistan. The post-1991 divide inside Arab politics is still alive, for understandable reasons. But what might become of it in the months and years to come depends above all on the quality of the U.S.' commitment to securing a transition to and consolidation of democracy in Iraq.

The State Department's report on human rights for 2008, released February 25, 2009, said that: "Insurgent and extremist violence, coupled with weak government performance in upholding the rule of law, resulted in widespread and severe human rights abuses."[7] Similarly, the report on International Religious Freedom attributed restrictions on the free exercise of religion (by religious minorities) to "terrorists, extremists, and criminal gangs," while praising the Iraqi government for endorsing free exercise of religious rights. The status of Christians was one major issue was that the Christians of Mosul (Nineveh Province) have blamed the Kurds for threatening them to leave the province in order to strengthen the Kurdish position there (Lewis, 2003). In the run-up to the January 2009 provincial elections, about 1,000 Christian families reportedly fled the province in October 2008, although Iraqi officials report that most families returned by December 2008 and the issue appears to have faded in 2009. Some Iraqi Christians blamed the attacks on Al Qaeda in Iraq, which is still somewhat strong in Nineveh Province and associates Christians with the U.S. UNAMI (United Nations Assistance Mission for Iraq) coordinated humanitarian assistance to the Christians and others displaced. Previously, some human rights groups alleged Kurdish abuses against Christians and other minorities in the Nineveh Plain, close to the KRG controlled region. Kurdish leaders deny the allegations. The FY2008 Consolidated Appropriation earmarked $10 million in ESF from previous appropriations to assist the Nineveh plain Christians. A supplemental appropriation for 2008 and 2009 (P.L. 110-252) earmarked another $10 million for this purpose. Before the latest rounds of violence in Nineveh, more than 100,000 Christians had left Iraq since the fall of Saddam Hussein. Christian priests have been kidnapped and killed; the body of Chaldean Catholic archbishop Faraj Rahho was discovered in Mosul on March 13, 2008, two weeks after his reported kidnapping. However, some Christians in Baghdad have felt safe enough to celebrate Christmas at churches in Baghdad since 2007. An attack on the Yazidis in August 2007, which killed about 500 persons, appeared to reflect the precarious situation for Iraqi minorities. U.S. military forces do not specifically protect Christian sites at all times.

Though the Iraq is a resource-rich country, yet workers hardly earn enough to feed their families. Economic revival has been slow and sporadic, and working Iraqis are seeing little in the way of progress after the long occupation and withdrawal (West, 2003). Sectarian violence means that travel to work can be a risk in many cities, and indiscriminate roadside bombs continue to kill people just trying to work to maintain their families. For retirees, the situation is worse; Iraqis describe the social security system as not providing enough "to pay for the taxi to pick up the check." While the government claims that unemployment has dropped to 11 per cent, unofficially it is estimated to be as high as 30 per cent. Employment for people who can find work is often unstable. Wages and salaries are not keeping up with inflation, and so living standards, instead of improving, continue to deteriorate for the Iraqi working class. While actual wages vary according to sector, skill, and location, most workers are not earning a sufficient wage to afford a decent standard of living. The official poverty rate was 23 per cent in late 2011. Many industrial facilities in Iraq were destroyed as a result of the war, and targeted bombing seriously depleted the productive economic sector. The lack of clean drinking water and electricity supply affects millions daily. Suhad Ibraheem, who works for the Ministry of Transport in Baghdad, said, "he started work in 1985 when the work conditions were very good, but things deteriorated significantly between 1991 and 2003. There have been some improvements since then, but salaries do not keep pace with inflation, especially affecting food, energy, housing, and transportation. And it is worse for many in the private sector." Unions report that the weakness of occupational safety and health laws and measures, along with the lack of labour inspection, leaves millions of workers at risk daily, especially in industrial facilities, where most workers have little or no safety equipment. Workplace accidents cause death and injury, and workers had exposed to hazardous materials while toiling for less than $1 an hour. Yet when they protest, unions still face the wrath of the courts. Sixteen workers in the Basra refining sector who organised a protest in October 2011 demanding worker rights were fined approximately $60,000 apiece for a work stoppage that lasted 17 hours, a harsh and draconian retaliation.

Iraq has suffered from internal violence resulting from the differences between the major political factions that have heightened the instability in the country. Throughout the war and related violence and instability, union groups have demanded change, only to see their efforts spurned (Fox, 2008). The right to real collective bargaining remains prohibited for most Iraqi workers. Its importance is manifest in cases where enterprises with no trade union representation are privatised and the ability to resist massive layoffs is considerably reduced. Unions say the proposed privatisation initiatives and deregulation in the major utility and transportation sectors, with a major port facilities being operated by Gulf companies, threaten to leave more Iraqi workers without employment and the country dependent on foreign ownership of crucial national interest. Underemployment meanwhile, was 43 per cent in rural areas and 21 per cent in urban areas in 2011, according to the government. With nearly one-fourth of the working population jobless, this means that roughly 55 per cent of the workforce was either out of work or working short-time.

Youth and rural unemployment remain huge causes of concern. More than 40 per cent of Iraq's population is younger than 15. According to a recent survey, 21 per cent of females and 23 per cent of males age 15-24 are unemployed; 33 per cent of youth who intend to migrate are looking for jobs. With the decline of agriculture, Iraqis are flocking to the cities, exacerbating unemployment. Women are even more economical disadvantaged. Across the country, only 14 per cent of all women are either working or actively seeking work, and of those, more than one in five is unemployed. Nine years on, the economy is dependent upon oil, which is not a labour-intensive industry. The government remains the largest employer, but corruption and political patronage are still major issues. Protests against corruption in management have become a frequent event over the last two years. Hashmeyya Muhsin Hussein, president of the Electrical Utility Workers Union in Basra, said, "With all the energy wealth Iraq has, we still cannot get a regular supply of electricity, and it is workers' families that suffer the most." Migrant workers, primarily from Asia, also are very vulnerable, facing high levels of exploitation. Given the lack of systematic inspection of work sites, it is difficult to estimate the amount of forced labour in Iraq (Clark, 2003). But anecdotal information suggests that migrant workers in the construction industry often work overtime without proper compensation. The only bright spot in this bleak economic picture, at least for private-sector workers, is Iraqi Kurdistan, but even that is dimming. Othman Sa'ad, president of the Construction Union in Sulaimaniya, said, "Since the fall of Saddam's regime in 2003, Kurdistan has established new work projects and the employment situation is better than in 2003. There are more opportunities in the private sector, and the trade unions have helped improve the terms and conditions of work. Working conditions have improved during the past two years, reflecting positively on the living conditions of workers. But the working conditions in the public sector are not as good; factories are closing, workers are being transferred, and the Kurdistan Regional Government is moving toward a more privatized economy."

Workers, meanwhile, are still subject to labour law from the Saddam Hussein era, and modifications affecting corporate law have removed trade union input into corporate decision-making. Most Iraqi workers hoped the fall of Saddam Hussein would enable them to recover their right to an independent union. In 1987, the regime reclassified most Iraqi workers, including those in large state enterprises, as civil servants, thus prohibiting them from forming unions and bargaining. Despite changes to much of Iraq's legislative structure, this decree remains in effect. And there is no indication as to where and when the rights of trade unions will be codified. Union leaders, with support from the international labour community, continue to press for worker rights, but neither U.S. nor Iraqi politicians have made this rights agenda a priority over the past nine years. Despite the Saddam-era labour decree, Iraq has seen a significant resurgence in trade union activity since the U.S. intervention. The country has a long and proud history of defiant trade unionism, as was manifest in its resistance to British imperial control decades ago. Unions have been formed in many sectors. They carry out official business, fight for improved terms and conditions of work, and campaign against corruption in the management of public companies. Trade union organisations across the country are striving for improvements despite the lack of a legal framework for their operation (Gilchrist, 2003). In 2011, Iraqi workers renewed protests about the poor public services and lack of employment. None of their demands have been met. In a major protest in 2011, Abdul Kareem Abdul Sada, vice-president of the General Federation of Workers' Councils and Unions in Iraq-Basra Branch, addressed the crowd: "We are demonstrating here to demand electricity, drinking water, essential services, and political reforms as the occupation has failed to do that. We are demonstrating for real democracy, social freedoms, and worker rights." Even though the protesters are increasingly met by armed security forces, workers and their unions are striking back against low wages, poor conditions, and dangerous work. Given the lack of bargaining rights, workers engage in mass protest activity, and even without legal status unions are finding ways to win some demands. Nine years after the fall of Saddam Hussein, workers are still struggling in Iraq-for decent jobs, for dignity, for security, for safety, for public services they once enjoyed, and for basic rights still denied them. But, they say, they will continue to call for a better environment for working people and for a better Iraq for all Iraqis.

Access to safe drinking water is a basic condition of good health and is also a human right (Stoltman, 1996). Unsafe drinking water can be a carrier of serious diseases such as cholera, typhoid, and diarrhoeal diseases such as amoebic and bacillary dysentery. Drinking water can also contaminated with chemical, biological and radiological contaminants with potentially harmful effects on human health. In addition to its association with diseases, access to drinking water is of great significance, especially in rural areas where children and women bear thc burden of carrying water often from great distances. The populations using improved drinking water sources are those who use any of the following types of water supply: piped water, public tap or standpipe, tube-well or borehole, protected well or spring, rainwater,

Following figure shows the main source of potable and consumable water based on population distribution, (Iraq, 2011).

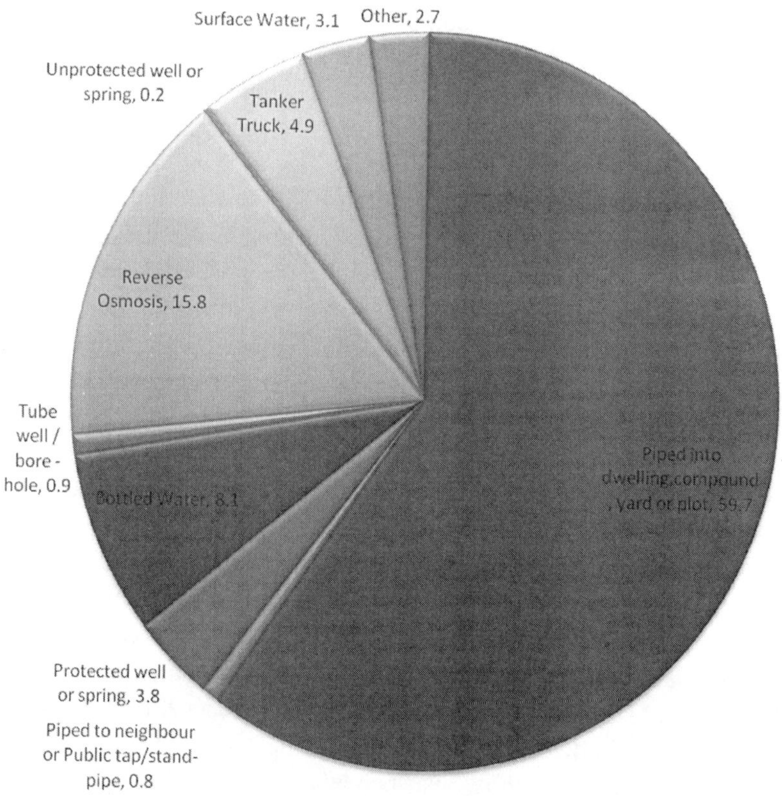

water treated with Reverse Osmosis, or bottled water (only if the water source used for cooking and hand washing is an improved one). About 89 per cent of the population has access to improved drinking water-97 per cent in urban areas and 76 per cent in rural areas. More than half of the population (53 per cent) has water piped into their dwellings. Water supply sources from the surface and tanker trucks are the main unimproved sources of unsafe drinking water, especially in rural areas (Furber, 2004). The sources of drinking water vary greatly by area of residence: about 47 per cent of the population uses drinking water piped into their dwellings or to the house courtyard in rural areas, while 67 per cent in urban areas have these water sources in urban areas.

Human rights abuses in Iraq are as bad as they were under Saddam Hussein if not worse, compared to occupation period, former Prime Minister Ayad Allawi has said. "People are doing the same as in Saddam's time and worse," Allawi said in an interview published in Britain on. "It is an appropriate comparison," Allawi told The Observer newspaper. "People are remembering the days of Saddam. These were the precise reasons that we fought Saddam and now we are seeing the same things" (Stockman, 2005). Allawi's comments come as Hussein's trial was all set to resume in Baghdad. The remarks also follow the discovery of an Iraqi government facility holding 170 prisoners, including some showing signs of torture. "They are hearing about secret police, secret bunkers where people are being interrogated," said Allawi, who was Iraq's first prime minister of the post-Saddam Hussein era. Allawi, a secular Shiite and former Ba'athist, is standing in parliamentary elections scheduled for December 15. He failed to win January's election, which brought Prime Minister Ibrahim Jaafari, an Islamist Shiite, to power. "A lot of Iraqis are being tortured or killed in the course of interrogations," Allawi said. "they are even witnessing Sharia courts based on Islamic law that are trying people and executing them." The Ministry of the Interior is at the heart of the matter," Allawi said. "I am not blaming the minister himself, but the rank and file are behind the secret dungeons and some of the executions that are taking place." Allawi warned that if no action was taken, "the disease infecting (the ministry) will become contagious and spread to all ministries and structures of Iraq's government." In a news conference, Interior Minister Bayan Jabr defended the prison facility, saying it held "the most criminal terrorists" and that "nobody was beheaded or killed."

Iraq's National Commission for Human Rights

On several occasions since the 1990s, powerful international actors have created NHRIs (National Human Rights Institutions) in post-conflict or post-transitional polities (Cardenas, 2005). On March 2004, the Iraqi Governing Council signed an Interim Constitution or Transitional Administrative Law. The Iraqi Transitional Government shall establish a National Commission for Human Rights for executing the commitments relative to the rights set forth in this Law and to examine complaints pertaining to violations of human rights. The Commission shall be established in accordance with the Paris Principles issued by the U.N. on the responsibilities of national institutions.[8] This Commission shall include an Office of the Ombudsman to inquire into complaints. This office shall have the power to investigate, on its own initiative or on the basis of a complaint submitted to it, any allegation that the conduct of the governmental authorities is arbitrary or contrary to law. Regardless of the Iraq war's controversial nature, the country's subsequent institutional reconfiguration demonstrates the ongoing currency of NHRIs as political innovations. Occupation authorities also created a Ministry of Human Rights, headed by a Kurd, Bakhtiyar Mustafa Amin. The U.N.'s Office of the High Commissioner for Human Rights has supported the Ministry's work by offering training workshops for state officials and assisting with a human rights documentation centre. Moreover, the Ministry has opened an office in Abu Ghurayb Prison, formed a special committee to investigate Iraqi prisons, and arranged human rights training. This limited activism is a slight improvement from 2003, when Ministry officials were denied access to prisoners held by the U.S. According to the Ministry's director general at the time, 'Ali al-Ka'bi, "the Coalition forces do not allow the ministry to do its job. He is trying to do his best, but they're not helping him get the information and he was angry. This will never satisfy the people in Iraq." Whether the National Commission, if established by the Iraqi Transitional Government, will fare any better than the Ministry remains to be seen, but regional experience suggests the importance of building NHRIs on solid domestic foundations. Much will depend on political developments in a country likely to be wracked by violence for the foreseeable future. Still, even a weak institution may further efforts at democratisation by shifting national discourse, legitimising human rights norms, and redefining the state's agenda. U.S. occupation forces violated the fundamentals of international human rights law in their treatment of prisoners. The simultaneous violation and affirmation of human rights, whether by state authorities or their occupation surrogates, can no longer be seen as inconsequential hypocrisies.

The creation of state human rights institutions in the Middle East has gone largely unnoticed. It began correcting this oversight by offering a preliminary survey of the 10 NHRIs that are planned or currently exist in the region (Monshipouri, 2009). To conclude, summarise four principal findings: the role of international pressure, the consequences of these institutions for civil society, the challenges of institutional design, and the discursive dynamics they engender. These conclusions should suggest future lines of inquiry for regional specialists. A prominent dynamic evident across the region is the importance of international pressure, which helps to explain why only some states have created these institutions. In fact, whole lands, institutional innovators in the Middle East have been motivated partly by international considerations. International pressure itself can be direct and targeted (as external actors do link relations to human rights conditions) or indirect and diffuse (as regional contagion leads neighbouring governments to worry about their reputations). The policy implications for international actors are therefore at least partly clear: in cases where state institution-building coincides with rising human rights violations, international actors should apply firm and specific pressure to assure that state hypocrisy produces at least some benefit for the victims of abuse. Only when international actors call on states to close the gap between rhetoric and practice is reform likely to be constructive and meaningful.

One of the most interesting effects of NHRIs is their influence on domestic social groups, whether intended or not. Many states in the region have created these institutions to co-opt and control social groups and the issues animating them. In some cases, states have been remarkably successful in using these institutions to undercut domestic human rights opponents. Whether the creation of a NHRI will backfire may depend on the number and strength of domestic human rights groups. Regardless, new state institutional actors invariably become implicated in state-society struggles, the outcomes of which are not fully transparent or predictable (Wolf, 2006). The findings also have implications for improving institutional design in this area. First, non-state funding appears to be the most important assurance of organisational independence. It is no coincidence that the most effective NHRI in the region is the Palestinian one. Although the Palestinian Authority is plagued by corruption and weakness on most fronts, a steady flow of foreign funding for its NHRI has contributed to the agency's relative efficacy. Second, having prominent members serve on NHRIs may be helpful, but it does not guarantee institutional effectiveness. Energetic, high profile members in Yemen and Palestine's institutions, and more recently in Morocco, explain some of their activism; but the appointment of Boutros-Ghali in Egypt has generated more domestic controversy than anything else. While prominent appointments may satisfy some international observers, members must also enjoy domestic legitimacy and be dedicated to their work in ways associated with lower-profile human rights professionals. Third, it is unclear how useful it is to build multiple official human rights bodies. The practice of institutional replication is evident in virtually every country examined, but wasteful inefficiencies occur when governments create multiple institutions simply to placate human rights critics. This question is difficult to answer in the short-term, demonstrates that if virtuous even hypocrisy can have unintended consequences. While the promise of human rights protection and promotion in the Middle East has not been fulfilled, in almost all cases the act of creating state institutions has had noticeable social and political effects. Even when institution-building is a symbolic gesture, it can set in motion a complex set of dynamics. As Susan Waltz has observed of the Maghrib, "in adopting the language of human rights, state leaders reset the parameters of what may be considered legitimate political concerns." One certainty, therefore, is that state human rights institutions in the Middle East should not be overlooked or dismissed as simple mouthpieces for propaganda. At a minimum, they can reconfigure national discourse and alter how state and society interact in defining the human rights agenda. Under the best of circumstances, they may contribute to the process of democratisation and the protection of human rights in the region (Cardenas, 2005).

Reported Removal of Prisoners from Iraq in late October 2004, there were press reports that the Central Intelligence Agency had transferred as many as a dozen non-Iraqi prisoners out of Iraq for interrogation elsewhere.' According to these accounts, the former head of the Office of Legal Counsel (OLC) of the Department of Justice prepared a draft legal opinion dated March 19, 2004, concluding that it was lawful to take non-Iraqi detainees out of the country for interrogation for a "brief but not in-definite period." The memorandum reportedly also concluded that it was lawful to remove permanently from Iraq the non-Iraqis who were present there in violation of local immigration law (Tenet, 2007). The U.S. position has been and remains that the Geneva Conventions apply in Iraq, including the Third Convention (protecting prisoners of war) and the Fourth (protecting civilians during armed conflict or occupation). The Fourth Convention contains a broad prohibition on transfers out of occupied territory. Article 49 states that "individual or mass forcible transfers, as well as deportations of protected persons from occupied territory to the territory of the Occupying Power or to that of any other country, occupied or not, are prohibited, regardless of motive." There is a narrow exception allowing transfers outside of occupied territory "if the security of the population or imperative military reasons so demand," but only "when for material reasons it is impossible to avoid such displacement."

Amnesty International published detailed evidence of the torture of political prisoners in Iraq. Ten years after the US-led invasion that toppled the dictatorship of Saddam Hussein, Iraq remains mired in human rights abuses. Thousands of Iraqis are detained without trial or serving prison sentences imposed after unfair trials, torture remains rife and continues to be committed with impunity, and the new Iraq is one of the world's leading executioners. The government hanged 129 prisoners in 2012, while hundreds more languished on death row. Yet, when he launched the campaign of "shock and awe" in March 2003, that swept away Saddam Hussein's regime within just four weeks, then US President George W Bush justified the military intervention partly on human rights grounds, pointing to the many grave crimes committed under the Iraqi leader (Amnesty Report: 2013). Besides the executions in Iraq and Iran, the death penalty also carried out. In Syria and Iraq, extra-judicial executions were reported. Libyan authorities appeared to encourage the killing of Libyan citizens abroad (Amnesty International Report, 1982). In 1992, HRW in conjunction with the Boston-based Physicians for Human Rights (PHR) sent a mission to Iraqi Kurdistan to investigate allegations of chemical weapons use. With the help of the Chemical and Biological Defence Establishment in the U.K., HRW and PHR were able to prove that the Iraqi regime had used mustard and nerve agents against the Kurdish village of Birjinni. Human Rights Watch was also able to document more than forty other Iraqi chemical attacks on Kurdish villages during field research in northern Iraq in 1992 and 1993. The Human Rights Watch Arms Project would like to build on that success to ensure that regimes that do employ these weapons are exposed and held accountable for their crimes (Human Rights Watch, 1995, 115). Several NGOs, committing them particularly to the improvement of the human rights situation in Iraq wrote this statement for the 7th session of the Human Rights Council in Geneva. It outlines the disastrous situation in Iraq, which has to be regarded as a direct consequence of the occupation of the U.S. and the "alliance of the willing". In this statement the NGOs demand of the Human Rights Council to commit them to improving this situation and to act. International Youth and Student Movement for the United Nation (ISMUN), Women's International League for Peace and Freedom (WILPF), The International Organisation for the Elimination of All forms of Racial Discrimination (EAFORD), General Arab Women Federation, International Educational Development-Humanitarian Law Project etc. are the few non-governmental organisations had worked for the improvement of the human rights situation in Iraq.

A series of recent U.N., ICRC, and NGOs reports point out the grave deterioration in the humanitarian situation in Iraq. The scale of death, destruction, systematic human rights violations and oppression following the invasion of 2003 continues. Iraqis are left without basic healthcare, education, drinkable water and adequate sanitation. The rights of women and children are totally ignored. Iraq, once among the most advanced countries of the region, has been reduced to the level of destitution (Hargreaves, 2003). The systematic abuse, mistreatment and torture continue in addition to the daily killings. Despite of all these circumstances, the HRC has never discussed the human rights situation in Iraq, nor has the High Commissioner brought it to the attention of the Council, in accordance with her mandate, although there are lot of U.N. reports, especially by the U.N. human rights office for Iraq. In its update of December 2007, the U.N. Office for the Coordination of Humanitarian Affairs (OCHA) described the situation as "one of the most complex and violent situation in the world, characterised by grave violations of human rights and international humanitarian law." It added that the basic human rights (the right to life and security) are the main concern for Iraqi civilians. Iraq faces a growing humanitarian emergency, with an unprecedented increase in poverty and unemployment. The U.N. estimates that upto eight million people are in need of immediate assistance. According to UNAMI reports, 54 per cent of the population is barely surviving on less than one U.S. dollar a day, while 15 per cent must endure extreme poverty, with less than 50 U.S. cents a day. The Iraqi Central Statistical Bureau confirms that 43 per cent of Iraqis suffer from "absolute poverty". Under the occupation, billions of dollars vanished from Iraq's fund. Corruption is a wide, open phenomenon in today's Iraq. The Iraqi state never knew such an extreme phenomenon before the occupation. In its reports, Transparency International cited Iraq among the worst countries in corruption. The U.N. agencies continue issuing appeals regarding the massive number of refugees and internally displaced persons. In its report, UNHCR estimates that there are 4.4 million Iraqis half of them are refugees. Iraqi intellectuals have been targeted since the very beginning of the 2003 invasion (Borshchevskaya, 2010). It is estimated that more than 500 Iraqi intellectuals were assassinated during the past five years. All these are part of the consequences of the invasion and occupation.

Several U.N. resolutions assign a role for the U.N. in post-Saddam reconstruction and governance. Resolution 1483 (cited above) provided for a U.N. special representative to Iraq, and "called on" governments to contribute forces for stabilisation. Resolution 1500 (August 14, 2003) established U.N. Assistance Mission for Iraq (UNAMI).[9] Now largely recovered from the bombing of its headquarters in 2003, UNAMI is headed by Ad Melkert (July 7, 2009), who replaced Swedish diplomat Staffan de Mistura. UNAMI staff exceeds 120 in Iraq (80 in Baghdad, 40 in Irbil, and others in Basra and Kirkuk), with equal numbers "offshore" in Jordan. UNAMI's responsibilities are expanding. U.N. Security Council Resolution, 1770, adopted August 10, 2007 and which renewed UNAMI's mandate for another year, enhanced its responsibility to be lead promoter of political reconciliation in Iraq and to plan a national census. UNAMI also played a major role in helping prepare for provincial elections by updating voter registries. It is extensively involved in assisting with the constitution review process (Pipes, 2011). U.N. Resolution 1830 of August 7, 2008, renewed UNAMI's expanded mandate until August 2009. (In Recommendations 7 and 26 and several others the Iraq Study Group calls for increased U.N. participation in promoting reconciliation in Iraq).

The conditions of Iraqi people in post-invasion period have been the subject of concern and controversy (Roberts *et.al.*, 2004). Concerns have been expressed about conduct by insurgents, the U.S.-led coalition forces and the Iraqi government. In the summer of 2003, the multinational forces focused on hunting down the remaining leaders of the former regime. Most significantly, Saddam Hussein himself was captured on December 13, 2003, on a farm near Tikrit. Shortly after the capture of Hussein, elements left out of the CPA began to agitate for elections and the formation of an Iraqi Interim Government (Otterman, 2004). The CPA opposed allowing democratic elections at this time. The insurgents stepped up their activities. The two most turbulent centres were the area around Fallujah and the poor Shia sections of cities from Baghdad (Sadr City) to Basra in the south. Toward the end of 2003, the intensity and pace of insurgent attacks began to increase. A sharp surge in guerrilla attacks ushered in an insurgent effort that was termed the "Ramadan Offensive", as it coincided with the beginning of the Muslim holy month of Ramadan.

Violence did increase during the Iraq Spring Fighting of 2004 with foreign fighters from around the Middle East as well as al-Qaeda in Iraq (an affiliated al-Qaeda group), led by Abu Musab al-Zarqawi helping to drive the insurgency. As the insurgency grew there was a distinct change in targeting from the coalition forces towards the new Iraqi Security Forces, as hundreds of Iraqi civilians and police were killed in a series of massive bombings. An organised Sunni insurgency, with deep roots and both nationalist and Islamist motivations, was becoming more powerful throughout Iraq. The Shia Mahdi Army also began launching attacks on coalition targets in an attempt to seize control from Iraqi security forces. The southern and central portions of Iraq were beginning to erupt in urban guerrilla combat as multinational forces attempted to keep control and prepared for a counter offensive. Another major event was the revelation of widespread prisoner abuse at Abu Ghraib, which received international media attention in April 2004, U.S. military personnel taunting and abusing Iraqi prisoners

(Synovitz, 2013). These revelations dealt a blow to the moral justifications for the occupation in the eyes of many people, especially Iraqis, and a turning point in the war.

Iraqis elected the Iraqi Transitional Government in order to draft a permanent constitution. Although some violence and a widespread Sunni boycott marred the event, most of the eligible Kurd and Shia populace participated (Pan, 2005). The summer of 2005 saw fighting around Baghdad and at Tall Afar in northwestern Iraq as U.S. forces tried to seal off the Syrian border. This led to fighting in the autumn in the small towns of the Euphrates valley between the capital and the border. The beginning of 2006 was marked by government creation talks, growing sectarian violence, and continuous anti-coalition attacks. Sectarian violence expanded to a new level of intensity following the al-Askari Mosque bombing in the Iraqi city of Samarra, on February 22, 2006. The explosion at the mosque, one of the holiest sites in Shi'a Islam, believed to have caused by a bomb planted by al-Qaeda. Although no injuries occurred in the blast, the mosque was severely damaged and the bombing resulted in violence the following days. Over 100 dead bodies with bullet wounds were found on February 23, and at least 165 people were thought to have been killed. In the aftermath of this attack the U.S. military calculated that the average homicide rate in Baghdad tripled from 11 to 33 deaths per day. In 2006, the U.N. described the environment in Iraq as a "civil war-like situation."

The withdrawal of U.S. forces began at the end of June 2009, with 38 bases to hand over to Iraqi forces. On June 29, 2009, U.S. forces withdrew from Baghdad. On November 30, 2009, Iraqi Interior Ministry officials reported that the civilian death toll in Iraq fell to its lowest level in November, since the 2003 invasion (Raphaeli, 2004). This political exclusion has come against the backdrop of strong sectarian violence, mainly between Sunnis and Shias, which reached a peak in the period between 2006 and 2008. The withdrawal of U.S. troops at the end of 2011 left a large power vacuum in Iraq, leading to a sharp escalation in sectarian violence and the ascent of several militant groups. During this period, much of the violence was perpetrated by state actors. Human rights violations committed by the Iraqi armed forces were routinely classified as 'anti-terrorist' operations. At the same time, militant and rebel groups in both Iraq and neighbouring Syria have grown at an alarming rate. In early June 2014, the Sunni militant group known as the Islamic State in Iraq and Syria (ISIS) led a rapid, highly coordinated, and violent insurgency, taking control of large swaths of territory primarily in Iraq's north and west Sunni-majority territories (Garfield, 2007). On 30 June 2014, ISIS declared the establishment of an Islamic caliphate, adding that the group should hereafter be referred to only as the "Islamic State". Abu Bakr al-Baghdadi is the self-proclaimed caliph of the "Islamic State".

In December 2007, the Iraqi government reported that there were five million orphans in Iraq-nearly half of the country's children. Iraq's health has deteriorated to a level not seen since the 1950s, said Joseph Chamie, former director of the U.N. Population Division and an Iraq specialist. "They were at the forefront", he said, referring to health care just before the 1991 Persian Gulf War. "Now they are looking more and more like a country in sub-Saharan Africa." Malnutrition rates have risen (Roug, 2006). Iraqi children are suffering from psychological problems too. Iraqis have no access to safe drinking water. A cholera outbreak in northern Iraq thought to be the result of poor water quality. Half of Iraqi doctors have left the country since 2003. During the entire Iraq war, there have been human rights abuses on all sides; by the Iraqi government, and mainly the torture by Iraqi security forces. The Iraqi police from the Interior Ministry were accused of forming Death Squads and committing numerous massacres and tortures of Sunni Arabs. The police collusion with militias in Iraq have compounded the problems (Lapkin, 2004). Human right abuses by the Coalition forces and private contractors, such as Abu Ghraib torture and prisoner abuse, use of white phosphorus in Iraq (Steinberg, 2013). Controversy continued over disproportionate force used, during the assaults by Coalition and mostly Shia and Kurdish Iraqi government forces on the Sunni insurgent stronghold of Fallujah in 2004 (Schleifer, 2005).

In a move to legitimise the existing Iraqi government, U.N. lifted the Saddam Hussein era restrictions on Iraq. These included allowing Iraq to have a civilian nuclear programme, permitting the participation of Iraq in international nuclear and chemical weapons treaties, as well as returning control of Iraq's oil and gas revenue to the government and ending the Oil-for-Food programme. There have been major criticisms by numerous human rights organisations and Shiite officials that currently Sunnis have systematically kidnapped, tortured and killed Shiites or those who they deem the enemy (Rubin, 2006). Casualties of the Iraq War, which has casualty numbers for coalition nations, women, non-Iraqi civilians, journalists, media helpers, aid workers, contractors wounded, etc. There have been several attempts by the media, coalition governments and others to estimate the Iraqi casualties (White, 2003). The table below summarises some of these estimates.

Source	*Iraqi Causalities*	*March 2003 to 2010*
Iraq Family Health Survey	1,51,000 violent deaths	June 2006
Lancet Survey	601,027 violent deaths out of 654,965 excess deaths.	June 2006
Opinion Research Business Survey	1,033,000 violent deaths from the conflict	August 2007
Associated Press	110,600 violent deaths	August 2009
Iraq Body Count	113,494-122,483 violent civilian deaths from the conflict (including new deaths added from the Iraq war Logs)	October 2010

Source: Griffis, Margaret Casualties in Iraq- The human Cost of Occupation, Antiwar.com. http://www.antiwar.com/casualties/.And Military- Casualties of the Iraq War. http://military.wikia.com/wiki/Casualties-of-the-Iraq-War.

After the invasion, the conditions of the Iraqi people grew worse as their roads, schools, hospital, homes, museums and other tourist attractions were blown up. The death rate in Iraq increased after the war and the new born came out deformed (Stiglitz and Linda, 2012). Diseases and illnesses also reached unbelievable catastrophic proportions (Lynch, 2006). The reason to these was type of destructive weapons used by the U.S. during the war. Even their sources of electricity and water supply were destroyed during the invasion. The war generated an increase in the number of fatal jihadist attacks, amounting to literally more additional terrorist attacks causing thousands of innocent civilians to lose their lives.

Simply every one can identify that U.S. acted on the pursuit of its 'primacy' and not to secure international peace and security. There is evidence that before the war, the price of crude oil was on the rise.

The U.S. being the highest importer of crude oil products in the globe saw this as a threat to its economy because U.S. citizens will have to spend more of their daily income on gasoline and heating than before (Stiglitz and Linda, 2008). To make things worse, Saddam Hussein converted the currency for crude oil transactions from the U.S. dollar to the European euro currency and this increased the pressure for the invasion of Iraq. The Bush Administration also saw the period, as a golden opportunity to finish up what was started during the First Gulf War with Iraq. The U.N. should have stopped the aggression of U.S. if failed because they rely on the U.S. to carry out some of their laws. U.N. was created after League of Nations failed because of lack of support from the U.S. and other great powers of the European nation. It was meant to act as an international organisation whose aims include conducting cooperation of international law and security to achieving world peace. But it failed to prevent the aggression of U.S. on Iraq, while pursuing their 'primacy'. The question now arises 'Does the U.S. government pick and choose laws of U.N. to be obeyed?' For U.N. providing international laws is not what makes it an active organisation, but the implementation of the laws they make. Saddam Hussein was accused wrongly of possessing Weapons of Mass Destruction (WMD) because U.S. had interest in Iraqi oil. The cost of the war affected U.S. economy which led to the establishment of the Central Bank in order to recover for the huge money spent in sending troop to Iraq. Thousands of people have died as a result of the 2003 war and its aftermath. U.S. pursuit of 'primacy' resulted to severe violence which accounted for these deaths, particularly during the air strikes by the coalition forces. The Iraqi people had faced wars after wars, but the invasion of 2003 worsened the threat to health posed by the damage inflicted by previous wars, tyranny and sanctions. In general, the war created further decline of infrastructure, road, schools, hospital and homes of the Iraqi society (Bilmes and Joseph, 2011). Today, there is lack of suitable system to determine the real numbers of the Iraqi troops that died during the war because U.S. disbanded their army after the war.

Iraqi Death Estimates During Post-Invasion Period

Possible estimates on the number of people killed in the invasion and occupation of Iraq vary widely, and are highly disputed

(Knapp 2014). The following table provides casualties during the 2003 invasion of Iraq and its aftermath:

Iraq war logs	Classified US military documents released by Wiki Leaks in October 2010, record Iraqi and Coalition military deaths between January 2004 and December 2009.[10] The documents record 109,032 deaths broken down into "Civilian" (66,081 deaths), "Host Nation" (15,196 deaths), "Enemy" (23,984 deaths), and "Friendly" (3,771 deaths).
Iraqi Health Ministry	The Health Ministry of the Iraqi government recorded 87,215 Iraqi violent deaths between January 1, 2005, and February 28, 2009. The data was in the form of a list of yearly totals for death certificates issued for violent deaths by hospitals and morgues (Stafford, 2010). The official who provided the data told the *Associated Press* said the ministry does not have figures for the first two years of the war, and estimated the actual number of deaths at 10 to 20 per cent higher because of thousands who are still missing and civilians who were buried in the chaos of war without official records.[11]
The Associated Press	*Associated Press* stated that more than 110,600 Iraqis had been killed since the start of the war to April 2009. This number is per the Health Ministry tally of 87,215 covering January 1, 2005, to February 28, 2009 combined with counts of casualties for 2003-2004, and after February 29, 2009, from hospital sources and media reports.[12]
Iraq Body Count	The Iraq Body Count project (IBC) figure of 110,937 - 121,227 civilian deaths from violence up to December 2012 includes reported civilian deaths due to Coalition and insurgent military action, sectarian violence and increased criminal

	violence. The IBC site states: "it should be noted that many deaths will probably go unreported or unrecorded by officials and media." The IBC website currently states that, "Further analysis of the WikiLeaks' Iraq War Logs may add 12,000 civilian deaths."[13]
Iraq Family Health Survey (with WHO)	Iraq Family Health Survey for the World Health Organisation. On January 9, 2008, the World Health Organisation reported the results of the "Iraq Family Health Survey" (Alkhuzai *et.al.,* 2008). The study surveyed 9,345 households across Iraq and estimated 151,000 deaths due to violence (95 per cent uncertainty range, 104,000 to 223,000) from March 2003 through June 2006. Employees of the Iraqi Health Ministry carried out the survey.[14]
Opinion Research Business (ORB) poll	Opinion Research Business (ORB) poll conducted August 12-19, 2007, estimated 10,33,000 violent deaths due to the Iraq War. The range given was 946,000 to 1,120,000 deaths. A nationally representative sample of approximately 2,000 Iraqi adults answered whether any members of their household (living under their roof) were killed due to the Iraq War. 22 per cent of the respondents had lost one or more household members. ORB reported that "48 per cent died from a gunshot wound, 20 per cent from the impact of a car bomb, 9 per cent from aerial bombardment, 6 per cent as a result of an accident and 6 per cent from another blast/ordnance."[15]
U.N.	The U.N. reported that 34,452 violent deaths occurred in 2006, based on data from morgues, hospitals, and municipal authorities across Iraq.[16]
Lancet studies	The Lancet study's figure of 654,965 excess deaths through the end of June 2006 is based on household survey data. The estimate is for all

	excess violent and nonviolent deaths. That also includes those due to increased lawlessness, degraded infrastructure; poorer healthcare etc. 601,027 deaths (range of 426,369 to 793,663 using a 95 per cent confidence interval) were estimated to be due to violence. 31 per cent of those were attributed to the Coalition, 24 per cent to others, 46 per cent unknown. The causes of violent deaths were gunshot (56 per cdent), car bomb (13 per cent), other explosion/ordnance (14 per cent), airstrike (13 per cent), accident (2 per cent), unknown (2 per cent). A copy of a death certificate was available for a high proportion of the reported deaths (92 per cent of those households asked to produce one).
Ali al-Shemari (earlier Iraqi Health Minister)	Concerning war-related deaths (civilian and non-civilian), and deaths from criminal gangs, Iraq's Health Minister Ali al-Shemari said that since the March 2003 invasion between 100,000 and 150,000 Iraqis had been killed. "Al-Shemari said on Thursday [*November 9, 2006*] that he based his figure on an estimate of 100 bodies per day brought to morgues and hospitals - though such a calculation would come out closer to 130,000 in total." For more info see farther down at Iraq Health Minister estimate in November 2006.
Costs of War Project	176,000-189,000 people were killed in violence in the Iraq war, including 134,000 civilians, according to the findings of the Costs of War Project, a team of 30 economists, anthropologists, political scientists, legal experts, and physicians assembled by Brown University and the Watson Institute to study the effects of wars involving the U.S. since 2001. The project also examined the economic costs of the Iraq war, as well as the human and economic cost of war in Afghanistan and Pakistan.

Following figure illustrates, the peak of violent civilian death occurred between 2003 and 2013. The war's violence diminished after 2008, although it certainly did not end for civilians. In addition to the civilian toll through December 2011, more than 10,000 Iraqi police and Iraqi military forces were killed by insurgents or in friendly fire incidents from June 2003 through July 2011. Iraqi military and insurgent deaths number more than 30,000 additional deaths. At its current rate, an additional 3,500-4,000 people were killed in Iraq in 2013.

Number of Iraqi Violent Civilian Death Due to War 2003-2013.[17]

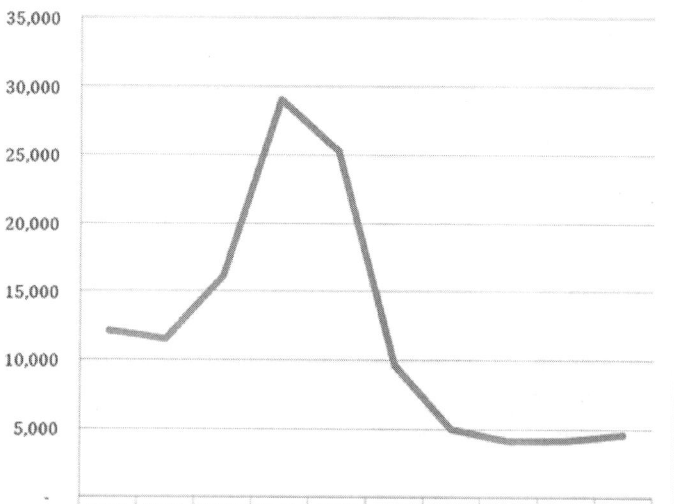

	2003	2004	2005	2006	2007	2008	2009	2010	2011	2012
Violent Deaths	12,109	11,524	16,116	29,027	25,284	9,630	4,970	4,099	4,144	4,568

Source: Civilian Death and Injury in the Iraq War, 2003-2013.[18]

In addition, likely several times that number of Iraqi civilians have died due to the effects of war, the so-called 'indirect deaths' that are a consequence of the destruction of Iraqi infrastructure and other war-induced or war-related conditions such as internal displacement and starvation. A reasonable estimate is that indirect deaths number two to four times the number of direct deaths. The indirect death toll had been much higher than that of the direct. This is because, despite the relatively sophisticated state of Iraq's healthcare and physical infrastructure before the 2003 war, the 1991 war, and the years of sanctions that followed, had already crippled Iraq's healthcare system and weakened its people. While the years of war following the 2003 invasion further devastated Iraq's medical and physical infrastructure.[19] The extra burden to Iraqis wrought by a decade of war and subsequent unrest- of physical and emotional stress, malnutrition, disease, environmental pollution, loss of medical personnel, and destruction of medical facilities- has translated into a miserable environment for many Iraqis. Although it is difficult to estimate with precision, indirect deaths, in other wars, tend to outnumber direct deaths. Beth Osborne Daponte estimated in 1993 that of the total deaths from the Gulf War in Iraq, civilian wartime deaths comprised less than two per cent of all deaths due to the war. 'In the Gulf war, far more persons died from post-war health effects than from direct war effects.'[20] The Iraq war begun in March 2003 was more devastating than the relatively short Gulf War a decade earlier. It would not be surprising then that indirect war death in Iraq from 2003 to 2013 was very high. Moreover, as with other wars, the indirect health effects of Iraq's most recent war and occupation will continue for many years after the war ends.

Summary

More than eighty years of hegemony by the central government left its imprint on peoples' psyche, making devolution of power to the provinces which seems to be irrelevant or even fraudulent. Visible improvements in the security situation in 2008 raised hopes that some kind of national reconciliation may follow and result in a peaceful compromise. The history of the Iraqi state is one of the muscular central governance. Throughout the state's existence, it was the midpoint that possessed supremacy and controlled resources, and provincial government had little role away from make possible central jurisdiction. Still what remains uncertain is whether the future Iraq would much resemble the unified political and geographic entity that the British sowed together in 1921 and which survived more or less intact under various monarchical and republican rulers until 2003. Considerable resources were invested to discourage Iraqis from fillet their country. Yet the gaping grazes acquired on the way to seeming national destruction would not heal lightly.

Notes

1. *Iraq: Saddam's Capture a 'Coup' for the Coalition*, Saddam's capture is a "political and psychological triumph" for the U.S. and coalition; Optimists view the arrest as a turning point for Iraq and an opportunity for reconciliation. Critics say nabbing Saddam doesn't solve Iraqi crisis, rather it could "inflame" the resistance. Global media call for justice not revenge; most want Saddam to be tried in an Iraqi court. Available online at http://www.globalsecurity.org/wmd/library/news/iraq/ 2003/12/wwwh31215.htm, accessed on 15/12/2003.
2. Nancy Gibbs, "Unfinished Business," *Time*, 28 April 2003, 41. During times of peace-the Coast Guard operates under the Department, although the Guard utilizes many part-*time* personnel with military training, it is a major, *Gibbs, Nancy*. "*Unfinished Business*: America's War With Iraq Won't Be Complete Until U.S. Forces Can Resolve Three Key Questions." *Time, 28 April 2003* Available online at http://www.referenceforbusiness.com/industries/Public-Administration/ National-Security.html.
3. C. David Welch, assistant secretary of state for international organization affairs testimony before the House International Relations Committee, March 23, 2000.
4. Tim Murphy GOP Congressional Candidate Insists We Found Saddam's *WMD* program -but says the war had nothing to do with *WMDs*. Available online at http://www.motherjones.com/politics/2014/06/steve-russell-saddam-hussein-oklahoma-congress accessed on 11.8.2014.
5. Kenneth Katzma, Iraq; transition to Soverignty. CRS Report (Congressional Research Service). CRS Report for Congress. Updated July 21, 2004The text of the TAL can be obtained from the CPA. Available online at http://cpa-iraq.org/government/TAL.html. accessed on 12.08.2004.
6. The *Iraq Interim Government* of 2004 was created by the US led coalition. The Iraqi *Interim Government*, led by Prime Minister Ayad *Allawi*. Available online at *www.globalsecurity.org/military/world/iraq/allawi.htm accessed on 20.05.2014*
7. "Saddam Hussein's Human Rights Record." Human Rights Abuses of Saddam Hussein's Regime 1991-2003 (Congressional Research Service (CRS), July 9, 2003). The most comprehensive treatment of *human rights abuses* in the period between 1991 and 2003 was contained in the State Department's unclassified annual Country Reports on Human Rights Practices. Available online at *www2.gwu.edu/~nsarchiv/NSAEBB/NSAEBB129/part17-saddam-hr.pdf*
8. "Suicide bomber attacks police recruitment centre." CNN. 12 November 2006. Baghdad, Iraq (*CNN*) — Two *suicide bombers* strapped with explosives killed at least 35. The victims were among dozens waiting to join the *police* force outside the *recruitment centre* in the Qadessiya district.

Available online at http://www.*cnn*.com/*2006*/WORLD/meast/11/*12*/iraq.main/index.html, accessed on 22.09. 2012.

9. Report on Human Rights in Iraq: July- December 2012. *Office of the* High *Commission for Human Rights*. Religion, political or other opinion, *national* or social origin, birth or other status. UNAMI Human Rights Office and Human Rights office of the High Commissioner for Human Rights. U.N Assistance Mission for Iraq Human Rights office. Available online at http://www.protectingeducation.org/sites/default/files/documents/hro_july-december2012report.pdf accessed on 11.06.2013.

10. Rogers, Simon (October 23, 2010). "Wikileaks Iraq: Data Journalism Maps Every Death-Data Journalism Allows Us To Really Interrogate the Wikileaks Iraq War Logs Release. Here Is the Statistical Breakdown - and Data for You To Download". *Data Blog -Facts Are Sacred* (blog on *The Guardian*). November 20, 2010, tiff writer (October 24, 2010). "Secret Iraq Files - US Turned Blind Eye To Torture." Al Jazeera. Retrieved November 21, 2010. "Iraq War Logs - Related Articles, Background Features and Opinions about this Topic" (gateway/portal page of site). *Der Spiegel*. Retrieved November 21, 2010.Staff writer (October 23, 2010). "Iraq War Logs: What the Numbers Reveal." Iraq Body Count. accessed on 20.11. 2010.

11. Gamel, Kim (April 14, 2009). "AP Impact: Secret Tally Has 87,215 Iraqis Dead". Associated Press (*via* Boston Herald). Full article.

12. For more information, see farther down at *The Associated Press and Health Ministry*. See Gamel, Kim (April 14, 2009). "AP Impact: Secret Tally Has 87,215 Iraqis Dead". Associated Press (*via* Boston Herald).

13. "Iraq Body Count database". Iraqbodycount.org. July 24, 2012. Iraq Body Count project. Source of IBC quote on undercounting by media is here. accessed on02.09.2012.

14. More details, Press release (January 9, 2008): "New Study Estimates 151,000 Violent Iraqi Deaths Since 2003 Invasion".World Health Organization (WHO). WHO Country Office in Iraq. Iraq Family Health Survey"(WHO). September 2, 2010. Boseley, Sarah (January 10, 2008): "151,000 Civilians Killed Since Iraq Invasion - Figures Up to June 2006 from Household Survey - Government Accepts New estimate on Death Toll. *The Guardian*. September 2, 2010. Brown, Davia; Partlow, Joshua (January 10, 2008). "New Estimate of Violent Deaths Among Iraqis Is Lower". *The Washington Post*. accessed on 02.09.2010.

15. "Update on Iraqi Casualty Data" by Opinion Research Business. January 2008. "More than 1,000,000 Iraqis Murdered". September 2007. Opinion Research Business. PDF report. Susman, Tina (September 14, 2007). "Poll: Civilian Death Toll in Iraq May Top 1 Million". *Los Angeles Times* (*via* commondreams.org). accessed on September 2, 2010. Beaumont, Peter; Walters, Joanna (September 16, 2007). "Greenspan Admits Iraq Was About Oil, As Deaths Put at 1.2 Million". *The Observer* (*via* commondreams.org).

Retrieved September 2, 2010. Staff writer (September 18, 2007). "The Media Ignore Credible Poll Revealing 1.2 Million Violent Deaths In Iraq". *Media Lens*. accessed on 02.09.2010.

16. See: Tavernise, Sabrina (January 17, 2007). "Iraqi Death Toll Exceeded 34,000 in '06, United Nations Says". *The New York Times*. Available online at www.Casualties-of-the-Iraq-Warcite-ref-nytimes-31-1.
17. Based on data in http:// www.iraqbodycount.org/database/.Accessed on 6 March 2013, IBC believes about 12,000 additional deaths will be recorded after the Wikileak files have been fully integrated into its database.
18. Crawford, Neta. C (2013): Civilian Death and Injury in the Iraq War, 2003-2013, Boston University,This paper updates and expands analysis in Neta C Crawford, "Civilian Death and Injury in Iraq, 2003-2011," Costs of War, September 2011 and relies on work from Neta C. Crawford, Moral Responsibility for Civilian Casualties.
19. See Mac Skelton, "Health and Health Care Decline in Iraq" Costs of War, march 2013.
20. Beth Osborne Daponate, "A Case Study in Estimating Casualties from War and Its Aftermath: The 1991 Persian Gulf War," Physicians for Social Responsibility Quarterly, 3 (1993). 57-66. *Medicine and Global Survival*, Available online at http://ippnw.org/Resources/MGS/PSQV3N2Daponate.html.

5

Human Rights Violations Against Iraqi Women

Introduction

The thirteen years of continued war and economic sanction enforced on Iraq mainly under American and British influence led to two million deaths, mostly children and women. Women's rights should be considered as the most important aspect in the human rights framework (Hannum, 2006). This chapter attempts to highlight the impact of continued military interventions and economic sanctions on the innocent Iraqi people, especially women and children. The chapter also highlights the social and cultural impacts, economic and health impacts etc.. The coalition forces violated all human rights norms and laws for enforcing their vested interests. The general picture arrived at is that of women being pushed further into the background and back into their homes. Women are suffering in terms of a deteriorating humanitarian situation and an enduring lack of security on the streets. The invasion of Iraq in 1991 led to more than 150,000 deaths, most of them women and children. The recognition of women as a social group is especially valuable in cases where women claim refugee status because of the absence of state protection from internal violence (Macklin, 2005).

VI. Iraqi Women-A Historical Study

Women in the Middle East are enforced to negotiate a path due to a variety influences -some of them contradictory. They are expected, for example, to be the bearers of authentic national identity but also the objects of modernity. In the words of the scholar Nadje Al-Ali, 'Caught between the pursuit of modernisation, attempts at liberalisation, a pervasive nationalist rhetoric of authenticity and ongoing imperialist encroachments, women are often the focus of conflicting and ambiguous interests' (Al-Ali, 2000). In exploring the lives of women, scholars investigate not only what shapes women's lives but also how women negotiate those forces to shape their own lives. Several socio-political research reports revealed the following facts about the conditions of the majority of women in the Middle East:

1. Women's political participation in most of the Middle Eastern countries is out of proportion to their population number, which is approximately 50 per cent (Lambert, 2011).
2. Middle Eastern societies tend to trap women in certain kinds of jobs, mainly as housewives, teachers, nurses, or unpaid helpers in rural areas (Makar, 1998).
3. Working women are paid less than men for the same kind of work (Moghadam, 1988).
4. Certain cultural traditions and social practices prevalent in Middle Eastern societies work against the health, happiness, and social and personal progress of women (Keddie and Beth, 1991).
5. Women in the Middle East, whether Muslim, Christian or Jewish, resent men's patriarchal control of the interpretation of the religious texts and traditions (Nashat, 1982).

These are sociological facts that are prevalent throughout Middle Eastern societies, as diverse as they are in ethnic composition of the population, religious affiliations, and economic and political systems (Barzilai, 2003). In all Middle Eastern countries, there is a need for legal reform with respect to inheritance, marriage, divorce, and custody of children. Diversity also exists in women's reactions to their status in their respective societies (Smihula, 2009).

Women in the Middle East respond to the discrimination and the inequality that is deeply rooted in the traditions of their societies and in the attitude and behaviour of men towards them and their vital roles in these societies. In general, nationalism in the nineteenth century and twentieth century mobilised women in most of the countries in the Middle East. However, once States gained independence from colonial powers, women more often lost their role in the process. At present, there is a women's movement in every Middle Eastern country. There are women leaders in these movements who have devoted all of their lives to the goal of achieving equal opportunity and dignity for their sisters. Some of them are more successful than others in their respective countries (Makar, 1998). In Algeria, women played a very important role in the war of independence in the 1950s and 1960s. In the 1990s however, they were subjected to the harsh policies and terrorist actions of the militant fundamentalists. Women in Tunisia enjoy a much better position because the governmental anti-fundamentalist efforts are supported by a legal, secular and civic group's network. Through the women's associations and the very active role of the National Union of Tunisian Women, the influence of conservative militant fundamentalism is minimal (Makar, 1998). In Morocco, the women's movement is invigorated by the leadership of the scholar feminist Fatima Mernissi. Her most recent book, 'Women's Rebellion and Islamic Memory', covers not only Morocco, but also the whole Middle East in the post-Gulf War period. It is her view that the oppression of women by militant conservatism is in fact oppression of all democratic values and the values of the civic society.

Saudi Arabian woman Professor, Saddeka Arebi of anthropology, who teaches in the U.S., has written the most important book about the women of her country. In "Women and Words in Saudi Arabia: The Politics of Literary Discourse", she studies a selected group of Saudi women writers who used "the word" to promote the women's cause in their society (Arebi, 1994). In Turkey, women have enjoyed theoretically the same legal rights as men since the earliest days of the country's new republic, which was founded in 1923. But the change has not been universal. The main problem is the obvious difference between the cities and the rural areas, as is the case in all of the Middle East. In the rural areas, women are not educated, and they are subservient to men and fundamentalist traditions. The women's movement in Egypt goes back to the nineteenth century. It was started by Rifcah al-Tahtawi, who called for the education of women because he knew that literacy was the key to improving the status of women. In 1984, a famous Christian lawyer, Morqus Fahmi, wrote a play about the ideal relations between men and women, which, in his view, should be based on equality, cooperation, and mutual respect (Makar, 1998).

Despite the diverse conditions of women in Middle East and the various responses of women to their lower social and economic status, there is something in common among all the women, that is, their rights are human rights. Women's rights advocates worldwide are in agreement as to the importance of internationalising women's rights as human rights. When little girls get less food, less medical care, less education, and more work than little boys, when women cannot travel, marry or leave home without some man's permission, when rights to vote, meet and speak out are restricted, when children's custody is given only to the father and when women are denied the right to control their bodies, they are actually being denied their human rights (Makar, 1998). The Nobel Women's Initiative (NWI) was created in 2006 by six female winners of the Nobel Peace Prize to support women's groups around the world in campaigning for justice, peace and equality. It was also a response to a suggestion by Iranian laureate Shirin Ebadi that women recipients of the Peace Prize should collectively endeavour to use the power and influence concomitant with being Nobel laureates to advance the cause of women internationally, by bringing their voices and experiences to the direct attention of the international community and media sources (Barlow, 2008).

The First International Conference of the Nobel Women's Initiative, "Women Redefining Peace in the Middle East and Beyond", was held in Galway, Ireland, on May 29-31, 2007. This was a gathering of over 80 of the world's leading activists and scholars on women's empowerment and gender equality. It provided women from more than 40 countries an opportunity to share their experiences of discrimination and oppression, exchange strategies that have improved women's conditions, and discuss how best to work together to demand a central place for women at the negotiating table of the peace process and political liberalisation. The Middle East was chosen as the contextual focus of the conference precisely because the region is widely characterised by conflict and political repression. Under such circumstances, women's rights and human security are readily sacrificed on the altar of "national security" and unqualified allegiance to the nation-state (Falk, 2008). Importantly, the conference was designed to challenge the stereotype that women are the exclusive "victims" of conflict, and passive subjects of systematised oppression. Despite spiralling violence in the Middle East, women have demonstrated positive responses of resilience and non-violent creativity. NWI believes that these kinds of responses "can serve as a lens that can offer ways women's rights, human security, and peace issues can be addressed globally."[1]

The practice of purdah explains the lower employment rates in Islamic countries. Purdah, meaning curtain, is most commonly associated with the system of restraints obliging women to behave with utmost modesty and enforcing sex segregation outside the family that severely restricts the activity of women (Winter, 2006). In Islamic countries, fewer women than men attend school, and those who do, receive an inferior education (Bunting, 2005). For example, the University of Riyadh bans women from the library; books must be brought out to them. Yet, today the situation is changing 6.6 per cent of Saudi Arabia's female college students study management and economics, and women in all the Arab countries do hold managerial or administrative positions. Although Israel's female participation rate exceeds that of her Arab neighbours, equality of opportunity is not a reality there. One-third of all Israeli women, compared with over 80 per cent of Israeli men, work outside the home.

Following Table shows the labour force participation rates of women in few majority Muslim countries. Until now unbreakable barrier that keeps minorities and women from rising to the upper rungs of the corporate hierarchy, despite of their qualifications or achievements. Women can see their privileged positions but cannot reach them (Davies, 1998 and Cotter *et.al.*, 2001). Majority Muslim countries are defined as states in which more than 50 per cent of the population identifies with the Islamic faith. Of these countries, Bangladesh and Indonesia had the highest rates of female participation in the labour force in 2010 with 57 per cent and 51 per cent, respectively. Syria, Iraq, and Afghanistan have the lowest rates of female labour force participation among these nations with 13 per cent, 14 per cent, and 15 per cent, respectively. Afghanistan's female labour force participation rate, for example, was 15 per cent in 2010 according to World Bank figures. That percentage nearly doubles to 28.9 per cent if data from UNESCAP is cited. The same discrepancy is true for figures

Female Labour Force Participation Rate

Country/Year	*Afghanistan*	*Egypt*	*Syria*	*Iran*	*Iraq*	*Indonesia*	*Bangladesh*	*Saudi Arabia*
2008	15 per cent	23 per cent	14 per cent	15 per cent	14 per cent	51 per cent	56 per cent	17 per cent
2009	15 per cent	24 per cent	13 per cent	15 per cent	14 per cent	51 per cent	57 per cent	17 per cent
2010	16 per cent	24 per cent	13 per cent	16 per cent	14 per cent	51 per cent	57 per cent	17 per cent

Source: Global Gender Gap Report 2012, World Economic Forum.

for Iran for which the World Bank lists its female participation rate at 16 per cent in 2010 and UNESCAP lists it as 26.9 per cent.

Muslim jurists claim, and all Muslims believe, that justice and equality are intrinsic values and cardinal principles of Islam and the Sharia. To a person for whom God's word has been absolutely revealed and whose law has developed under God's guidance, change is a slow and problematic process. When it does come, Muslim men and women agree, it must be within the framework of that revelation. Equality will carry an Islamic, not a Western, definition, and in the Muslim mind the role of women must evolve into a pattern consistent with God's ordered plan for humankind (Smith, 1979). The questions have acquired a fresh urgency in a new century that has brought an aggressive unilateralism in the policies of the sole remaining superpower towards the Middle East and Southwest Asia, rhetoric of "promoting democracy" and "human rights" to support military interventions in places so far as Afghanistan and Iraq. In Afghanistan, the invasion was a reaction to the Al-Qaeda attacks of 11 September 2001. It succeeded in bringing down the Taliban government which was not responsible for the attacks but not in capturing the Al-Qaeda leadership. The invasion, occupation, and "regime change" were in part justified to the U.S. (and world) public as rescuing Afghan women from oppression, vividly represented in their all-enveloping cover, the *chadri* or *burqa* (a shroud which covers the body from head to foot, usually worn by females in Islamic countries). Many observers were consequently surprised and disappointed that the downfall of the Taliban did not lead to Afghan women's mass abandonment of the burqa (Abirafeh, 2003). Its persistence was quite rightly judged, however, to reflect the persistence of traditional patriarchal values and norms that the Taliban had merely enforced in an extreme form, norms and values that most Afghan women and men continue to associate with Islam and that few of them are yet ready to abandon in the absence of any credible or palatable alternative set of values. Indeed, the family law established in the years since the invasion enshrines the very same values despite the emergence on the political scene of a significant number of brave Afghan women (Hosseini, 2006).

During the first half of January 2004, a violent conflict burst out over the veiling of young girls in the public schools of France. The French authorities had announced that in defence of their traditional secular system they were preparing to pass a law which banned young girls and boys from wearing visible religious accessories or apparel which denoted their belonging to a particular religious faith. This ban would include such things as the Christian crucifix, the Jewish skull-cap and the Islamic veil. Following this announcement a wave of protests broke out in the Arab world. The argument was that wearing the veil by girls and women who were Muslims was ordained by divine law and no woman or girl could be forced to disobey what Allah had commended her to do (Ahmed, 1992). Religious dignitaries and sheikhs, Islamic thinkers and scholars, heads of political parties or movements like the "Muslim Brotherhood" and the "Jihad," parliamentarians, journalists joined in the general clamour as though some terrible catastrophe had befallen the Islamic faith and its followers, although in the Qur'an there is absolutely nothing to indicate that the wearing of the veil is a divine command.

No more than the age-old patriarchal struggle over women's heads, the fear that they might begin to think and throw off the bonds of slavery, of inferiority enforced on them in all religions and in all societies. For the Muslim men who raised their voice in protest this was an integral part of their struggle to maintain men's control over women, men's control over their minds. This was above all the desire of Islamic fundamentalists to preserve the political power they exercise in society, a cornerstone of which has always been power over women (Saadawi, 2008). But in this political fray there were other players using women rights or lack of rights to their own ends. Young women in the streets of Paris and Cairo and other cities demonstrating against the French government's announcement in defence of their right to wear the veil, and of God's divine commandments in defence of this symbol of their servitude. This is a signal example of how "false consciousness" makes women enemies of their freedom, enemies of themselves, an example of how they are used in the political game being played by the Islamic fundamentalist movement in its bid for power (Saadawi, 2008). A group of *Iraqi women* in New York was astounded when they expressed their happiness at the 'liberation of Iraq' and its occupation by U.S. troops. Perhaps they or their families had suffered at the hands of Saddam Hussein and his tyrannical regime but how could they fail to realise that the Iraqi people, and with them Iraqi women and children, would suffer at the hands of a colonial military occupation even more than ever before (Raphaeli, 2007). The slogan raised by the girls and young women who demonstrated against the announcement made by the government of France was, "The veil is a doctrine not a symbol." This was the same argumentation defended by the religious leaders of the Islamic movement and the sheikh of Al-centre (Mernissi, 1991). Another argument used as a part of the brainwashing process is to consider the veil an integral part of the identity of Islamic women and a reflection of their struggle against Western imperialism, against its values, and against "cultural invasion" of the Arab and Islamic countries aimed at enforcing complete domination over them. Yet, in these demonstrations the young women and girls who marched in them wearing the veil were often clothed in tight fitting jeans, their faces covered with layers of make-up, their lips painted bright red, the lashes around their eyes thickened black or blue with heavy mascara (Dawisha, 2003). They walked along the streets swaying over high heeled shoes, drinking out of bottles of "Coca Cola" or "Sprite." Their demonstration was a proof of the link between Western capitalist consumerism and Islamic fundamentalism, how, in systems money and trade ride supreme, bend to the rule of corporate globalisation. It was an illustration of how a "false consciousness" is shot with contradiction.

In Muslim belief, Sharia-revealed law, literally 'the way'- is the totality of God's will as revealed to the Prophet Muhammad. *Fiqh*-the theory or the philosophy of Islamic law, based on the teachings of the the Koran and the traditions of the Prophet. *Hadith*- a collection of traditions containing sayings of the prophet Muhammad which, with accounts of his daily practice (the Sunna), constitute the major source of guidance for Muslims apart from the Koran. In other words, while the Sharia is sacred, universal, and eternal, fiqh is human and-like any other system of jurisprudence subject to change. Fiqh is often mistakenly equated with sharia, both in popular Muslim discourses and by politicians and academic and legal specialists, and often with ideological intent; that is, what Islamists and others assert to be a Sharia mandate (hence divine and infallible) is the result of fiqh, juristic speculation and extrapolation (hence human and fallible). Fiqh texts, which are patriarchal in both spirit and form, are frequently invoked as God's law, as a means to silence and frustrate Muslims' search for legal justice and equality, which are intrinsic to this-worldly justice (Hosseini, 2006).

In Iraq, when the primary reasons for the necessity of a "regime change" (Saddam's supposed weapons of mass destruction and links to al-Qaeda) were discredited, the invaders resorted to magnifying the tyrannical nature of the Ba'ath regime, failing to justify why they had chosen to attack this tyranny rather than the many others, far and near. The subsequent occupation and attempts to institute "freedom" and "democracy" have resulted in the strengthening of traditionalist religious forces intent on bringing family law in line with their interpretations of the sharia and on dismantling the Iraqi Family Code, which stands among the most progressive in the Muslim world. As in Afghanistan, it seems that most Iraqi Muslims see the neo-imperialist intervention as a direct assault on their religion, which has given a new legitimacy to radical Islamist groups and undermined the position and discourse of progressive forces (Hosseini, 2006). Three hundred Islamic women from around the world met at the first international congress in Madrid on Islamic feminism. The organisers said there should be a "gender jihad" to work for equal rights for women and to promote interpretations of the Koran that support equal rights. Fundamentalists who curtail women's rights are distorting the Koran because of their own misogyny. (Verma *et.al.*, 2005). The organisers said they held the conference in Spain to reach out to the increasing number of Muslim women in Europe.

By the late 1980s in Iran, the ideological, theological, theoretical, and practical problems brought by the experience of administering pre-modern interpretations of fiqh had led to the formulation of a new approach. The main architect was Abdolkarim Soroush, whose interpretative- epistemological theory of the evolution of religious knowledge- known as the contraction and expansion of sharia- posed a serious challenge to both traditional and ideological constructions of the sharia. Soroush made a distinction between religion and religious knowledge and argued that, whereas the first is sacred and immutable, the second - including Islamic law- is human and evolves in time because of forces external to religion itself, discourse became the intellectual backbone of the reformist movement that emerged in 1997. It is part of an older trend of thought that remained dormant during the first decade of the Islamic Republic, which was then engaged in a war with Iraq. Its advocates now display a refreshingly pragmatic vigour and a willingness to engage with nonreligious perspectives. They do not reject an idea simply because it is Western, nor do they see Islam as having a built-in blueprint for solving the social, economic, and political problems of the Muslim world (Hosseini, 2006). They contend that the human understanding of Islam is flexible, that Islam's tenets can be interpreted to encourage both pluralism and democracy, and that Islam allows change in the face of time, space, and experience.

While women of elite background were encouraged by their families to obtain education, neither the Iraqi state nor its British advisers actively promoted women's education or women's rights. Women even before the creation of the Iraqi state adopted nationalism as a liberating discourse, which is in the 'awakening stage'. It appears that the 'awakening stage' in Iraq came relatively late the intellectual debate on women's status began only in the twentieth century; and the first women's organisation and the first women's magazine were established only in 1923; and so on. It also said that developments ascribed to this stage were of a relatively limited scope a separate women's press never evolved, women's participation in the debate on their position was limited, women established only one private girls' school and there were relatively few women's organisations. It also seems that unlike other Arab countries, religiously-based charitable societies did not precede secular and more overtly social and political organisations. The first women's organisation was secular and a variety of organisations later developed in parallel. In addition the emergence of new women's organisations at the 'nationalist stage' had less to do with 'periods when nationalist feelings were at their peak' and more to do with governmental control (Wilbanks, 2010). While these comparisons may raise expectations for conclusions, it would be premature to make them on this basis. Relatively late beginnings in the 'awakening stage' may be attributed to the fact that much of the source material regarding the development of the women's movement was written after the creation of the new state. Developments not considered 'purely' Iraqi, such as the establishment of externally inspired or Ottoman women's organisations, might have been omitted. Mostly male reformers also addressed the subject of the veil which they perceived to be a major symbol of cultural backwardness and subordination. Sources have indeed hinted at earlier beginnings, as in the question of whose voice was first raised in the debate on women's position and the case of the first girls' school.

Since the 1940's, the number of Iraqi women who left the nation was huge. Most of them had left due to political repression or fear of persecution. Others left to escape war and destruction. Economic betterment as well as the wish to pursue higher education were other reasons for the mass migration. During the period of economic sanctions (1990-2003), simple categories of voluntary versus forced migration did become blurred as hundreds of thousands of Iraqis left in the context of a severe economic crisis and ongoing political repression. Efforts to draft such a law were made in the second half of the 1940s and the beginning of the 1950s. At that time, however, women were not included in the legislative process. Legislators were rarely concerned with improving women's status and the demands of women's organisations were largely ignored. Women activists expressed concern about child marriages and polygamy. They criticised the ease with which a man could divorce his wife and her difficulty in dissolving her marriage and in maintaining custody of her children. Drafts debated in Parliament during the 1940s and 1950s contained only minor reforms, mainly regarding divorce and child marriages. These drafts never became law, mainly because of the objections of Sunni and Shi'ia 'ulama'. The 'ulama' were apprehensive that codifying provisions of the Shari'a would permit judges to administer this code without recourse to expert opinion. Thus, the prestige and income of the 'ulama' would suffer. Shi'ia opposition was even stronger they saw the code as an encroachment on the realm of their mujtahids. The outstanding features of the status quo prior to 1958 were the following the proposed Personal Status Law had not passed; procedurally, contracting or registering marriages in state courts was not required; and the "Sharia' Courts Law" actually recommended referral of certain suits to the 'ulama'. Hence, the field of personal status in this period, to a large extent, remained in the hands of the 'ulama' (Efrati, 2008). In the context of the general history of the women's movement in the Middle East. The women's movements in Iraq face preliminary comparisons. As in most of the rest of the world, at the time women were almost completely excluded from formal political institutions and processes, but from the 1920s onwards established a growing number of humanitarian, social and political organisations that were part of an emerging Iraqi 'civic order'. The first Iraqi women's movement called Women's Awakening (*Nadi al-Nahda al-Nisa'iyya*). Baghdadi elite women embraced the idea of 'the new woman'. During the 1930s, women's associations set up charitable organisations, including shelters for orphans and health centres, to address the growing 'social question' and lack of state welfare provision (Coleman, 2006) issues that were only seriously debated in Western Europe after World War II. Women's education, the need for enlightened mothers and housewives, suffrage and entry into the labour force became subjects of debate.

Concerning the limited scope of developments in Iraq, here too, caution is required. Regarding women's participation in the earlier stages of the intellectual debate, for example, research on neighbouring countries has taught that preoccupation with the role of individual male thinkers diverts our attention from a wider intellectual milieu and thus from intellectual women's contribution to the discussions. Fleischmann has indeed identified central characteristic features of the women's movements in the Middle East. Many were noted regarding Iraq the emergence of intellectual debate on women's status, establishment of a myriad of women's organisations, evolution of a women's press, women's efforts to enhance girls' education, women's participation in the nationalist struggle, the adoption of nationalism as a liberating discourse and development of pan-Arab feminism. These features facilitate portrayal not only of an expanded picture of the emergence of the women's movement, but also its integration into the general history of women's movements in the Middle East (Townsend, 2003). Assignment of features to different stages, however, proved less useful. As cautioned by Fleischmann, stages may not follow a linear chronology and may overlap with lines of demarcation, which are often obscured.

The most dangerous and pervasive forces in the war on women's minds are those of political religious fundamentalism at home in the traditionalist, conservative social structure of our societies. For it serves to conceal, to perpetuate, to reinforce and to rationalise the economic, political, social and cultural exploitation of international corporate capital and U.S. imperialism, made easier by the adaptability and versatility resulting from new technologies in the field of information and communication (Saadaw, 2008). Since the toppling of Saddam Hussein by the U.S.-led coalition, the threat of abolishing Iraq's progressive Personal Status Law, in force since 1959, has hung like a dark cloud over the heads of many Iraqi women. Recent attempts to introduce clauses into the permanent constitution that would effectively repeal the law were preceded by similar efforts in 2003. In both cases women's voices resonated in protest (Efrati, 2008).

Women in Saddam Hussein's Period

Valentine argues that women were the first whose social life was affected by the economy and in cases of war. He says that, the "onset of the war with Iran brought about a toughening of the state's position on women." Women were not allowed to travel without their husbands, fathers, or guardians and their role was to bear children (Moghadam, 1993). In general in cases of war, "women carried the conflicting double burden of being the main motors of the state bureaucracy and the public sector, the main breadwinners and heads of households but also the mothers of 'future soldiers' (Al-Ali, 2007). Moreover, Saddam Hussein, "in an attempt to maintain legitimacy after the Gulf War by appeasing conservative patriarchal constituencies, brought in anti-woman legislation, such as the 1990 presidential decree granting immunity to men who had committed honour crimes" (Al-Ali, 2007). By legalising these so called honour killings women's roles and their social status in the society, were further undermined during Saddam Hussein's presidency. As noted by Yasmine Hussein, author of Women in Iraq, the traditional role of women in Iraq is confined mainly to domestic responsibilities and nurturing the family. The wide scale destruction of the Iraq's infrastructure (i.e., sanitation, water supply and electricity) as a result of war and sanctions worsened their situation. Women in the process assumed extra burdens and domestic responsibilities in society, as opposed to their male counterparts (Hussein, 2008). Like in many Muslim societies, there has been strong resistance faced in the struggle to liberate women and their social status. Due to the Western media's obsession with women's oppression and symbols of Islam however, there has been some significant differences in women's current status, as opposed to the situation prior to the Iraq invasion.

Religious and patriarchal values weighed more heavily on rural and impoverished women than on their more secular, educated, and urban peers. From 1958 to the 1990s Iraq provided relatively more rights and freedom for women and girls than most of its neighbours. Even after Saddam Hussein became president in 1979, at war with

Iran and unsparing with political repression, women's access to education and to waged labour continued to grow-mainly because the expanding economy increasingly demanded their labour. In 1959, Iraq broke somewhat from Shari'a by introducing a Personal Status Law that granted equal inheritance and divorce rights, relegated divorce, inheritance and marriage to civil, instead of religious, courts, and provided for child support. Shari'a was still allowed to adjudicate cases that the Personal Status Law did not cover, and polygamy was permitted under certain circumstances. In the early 1970s, the party established the General Federation of Iraqi Women (GFIW) to implement state policy. The only women's organisation allowed, the GFIW operated primarily through female based community centres to offer educational, job training, and other social programmes. The Iraqi Ba'ath party, which came to power in 1963, included its ideology provisions were for women's equality. The Ba'ath party's programme, which sought to cement loyalty to the state, penetrated as well into education, politics, and society. The Iraqi constitution of 1970 gave women equality and liberty in the Muslim world, but since the invasion, women's rights have fallen to the lowest in Iraqi history. In the 1980s, the government programme to eradicate illiteracy among Iraqi women was exceedingly successful. Traditionally, women in Iraq enjoyed freedoms not found in other Arab and Muslim countries. In addition, Iraq's Constitution was the most advanced in the Middle East, if not the Muslim World. Prior to the 1991 U.S. war and the 13 years of the sanctions of genocide nature, Iraqi women enjoyed unquestionable quality rights to education and health. Education and healthcare were free at all levels. Iraqi women had the most progressive human rights in the region and Iraqi women were the first Arab women to hold high positions in academia, law, medicine and government. After the disastrous eighty year Iran-Iraq war Saddam's regime moved away from Arab socialist ideals and closer to traditional interpretations of Islam in the region, including less tolerance for female autonomy in the public realm (Brown and David, 2006). During the Hussein presidency, women continued to work and study in the public sphere. Before the U.S. invasion and occupation of Iraq, Iraqi women made up 40 per cent of the public-sector work force. Men and women received equal pay for work; Before March 2003, many of the families in Iraq lived in nice apartments, women had good jobs, they were free to go to schools, universities and work, and to perform other duties. Due to security reasons and repression by the government, they are being forced to stay in their homes.

In the early 1970s, the Ba'ath party established the General Federation of Iraqi Women (GFIW) to implement state policy (Lasky, 2006). It also communicated state propaganda. In the late 1970s, the United Nations drafted a treaty Convention on the Elimination of All Forms of Discrimination against Women (CEDAW), for the protection of women throughout the world and a comprehensive human rights treaty to ensure women's equality. The government passed laws to encourage literacy for the entire population, female and male, between the ages of 6 and 45. Women were given the right to vote in 1980 and to be elected to the National Assembly and local governing bodies, although the number of female representatives remained small. Around the same time, laws on divorce, polygamy, and inheritance still further expanded women's rights. Women's basic rights under the Hussein regime were guaranteed in the constitution and-more importantly-respected, with women often occupying important government positions. Now, although their rights are still enshrined in the national constitution, activists complain that, in practice, they have lost almost all of their rights. Women's groups point to the new government, many members of which take a conservative view when it comes to the role of women. "When we tell the government we need more representation in parliament, they respond by telling us that, if well-qualified women appear one day, they won't be turned down," said Senar Muhammad, president of Baghdad-based NGO Woman Freedom Organisation (Mahmoud and Yanar, 2006). According to Senar, however, Shari'a has been misinterpreted by elements within the government and by certain religious leaders, which has resulted in the frequent denial of women's rights. This is particularly the case in matters pertaining to divorce. Women represent roughly 60 per cent of the population. Despite a 25 per cent representative presence in parliament, however, they are seldom entrusted with high government positions, while their contribution to political debate is rarely taken seriously.

VII. Humanitarian Impact of Women in Occupation Period

The military occupation of Iraq has deprived the people of their very basic needs and to a very large extent imperilled their personal security. In Baghdad, none had running water, guaranteed electricity, or adequate medical supplies (Ismael, 2014). The director of the best hospital in Baghdad does not have internet access or a means to telephone someone outside the hospital. Clean running water and adequate sewage are not assured, even in Baghdad. Electricity constantly turns on and off. The cycle is about three hours on, four hours off. In many respects, Iraq has become an instant third-world nation. Before March 2003, many of these families lived in nice apartments, had good jobs. Their children went to universities. After the invasion and the lift of the rent cap instituted by Saddam, rent rates quadrupled just when jobs were being obliterated. In Baghdad alone, thousands of families live in camps or on the streets. The effect of the lack of basic needs doesn't stop at the hospital or in the hungry belly. There are far reaching implications. Without their basic needs being met, the Iraqi people are not afforded the luxury to even begin thinking about women's political participation or the drafting of a constitution. The great majority are far too busy trying to find their next meal and place to sleep for the night to be concerned about the more abstract after-effects of the toppling of a dictator (Cunningham and Michael, 2004). The fall of Baghdad on 10 April 2003 brought Iraq and the women living there into an uncertain transition period. In the post II World War period, Iraq was often touted as one of the Middle Eastern countries that offered its women more liberties with regard to education and employment. The Iraqi Ba'ath party, which came to power in 1963, included in its ideology provisions for women's equality. Despite this, Iraqi traditional societies outside the major urban centre of Baghdad still relegated Iraqi women to a very inferior position vis-à-vis men. Additionally the repression that all Iraqis suffered under Saddam's regime, as well as the consequences of this wars, applied to the female half of the population as well.

Since the beginning of the U.S. occupation, there has been a dramatic increase in sexual assaults and violations of women's rights by U.S. forces in Iraq. In Iraq there are additional challenges in addressing crimes of a sexual nature. In many parts of the country when a woman or girl loses her "sexual purity" she could be defamed and subject to imprisonment or even death if she cannot prove, often with the testimony of four male witnesses, that the sexual incident was, in fact, rape (Jordan and John, 2004). Many women have been taken hostages tortured, and sexually abused. The sexual abuse, rape and torture against Iraqi women is not confined only to Western media-loved Abu Ghraib prison, but is "happening all across Iraq", said Amal Kadhim Swadi, an Iraqi lawyers representing women detainees at Abu Ghraib. "Sexualised violence and abuse committed by U.S. troops goes far beyond a few isolated cases", she added. Many people feel it is due to the ongoing terror wrought in this land that brings so much oppression to women (Hassan, 2005). Prior to the arrival of forces in Iraq, Iraqi women were free to wear whatever they liked and go wherever they chose. Since the invasion in 2003 "Iraqi women have been brutally attacked, kidnapped and intimidated from participating in the Iraqi society." Iraqi women's experiences of Ba'ath rule and of the occupations have varied immensely depending on social class, political affiliation, religious identity, place of residence and educational background (Al-Ali, 2009). She continues by arguing that "The first losers in all these were women". Arising from their fear of being raped and harassed, women have to wear not only the veil, but must also to wear the black dress in order not to attract attention. In an online edition of Guardian, the reporter Mark Lattiner reports that despite promises and hopes given to the Iraqi population that their lives were going to change, Iraqi women's lives "have become immeasurably worse, with rapes, burnings and murders now as a daily occurrence" (Mark, 2007).

Under the U.S. Occupation, the situation of Iraqi women has continued to deteriorate. In addition to torture and sexual violence perpetrated by U.S. Occupation forces, a great number of Iraqi women and girls are kept locked up in their homes by a very real fear of abduction and criminal abuse. Prior to the invasion of Iraq, Iraqi women had the most progressive human rights in the region and Iraqi women were the first Arab women to hold high positions in academia, law, medicine and government (Al-Ali, 2005). Before the U.S. invasion and occupation of Iraq, Iraqi women made up 40 per cent of the public-sector work force. Men and women received equal pay for work; education and healthcare were free at all levels. In the 1980s, a government programme to eradicate illiteracy among Iraqi women was exceedingly successful, and women have traditionally enjoyed freedoms not found in other Arab and Muslim countries. In addition, Iraq's Constitution was the most advanced in the Middle East, if not the Muslim World. Women's rights are enshrined in the Constitution, which was dissolved (together with Iraqi Police and Security) by the U.S. Occupation and replaced by a U.S.-crafted "Interim Constitution", produced without women's representation, which deprives Iraqi women of their rights and dignity. In today's Iraq, crimes and abuse against women were back to the levels before independence from colonial Britain 1958. The crime of rape was capital offence under Iraq's Constitution.

Social Conditions

The miseries of the Iraqi people have more than doubled in the last two years, and Iraqis viewed the occupation as the cause of their miseries. In addition to the crimes of sexual abuse, torture and rape committed by U.S. soldiers against Iraqi women, all other aspects of Iraqi women's rights have also deteriorated (Verma, 2005). Iraq had assent U.N. conventions regarding human rights but there had been no sufficient improvement of Iraqi women's rights. Women health and education have fallen significantly. Unemployment, prostitution and malnutrition, have increased dramatically, and are now widespread among Iraqi women today. Iraqi women have also suffered great loss of lives. U.S. serial bombing and destruction caused the death of great numbers of women and children. Most of the victims were innocent women and children killed by U.S. bombing of population centres. Especially following, the U.S.-led 2003 occupation of Iraq and the fall of the Ba'ath regime of Saddam Hussein, the status of women's rights in Iraq were expected to progress. But now the condition of women situation worsened because of continued and irregular violence and the adoption of the 2005 Iraqi constitution.. Moreover, Iraqi women and their children are being taken hostages by U.S. forces and used as 'bargaining chips'. On 11 April 2005, the Guardian reported, that U.S. forces were accused of violating international law by taking Iraqi women hostages to force their male relatives to surrender. Iraqi women are arrested, detained, abused and tortured not because of anything they have done, but to force their close relatives (spouses, sons and brothers) to collaborate with the occupation and to inform against the Resistance (Ismael, 2014). Contrary to the Geneva Conventions, which stipulate that no one can "be punished for an offence he or she has not personally committed." The practices, which have been condemned by the U.N. and human rights organisations, are widely used by the Israeli Army against Palestinian men, women and children in occupied Palestine.

The elections of 2005 and 2009 increased women's representation in national and provincial legislative bodies to 25 per cent, one of the highest levels in the region. The dismantling of the Iraqi Security and Police led to increase in violence and crimes against women. Women are no longer leaving their homes unaccompanied by relatives. Human Rights Watch documented a wave of sexual violence and abductions against women in Baghdad in the months following the invasion. It also documented during the invasion Iraq has made some efforts to improve the rights of women in recent years. The Bush administration's promotion of religious fundamentalism and sectarianism mean the worst for Iraqi women rights. U.S. foreign policy preys on religious fundamentalism. The miseries of the Iraqi people had more than doubled in the following years, and Iraqis viewed the occupation as the cause of their miseries. In addition to the crimes of sexual abuse, torture and rape committed by U.S. soldiers against Iraqi women, all other aspects of Iraqi women's rights also deteriorated (Enloe, 2006). This traumatic situation had significant psychological effects on the health and welfare of the mothers. Doctors in Iraq have reported a significant increase in deformities among newborn babies that could be due to radiation passed through mothers following U.S. wars of 1991-2003. "The depleted uranium left by the U.S. bombing campaign has turned Iraq into a cancer-infested country. Women health and education had fallen significantly. Unemployment, prostitution and malnutrition, have increased dramatically, and are now widespread among Iraqi women today. During the period of the U.N. sanctions, many women lost their jobs due to the deterioration of the economy.[2] Moreover, sanctions led to the dismantling of government social programmes and women suffered disproportionately.[3] As a result of the U.S. dismantling of the Iraqi state, many women lost their jobs. Unemployment among Iraqi women was more than 70 per cent and rising. During the U.S. led invasion in 2003 and the war that followed, many women started private businesses in their homes, but when electricity was cut they could not continue. Women who benefited from commerce in the informal market had also been forced to give up this source of income. Before the U.S. occupation, Iraqi women made up 40 per cent of the public-sector work force. Today, most women are unemployed. When the economy deteriorated, women were the first to lose their jobs. Today women's unemployment is at 70 per cent.[4] In addition, due to the climate of violence and fear, fewer children attend school and consequently, mothers or the oldest female in the family have had to stop working to take care of the children. As a result, women and children have fewer opportunities. The U.S. dismantling of the Iraqi state meant that many women lost governmental positions.

Political and Economical Situations

In several other aspects too Iraqi women's rights have deteriorated. Iraq suffered a lot; many women are widowed and others are abandoned. Iraqi women were not represented in the Iraqi ministries and in the judicial infrastructure (Eland, 2005). A report by Women for Women International reveals that 57 per cent of Iraqi women and their families do not have adequate healthcare, and that maternal mortality rate has tripled when compared to the period between 1989 and 2002. Iraq's infrastructure has been reduced to rubble. The healthcare services and the education system are on the brink of total collapse. Only 3 women were nominated to the interim Iraqi Governing Council in July 2003. Women were not included in either the nine-member rotating presidential council or the committee working on constitutional reform. The majority of Iraqi women doesn't trust political parties. All political parties are run by men. Many activists in women's organisations gathered to discuss violence against women, including Hanaa Edwar, the head of the Al-Amal Association, Suhaila Alaasm of the Iraqi Women's League and Athraa al-Hassani, the head of the Model Iraqi Woman Organisation. All of them noted that dozens of women have been killed by their husbands or other male relatives in horrible ways for not wearing the veil or over doubts concerning their morality (Bloom, 2010). For example, if a woman speaks on the phone late at night and her family does not know whom she is calling, this could raise suspicion. Even today, most women in Shiite areas of Baghdad do not dare to go out on the streets without wearing the veil and a black abaya.

Women Prisoners

The Red Cross estimates there are between 10,000-15,000 prisoners. The oldest prisoner is 75 and the youngest 11. None of them has been charged. American-led forces conduct daily raids, arresting men and women. Women are detained in most cases as hostages. There are no exact figures of how many women prisoners are in Iraq (Yacoub, 2010). The rape of a woman stigmatises her whole family. Historically, Iraqi women have not been confined to the private sphere and have attained high levels of educational and professional accomplishments in law, government, and medicine. During the Hussein presidency, women continued to work and study in the public sphere but during the period of the U.N. sanctions, many women lost their jobs due to the deterioration of the economy. Moreover, sanctions led to the dismantling of government social programmes and women suffered disproportionately. The CPA lay off hundreds of thousands of government workers.[5] Despite the amount of reconstruction work in Iraq, Iraqis themselves are not being employed. Instead, the U.S. has hired foreign contractors and flown in foreign workers for high and low skilled positions previously held by Iraqis. According to the household survey done by Women for Women International in August 2004, 84 per cent of the women surveyed had no income from formal or informal work. The women identified electricity, jobs, and water as the most pressing concerns. Despite Iraq's valuable oil reserves, 27 per cent of the population is estimated to live on less than $2 a day.[6] In a move that worsened the crisis exponentially, while imposing a privatised model of governance not chosen by the Iraqi people, the CPA cut the social safety net. Following the many wars Iraq has suffered, many women are widowed or abandoned. According to the U.N. and the World Bank, there were close to one million women heads of households in October 2003. As the U.S. increasingly pushes for privatisation and a 100 per cent free market state, this means that more women will inevitably suffer disproportionately compared to men in Iraq.

The Bush administration's promotion of religious fundamentalism and sectarianism meant the worst for Iraqi women rights. U.S. foreign policy preys on religious fundamentalism. In July 2003, some observers argued that Iraqi women did not have an adequate presence in the Iraqi ministries and in the judicial infrastructure. In December 2003, Khuzai and Chapouk enunciated their frustration with CPA, writing that "women are severely under represented in the leadership established for the transition. They asserted that, as plans for a new governing structure are developed, the Iraqi Governing Council and the CPA should ensure women their rightful place at the decision making table."[7] This criticism as some observers have noted, highlights one of the challenges facing U.S. officials working to include Iraqi women in all levels of the government. Prior to the formation of IGC Bremer reportedly promised that IGC would include a wide spectrum of Iraqis and would not be dominated by exiles. As a result one of the problems in appointing the local Iraqi women lay in identify experienced women, who had remained in Iraq but were not affiliated with the Ba'athist regime, to work within the interim government (Pratt and Nadje, 2008). As part of its 'de-Baahtification' policy, the CPA abolished the GFIW, which had been the only officially recognised organisation for women under Ba'athist rule. After its collapse, some of the GFIW's top leaders, who had been closely affiliated with the Saddam Hussein's regime, reportedly fled Iraq out of fear of prosecution.[8]

The U.S. appointed Iraqi Governing Council passed Resolution 137, which would have overruled the Iraqi Family Law that has been in effect since 1959. Resolution 137 would have placed several aspects of family law, including matters of marriage, divorce and inheritance, under Islamic law. Despite the concern over women's constitutional rights, there were no Iraqi women on the nine-member committee drafting the Transitional Administrative Law (TAL), which was signed by IGC, the TAL declares equal rights to all Iraqis regardless of gender, ethnicity, religion or nationality. It considers Islamic religion as a source of law; also, no provision in the TAL can violate Islamic principle. The TAL also contains a provision calling for targeted goal of 25 per cent representation for women in the transitional National Assembly.[9] It is not clear whether this provision will remain in effect after a permanent constitution is ratified. The Prime Minister of Iraq, Ibrahim al-Jaffari (a Shi'ia), stated that he supports women's rights, including the right to become President or Prime Minister (Osgood, 2005). Furthermore there is a widespread hope, among Iraqi women's group, that a new constitution will continue to stipulate wide-ranging, liberal rights for Iraqi women. Yet, here are some who caution against the belief that women are virtually guaranteed gender equality in the civil and legal spheres of Iraqi society. The issue of Islam's place in many Middle Eastern and predominately Muslim nations' legal codes is common and Iraq is no exception. Although modern Iraqi history is replete with liberal view towards women, Iraqi Shi'iaism and the wider culture of the country may create obstacles for women increasing their participation and visibility in Iraqi political and social life. In particular, some analysts are concerned that any Iraqi constitution may mirror the 'cosmetic' rights Saddam Hussein extended to women during his regime. These experts note that a Shi'ia dominated Iraqi political system will face challenges from secular Iraqis with regards to persistent social issues such as honour killing, harassment, polygamy and property ownership.

The Bush administration has continued to assert that the position of Iraqi woman has improved following the U.S. toppling of the Saddam Hussein's regime. In a speech on March 12, 2004, President Bush indicated that 'every woman in Iraq is better off because the rape rooms and torture chambers of Saddam Hussein is forever closed.[10] Nonetheless, a number of concerns have been raised over the past year regarding the role of women in a future Iraq and the status of U.S. efforts to promote women's rights. The concern for many is that any modest political gains Iraqi women have secured may be threatened by cultural forces and increased political authority of Shi'ia conservatism. Also, the question of equal distribution for women in local governance and judiciary may continue to resonate, despite any increases in the parliament. Furthermore, the continuing violence in Iraq affects 'at risk' populations, who often restrict themselves to their homes out of fear of physical harm, intimidation and abuse. A number of security concerns affect not only the involvement of women in the developing Iraqi political system but also the access of the Iraqi ordinary women to reconstruction programmes (Mingus, 2012). Some report that many Iraqi women, who work to advance political freedom, do so under threat of violence, and kidnappings. The lack of security has been cited as a major obstacle in the progress of reconstruction efforts aimed at advancing women's rights. One analyst wrote in 2004 that since the start of the occupation, 'life has not returned to normal' in Iraq. In places were kidnappings occur frequently, children must be accompanied and women escorted to the market and have taken to donning abaya (body-covering garments) to ensure greater self protection.

Subjugated Womanhood

Religious and cultural factors in Iraq also present challenges to reconstruction efforts targeting women. For example, there is a debate over the extent of the role that Islamic law or Shari'a should play in a future Iraqi government. Some Iraqi groups- including those who represented on the U.S. appointed Governing Council- are interested in instituting Islamic courts instead of civil courts to oversee matters related to marriage, divorce, property ownership and inheritance. These courts would be run by Muslim clerics- all of whom are male. Some analyst expressed concerns that the growing religious conservatisms within Iraqi society is threatening women who are liberal, secularist and non-Muslim or those Muslim women who do not wish to be ruled by religious-based law. There is also concern among Kurdish Iraqi women's group who feel that the strides made during years of relative autonomy (1990-2003) could be threatened by the inclusion of the Kurdish areas in what could become an Islamist-governed Iraqi state (Romano, 2006). Many Iraqi women, including Christian female students in Shi'ite Basra, have complained that they were forced to wear a head scarf. Other Iraqi women's groups, however, point out that Islamic law is not inherently contrary to the rights of women. A Baghdad-based group called the Islamic Women's Movements notes that Islamic scriptures accord women considerable rights-inheriting property, for example, or declining an unwanted husband. They say it's the way male authorities interpret those writings that keeps women from exercising them, 'adding that teaching women their rights under Islam would help end injustices against them.[11] One study of southern Iraq indicated that most Iraqi men and women do not fully support civil and political rights of the women, including freedom to move about in public and to participate in government.[12] The study mentions that 'lack of support for such rights for women may be related to implementation considerations, such as inadequate numbers of teachers, employment opportunities, and safety issues, among others. This may not reflect the opinion of Iraqis towards women in other regions of Iraq. Women in Northern Kurdish region have experienced greater freedom and more opportunities for political involvement in the past several years. The attitude of Iraqi towards women in larger urban centres, such as Baghdad, has yet to be fully investigated and might also reflect a range of opinions on women's rights.

Under U.S. occupation children are dying from malnutrition, a lack of clean water and a lack of medical equipment and drugs to cure easily treatable diseases. This traumatic situation has significant psychological effects on the health and welfare of the children's mothers. Electricity blackout is as long as 15 hours a day, much longer than that of pre-war level. To increase the atrocity, the U.S. provides its soldiers with "self-immunity" from prosecution making it very easy for them to kill Iraqis with institutionalised immunity, as if Iraqis were not human beings. In addition, evidence shows that the U.S.-British forces use banned weapons such as napalm and weapons of mass destruction (WMD), which contaminated and polluted Iraq's environment, and caused health hazards (Smallwood, 2011). As a result of armed conflict many Iraqi women had lost their husbands, generalised violence, and displacement. The resulting financial hardship has made them vulnerable to trafficking for sexual exploitation and prostitution. The parliament passed a counter-trafficking law that outlines government obligations and provides for prosecution of traffickers. Iraqi authorities announced the arrest of a Baghdad trafficking leader, but little has been done to prosecute other people accused of trafficking, or to take measures to prevent it. Victims of trafficking continue to report having passports confiscated and being prevented from obtaining visas and new identification papers, leaving them vulnerable to arrest and unable to access healthcare. In June 2011, the Kurdistan Regional Government (KRG) parliament passed the Family Violence Bill, which includes provisions criminalising forced and child marriages; abuse of girls and women; and a total ban on FGM. Implementation of the law is poor, and dozens of girls and practitioners said that they had either undergone or performed FGM since the law was passed. The authorities took no measures to investigate these cases.

Iraq witnessed a string of attacks against young people with socially non-conforming appearances, including gender non-conforming and gay men and those who identify as "emo"- a subculture characterised by distinctive clothes and musical tastes. Local human rights groups, community activists, and media reported numerous deaths of these youths. Rather than undertaking measures to protect targeted individuals, the Interior Ministry said reports of attacks on those suspected of homosexual conduct or who appeared "emo" were "fabricated" and "groundless" and took no measure to prosecute or arrest attackers. Iraq ratified the Convention on the Rights of Persons with Disabilities (CRPD) (UNTC, 2006). However, Iraq's government has failed to take the necessary steps to ensure that persons with disabilities do not face discrimination, as the CRPD requires, and to ensure access to their rights to education, employment, personal mobility, healthcare, and comprehensive rehabilitation services and programmes, among other things. Large numbers of Iraqis with disabilities-including those resulting from conflicts, disease, and non-war-related injuries-are unable to find support for integration into their local communities.

In January 2013, Prime Minister Nuri al-Maliki promised to reform the criminal justice system, beginning with releasing detained women who had judicial orders of release. The New York-based watchdog said the brutal tactics of security forces remain essentially the same and hundreds of women remain in detention illegally. Many of the 27 women who spoke with HRW described being beaten, kicked, slapped, hung upside-down and beaten on their feet (*falaqa*), given electric shocks, and raped or threatened with sexual assault by security forces during their interrogation. HRW found that Iraqi security forces regularly arrest women illegally and commit other due process violations against women at every stage of the justice system. Women are subjected to threats of, or actual, sexual assault, sometimes in front of husbands, brothers, and children. Failure by the courts to investigate allegations of abuse and hold the abusers responsible encourages the police to falsify confessions and use torture, Iraq's broken criminal justice system fails to achieve justice for victims either of security force abuses or of criminal attacks by armed groups, the watchdog said (Steinberg, 2013). Arrests and convictions documented by HRW appeared often to have been predicated on information provided by secret informants and confessions coerced under torture. "The abuses of women we documented are in many ways at the heart of the current crisis in Iraq," Stork said. "These abuses have caused a deep-seated anger and lack of trust between Iraq's diverse communities and security forces, and all Iraqis are paying the price." Violence in Iraq is some of its highest levels, with more than 1,000 people killed in the country.

Increased rates of miscarriages and developmental disabilities in children in Fallujah and Basrah to environmental toxins left by U.S. military operations in those areas. Human Rights Watch (HRW) reported that Iraqi authorities are detaining thousands of Iraqi women illegally and subjecting many to torture and ill-treatment, including sexual abuse. The report documents abuses of women in detention, based on interviews with women and girls in prison, as well as their families, lawyers and prison medical service providers (Evers, 2014). The report came at a time of escalating sectarian violence in Iraq, involving security forces and armed groups. "The vast majority of the more than 4,200 women detained in interior-and defense ministry facilities are Sunni, but the abuses HRW documents affect women of all sects and classes throughout Iraqi society. Iraq's large Sunni minority complains of large-scale discrimination by the Shiite led government in Baghdad. The report said that "Many women were detained for months or even years without charge before seeing a judge." Joe Stork Deputy Middle East and North Africa director at HRW mentioned "Iraqi security forces and officials act as if brutally abusing women will make the country safer." Doctors in Iraq have reported a significant increase in deformities among newborn babies that could be due to radiation passed through mothers following U.S. wars of 1991-2003. 'After studying family history of couples with deformed babies, they concluded that radiation and pollution caused by 'depleted' uranium dust, DU were the main causes of the deformity,' Dr Lamia'a Amran, a paediatrician at the Iraqi Red Crescent Society (IRCS) hospital in Baghdad, told Irin news (Hassan, 2005). "Since 1991 the number of children born with birth deformities has quadrupled", said Dr Janan Hassan, who runs a children's clinic in Basra in southern Iraq. If DU is the cause of the cancers, which is most likely, the crisis could become infinitely worse for women and children in Iraq. The U.S. and Britain used thousands of tonnes of DU in their wars on Iraq and over a wide range of areas. It took three to five years for the cancers to begin manifesting after the first Gulf crisis. Iraqi women and their newborn babies are expecting bleak future as a result of the U.S.-Britain use of WMD. The pretexts for the war were proved to be just lies. Iraq had no WMD and Iraq had no relations with terrorism. The war on Iraq was an illegal act of aggression, designed to increase the threat of terrorism and violence, in order to exert control (Pitt, 2002). The female suicide bombers are also violating the peaceful situation in Iraq. Mainly three types of terrorist or insurgent groups operate in Iraq. There are Al Qaeda-affiliated groups, Sunni nationalist organisations, and Shi'ite militias. The Al Qaeda affiliated groups are controlled and financed by non-Iraqis, it has both Iraqi nationalists and non-Iraqi fighters.

The Sunni nationalist groups are almost entirely made up of Iraqi nationals, and mainly target coalition forces and Shi'a elements. This groups work to end the U.S. occupation and secure political and economic resources; they infrequently use suicide tactics. Other terrorist groups are the Shi'a militias consist of groups such as Badr Corps and Mehdi Militia, and have attacked coalition and Sunni societal elements.The continuing occupation of Iraq is to rob Iraq of its oil resources, and enhance U.S. imperialist doctrine (Cleminson, 2003). So, as news of the appalling miseries of Iraqi women pile up, the setting up of an international war crimes tribunal to investigate and prosecute those who committed these crimes against the Iraqi people should be the aim of the world community. It will enhance human rights and democracy worldwide.

The depleted uranium left by the U.S. bombing campaign has turned Iraq into a cancer-infected country. "For hundreds of years to come, the effects of the uranium will continue to wreak havoc on Iraq and its surrounding areas", said Iraqi artist and author of 'Baghdad Diaries', Nuha Al-Radi before she died of leukaemia on August 13, 2004. The ccupation had both immediate and long-term negative implications for the safety of Iraqi women and for their participation in post-war life in Iraq (Anastasiou and Gould, 2007). Al Qaeda-affiliated groups use suicide terrorism primarily to attack Iraqi security forces and Shi'a civilians. The end of the Occupation is supposed to stop the chain reactions of violence, and may allow the victim's wounds to heal.[13]

The biggest and most important national challenge is to retain girls in school during their primary years, and particularly to ensure that they progress from grade 1 to grade 2 and from grade 5 to grade 6.[14] In Iraq there is also a major issue with the number of children in each grade who are over age. The decreased percentage of girls, the older a girl becomes, less likely she is to remain in school (UNICEF, 2013). Economic growth is a crucial component for sustainable development. However, in the context of war-affected countries like Iraq there is the added cost of reconstruction investment. Therefore, the simplistic notion that, in Iraq, oil revenues alone will pay for recovery fails to recognise that there is no supporting institutional and administrative infrastructure in place to ensure the trickle-down effect.

While many commentators, consider economic growth to be critical to ease the transition from the immediate post-war recovery to longer-term development (Hill, 1996). This does not mean simply promoting national 'economic growth' by employing liberal market strategies, as the World Bank and other financial institutions have had the tendency to advocate in the past. Such an emphasis, particularly when it is purely ideologically motivated, as now in Iraq, can often lead to extra pressure on emerging societies. Privatisation and restructuring can result in large job losses and wider grievances at a time when reconstruction should be creating hope through delivering tangible benefits to individuals and their communities. The public may not have the means to purchase the enterprises or the enterprises themselves may not be attractive to the private sector when they are not functional (Kubrusi, 2003). On the other hand, stimulating the economy through increasing the number of people employed has the added advantage of improving legitimacy and therefore security, as noted above. However, the U.S. strategy of inviting corporate U.S. business to tender for the large reconstruction contracts, and its intended oil privatisation, is more likely to lead to asset stripping than to the investment in the economy which is so crucial for encouraging employment. In addition, Iraq's $200 billion war reparations debt could seriously hinder any capital investment for economic and social development (Abdel-Fadil, 2003). This economic dislocation will continue as long as the U.S. remains obsessed with oil as the only form of economic salvation (Abdel-Fadil, 2003). Kubrusi argues that it is the agricultural sector, which has traditionally been an engine for growth, which should be seen as a priority and stimulated to complement oil revenue. This would not only restore the livelihoods of a substantial section of the population but also increase food security. Contrary to the economic reconstruction needs discussed above, the U.S. strategy neither addressed the immediate macro nor the micro economic priorities necessary to initiate development. At the macro level currency stabilisation, rehabilitation of the banking sector and national control of economic assets (oil) are not yet addressed (Corm, 2003 and Abdel-Fadil, 2003).

At the micro level the combined effect of debaathification, disbanding the army, privatisation of state enterprises, the dollarisation of the economy and the resulting insecurity has increased levels of unemployment across all classes of society. It has also failed to stimulate alternative income generation from small businesses and agriculture (Abdel-Fadil, 2003). According to Barton and Crocker the interim evaluation found that the continuing lack of economic opportunity and high levels of unemployment (Barton and Crocker, 2004). These lack of economic opportunity and high levels of unemployment combined with personal insecurity, are now the main concerns of the Iraqi public (Barakat, 2005).

Feminist Protest against War in Iraq

The National Women's Studies Association (NWSA) had joined hundreds of thousands of Americans in an unprecedented historic grassroots movement by sending a message to President George W. Bush and other elected officials urging the U. S. government to refrain from using military force against Iraq (Hudnall, 2003). NWSA, which adopted an anti-war resolution on 25 February 2003, speaks for thousands of women's studies practitioners and feminist organisations in the U.S. who are committed to resolving conflict through negotiation. The National Women's Studies Association is committed to resolving local and global conflicts through negotiation; hence, it urges the U.S. government to refrain from using military force to effect social and political change in Iraq. NWSA further urges the U.S. government to immediately and wholeheartedly commit itself to international conflict resolution processes that will lead to greater social justice and enduring peace worldwide. NWSA's position on the question of war against Iraq is based on feminist thinking about the causes, consequences, and solutions to violence against women. Feminist analysis shows that there is a connection between individual acts of violence directed against women and violence that women experience as the result of war. Feminist practice also demonstrates that working to eliminate oppression and establish social justice is more effective than military aggression in reducing interpersonal and state-sponsored violence (Anderson and Clack, 2004).

The penal law criminalises rape but allows the case to be dropped if the offender marries the victim, permits a maximum sentence of life imprisonment if the victim dies, and does not address spousal rape (Teague, 2010). There were no reliable estimates of the incidents of rape or the effectiveness of government enforcement of the law. Due to social conventions and retribution against both the victim and perpetrator, victims of sexual crimes did not usually pursue legal remedies. The U.N. Development Programme documented cases of families of rape victims sometimes demanding that the victim marry her perpetrator in order to maintain the family's honour, noting that in some cases when the victim refused the marriage, families asked judges to intervene and force the marriage between victim and perpetrator. Moreover, reporting by local and international NGOs and media indicated that domestic violence often went unreported and unpunished with abuses customarily addressed within the family and tribal structure. Harassment of legal personnel working on domestic violence cases and a lack of trained police and judicial personnel further hampered efforts to bring perpetrators to justice. June 2011 KRG Family Violence Law criminalises domestic violence, including physical and psychological abuse, threats of violence, and spousal rape. During the year the KRG mounted public awareness campaigns, issued directives to police; and trained judges on the provisions of the law. Provisions of the law creating a special police force to investigate cases of gender-based violence and a reconciliation committee within the judicial system was not implemented at year's end. The IKR's Iraqi Kurdistan Region (IKR) Council of Ministers (COM) established a Women's Rights Monitoring Board to address women's problems, including gender based violence.[15]

Feminist scholars were already questioning how a collapsed state able to guarantee basic policing utilities could possibly the individual right to women.[16] Women remained noticeably under-represented in party leaderships, the constitution-writing and review committees, positions outside the Ministry of Women's Affairs and backroom bargaining to form a government (Al-Ali and Nochola, 2006). The moral victory of a parliamentary quotas was devalued further in 2010 when stalemated elections were followed by protracted negotiations resulting in a conspicuously make government. Thus, instituting a quota for the representation of Iraqi women was a symbolic achievement but not necessarily a very sustentative one. Many Iraqi women seemed dubious about economic autonomy and parliamentary quotas. A former political prisoner of the Iraqi police state, an exile returnee observed that the enemy is not Islam, nor their families but the occupation itself (Zangana 2005). By 2006, female parliamentarian, officials and activists expressed ambivalence about gains amidst socio-economic deterioration.[17] Consistent with WWI (Women-to-Women International) eliminating violence against women paradigm, nearly fourteen Iraqi women murdered by other Iraqis between March and December 2004. They were two news reporters, two district council members, two translators, two women activists and a pharmacist whose body was dumped on a highway in a traditional headscarf she never wore. The headscarf incident presumably signified that all these crimes were cultural or religious rather than political or even criminal.

NGOs, CSOs, Human Rights and Women's Equality

The most basic tenets of democratic practice require broad acceptance by the state and civil society. Whether in Iraq or elsewhere, this is a complex, gradual and delicate process. The non-government and civil society sector, in Iraq has multiplied. Most of these growing human rights organisations are not yet sufficiently well established to operate effectively, nor are they in a position to influence public debate. Training and capacity building efforts by UN and its agencies and INGOs will continue to focus on training human rights organisations, CSOs and women's groups on the basic principles of human rights and gender equality. Women's groups appear to be active at the community level (Paffenholz and C Spurk, 2010). These groups provide basic community services such as health, education and family support. UN agencies are well placed to continue support of these institutions. However, the exodus of INGOs due to security reasons and the incapacity of local NGOs to operate at the community level due to similar reasons, jeopardize these institutions that are the pillars of grass-roots democratic movement.

The term civil society is used in connection with various non-governmental organisations and initiatives that deal with democracy, peace-building, human rights and gender equality. After the 2003 invasion, many local NGOs were formed in the hope of contributing and promoting welfare of people. As civil society was mostly suppressed during the Republican and Ba'athist phase, the newly formed local organisations are dependent on international support for training and knowledge. This led to a civil society that is less based on historical and cultural roots and more influenced by a Western concept. Furthermore, many of these local NGOs or CSOs are suspected to have close affiliations with political parties (Genot, 2010). That claim is based on two reasons: the first one is that the sources for funding and other support of the organisations are often not transparent. The second one is that political parties often create NGOs to implement social welfare programmes and as soon as elections lead to a change of power, these organisations vanish and new ones come into place. After the 2003-invasion, many of the new established NGOs were formed as a substitute for political parties as a reaction to the suppression of the Ba'athist government and to profit from the tremendous amounts of humanitarian aid that swept over the country. Although there are no claims against it, the accusations made by the NCCI[18] are not proven with any stated evidence or examples and, therefore, cannot be taken as a fact but rather as an expression of the organisations opinion. However, as the NCCI provides the only critical view towards the Iraqi civil society organisations, their expressed concerns and accusations are crucial for a critical and balanced treatment of the provided information.

Al-Mesalla Center for Human Resources Development is a nongovernmental and non-profit organisation for human resource development. It was founded in Baghdad in 2004, is dependent on voluntary work and has financial and administrative independence from the state. The financial independence is possible through revenues of organisational activities, donor support and contributions by other associates of the organisation. The major goals of Al-Mesalla are establishing a human rights culture, particularly women's rights (Parver and R Wolf, 2008). It is also promoting non-violence culture in order to fight against discrimination based on gender, religion or race. Its capacity building with special focus on youth and civil programmes. That is aimed at political, economic, social, and educational changes; and strengthening the role of former suppressed communities that had to suffer from violence and poverty and reintegrating them into society. Part of their programmes are *Enhancing Local Protection of Women and Girls,* Women Watch Projects-(1) Sewing Training Programme for Women-Small Investing Project with the focus on training poor women who faced violence, providing the needs of this programme for those women, joining those women with the society and erasing the violence trace on them. (2) Women Health Awareness Programme -the programme was broadcasted live via the local radio station in Erbil. This programme aimed at gives warning to women in Erbil city about women diseases, and encouraging them to take care of their health (Al-Mesalla, 2012).

The IIWO is a non-governmental civil society organisation that was established in Baghdad in 2003 by Iraqi women. The aspirations of the organisation are, inter alia, capacity building, to empower women socially, economically and also political, to fight against violence and discrimination, to cultivate a culture of human rights and peace, to take care of handicapped and paralysed women, to gain and teach expertise in conflict resolution and peace building. The activities of the organisation are for instance: 'designing and publishing flyers about hygiene, environment, culture and politics, holding cultural and hygienic meetings in many areas in Baghdad especially public areas. Conducting projects using art to express political themes, and leading advocacy campaigns concerning women issues, holding four successful conferences to bring together women to discuss important social issues such as unemployment and education' (Coleman, 2006).

The ICWRE a non-governmental, non-political and non-profit organisation, Janan Mubarak, head of ICWRE, according to him 'One of the biggest challenges facing Iraqi women at work is the spread of favouritism, especially in advanced administrative positions, because nominations to these posts are made by political parties' (Al-Ali, 2012). Although Articles 22 and 25 of the Iraqi Constitution of 2005 provided for equal rights and employment opportunities regardless of gender. There is no supportive legislation except for the quota system, which is only implemented in parliament and does not allow women to hold decision-making positions, which are controlled by political parties. ICWRE seeks to reach legislation regarding quotas for women in governmental positions (Al-Ali, 2014).

In March 2003, women's rights activists and organisations in London, founded the Iraqi Women's Rights Coalition in order to streamline their efforts to influence the policy-making of the new government in Iraq, and to ensure that womens equal rights to be secured and promoted (Enloe, 2004). These women use the Coalition as a vehicle for media publicity, to facilitate meetings with government officials, human rights and humanitarian organisations, and to network with peer organisations in the European Union. Coalition members established women's advocacy centres in Iraq in order to raise Iraqi women's awareness of the international standards of women's rights. They also established shelters to protect Iraqi women from domestic violence.

- In March 2003, the Kurdish Women Action Against Honour Killing sent an open letter to the UN, the US, and the European Union, expressing their concern that women were not being adequately represented and that their roles and rights were not being addressed by the pre-war Iraqi opposition, and demanding women's full participation in the future government of Iraq (Yildiz, 2004).
- In June 2003, women's networks in Afghanistan and Kosovo sent open letters to the women of Iraq, outlining their struggles to be heard in the reconstruction processes in their own countries, and urging Iraqi women to raise their voices and ensure that they play a significant role in the rebuilding of post-war Iraq (Amowitz *et.al.*, 2004).
- On 3 July 2003, hundreds of women demonstrated in Baghdad, demanding to be included in shaping the political future of the country.
- On 9 July 2003, more than 80 women from all parts of Iraq participated in the "Voice of Iraqi Women" conference in Baghdad- the first national women's conference since the fall of Saddam Hussein's government. Conference participants discussed strategies for how to increase women's role in the recovery and reconstruction of Iraq, including the status of women in the constitution, legislation, the democratic process, education, the health system, the economy, and social and cultural affairs (Carapico, 2014). The main conference also brought together Iraqi women who had remained in Iraq under the dictatorship, women from the diaspora, and women from the three Kurdish governorates who, for over ten years, were able to promote the participation of women in the emerging civil society. Representatives of the Coalition Provisional Authority (CPA) and several U.N. agencies also attended the conference discussions.
- In mid-December 2003, a group of prominent women's rights activists and organisations in Iraq sent a letter to

Ambassadors Bremer, Greenstock and the members of the Iraqi Governing Council to call attention to the gender-based discrimination that Iraqi women had faced under the Coalition Provisional Authority (Rubin, 2008).

- Iraqi women mounted a nation-wide campaign to repeal Resolution 137 of the Iraqi Governing Council, which cancelled the 1959 Personal Status Law and placed issues of family law, including marriage, divorce, custody and inheritance, under religious rather than civil jurisdiction (Ahmed, 2010). Iraqi women held massive street protests and conferences to denounce the resolution.
- Since the fall of Saddam Hussein in April 2003, more than 80 women's organisations have been formed in Baghdad alone, offering a new space for dialogue and empowerment for women (Brown and Shannon, 2003). According to Nesreen Barwari, Iraqi Minister for Municipalities and Public Works, NGOs have also been holding "discussion groups" with women across the country to generate interest in the democratic process and inform women of the importance of registering to vote (Barwari, 2005 and 2013).
- Iraqi women campaigned vigorously to ensure a 40 per cent quota for women's representation in the country's interim constitution (Bernard *et.al.*, 2006). As of February 2004, The Advising Committee for Women Affairs in Iraq (formerly the Women Experts Committee), headed by Nesreen Barwari (Iraq's only female Minister), held weekly meetings to organise a campaign for demands on quota of 40 per cent representation by women in the Transitional Council, constitutional committee, and caucuses. According to Barwari, "For Iraq to move forward faster it is essential for women to play stronger contributing roles. Women need to have opportunities to more actively participate in decision-making. In order for this to occur, an enabling environment to promote women's participation needs to be enshrined within the fundamental law of administration" (Barwari, 2005). However, the CPA and some members of the Iraqi Governing Council were strongly opposed to the establishment of any explicit quota.

In the end, a "target" of 25 per cent was included in the interim constitution, signed 8 March 2004.

- The Iraqi Women's Higher Council held three women's conferences in the Centre, North and South of Iraq between October 2003 and January 2004.The Basra Southern Women's Conference, held 28-29 January 2004 and sponsored by the CPA, included a petition campaign to collect signatures supporting women's demands for political participation and for this to be stated in the fundamental law which was to be released on 28 February 2004 (Duraila and Ali, 2004).
- On 30 April 2004, nine women delegates met with Ambassador L. Paul Bremer to discuss their concern over the success of the political process during the transitional period following the transfer of sovereignty planned for 30 June 2004.[19] The group was comprised of the Vice-Minister for Culture, a representative of UNIFEM and representatives of women's organisations in Iraq (including Women Without Borders, the Al Amal Association, the IWN, the ACWAI, the Assyrian Women's Union, and the Women's and Children's Union Baghdad). Among the issues they raised were the deterioration of security in Iraq and its effect on democracy, violations of human rights and especially women's human rights, the excessive use of force by the military against civilians and possibilities for women's participation in peace processes and transitional institutions (Kuehnast *et.al.,* 2012).

United Nations Iraq Assistance Strategy (Unias) 2008-14

As an integral part of UNIAS (2008-2010), all sectors have made commitments to incorporating gender-equality measures into their programmes and indicators to assess each sector's progress toward achieving these commitments. Gender as a cross-cutting issue recognises that, in offering protection and distributing aid to the people of Iraq, assistance providers must not lose sight of the fact that women, men, girls and boys often have different needs, face different threats and challenges and have different skills and resources on which to draw upon (GBV, 2010). Acknowledging this as well as the potential marginalisation of women and girls from political and public participation and decision-making forums, the UNCT will aim to ensure that programmes and projects do not emphasise this phenomenon by excluding them further in programme activities.[20] The challenge at hand is to operationalise gender-based commitments and to assist the various humanitarian development actors and stakeholders in identifying causal links between gender equality and sustainable, effective and peaceful humanitarian and development responses. In addition, the U.N. will strive to provide a robust and effective coordination structure that will integrate gender equality issues across all of its work with a specific focus on the Protection and Governance Sectors.

Iraq is going through a human rights crisis because almost all problems plaguing the country, no matter what label is attached to them can be characterised as emanating from a lack of, or disrespect for, fundamental rights- including the right to life. Violations of these rights, which are codified in international law, remain widespread and systematic. IDPs refugees, women, widows, children, detainees, detainee family members, religious and ethnic minorities, and certain professions such as journalists, lawyers, doctors, educators, politicians all face dangers, injustice or precarious living conditions (Al-Khalidi and Victor, 2006). Many individuals fall into multiple categories of vulnerability simultaneously. Their entitlements to human rights remain unfulfilled for four main reasons: lack of resources, lack of institutional or individual capacity or skills of duty-bearers, lack of political will, or policies by certain groups to deny human dignity to their perceived 'enemies'. Hammurabi Human Rights Organisation (HHRO) reported that some women prisoners were suffering from skin ailments and that the authorities were apparently unable to call on sufficient women police officers to manage transfers of female detainees.[21] To assist in improving the situation, The UNCT had promoted human rights and support sustainable human development in every aspect of its work. This is to be realised by pursuing policies that use the Human Rights Based Approach to programming, which incorporates empowerment of people to participate in key development projects and activities, not only with respect to outcomes but also on processes.

This UNDAF (2011-2014) had prepared by the UNCT in Iraq in consultation with the Government of Iraq and other partners, with the aim of improving the lives of the people of Iraq, and particularly the most vulnerable, in alignment with the national priorities and

Millennium Development Goals (UNDG-ITF, 2011). Five UNDAF priorities have been identified, providing the scope and strategic direction of the UN system is supported to Iraq for the last four years (WFP, 2011), namely:

1. Improved governance, including the protection of human rights.
2. Inclusive, more equitable and sustainable economic growth.
3. Environmental management and compliance with ratified international environmental treaties and obligations.
4. Increased access to quality essential services.
5. Investment in human capital and empowerment of women, youth and children.

The UNDAF had focused on women especially widows and female heads of household, youth and children, who comprise a majority of the total population in Iraq and represent the future human resources that Iraq depended upon for its long-term socio-economic development. Support had provided to further develop policies and planning processes at national and sub-national levels to create the necessary environment for the empowerment of women, youth and children, while maintaining strong programmatic linkages with the UNCT's work under UNDAF Priority. The NDP specifically acknowledges the role of women and youth as critical assets in the ongoing state building process, as their exclusion undermines not only Iraq's efforts towards the MDGs but also its international commitments. This is also reflected in two of the six PRS objectives, namely higher income for the poor from work and less inequality between poor women and men. The human rights situation is poor particularly for minorities and women. Fundamental human rights such as the right to life and to physical integrity, the right to liberty and security have in the past been severely violated, particularly for populations living directly in zones of conflict or in areas discriminated by previous government policy due to religious or tribal orientations. Structural human rights issues need improvement and reform and awareness among the population of their constitutional and legal rights needs improvement.

Through several entities, U.N. is helping Iraq to combat and end violence against women in the country. GoI is taking steps to address violence against women including drafting a Domestic Violence Bill, establishing an inter-ministerial to address issues of violence against women. With the support of UNICEF, the GoI is developing policies and assessments on gender-based violence and violence against children, with particular sensitivity towards the needs of girls. In the Kurdistan Regional Government, the government is working closely with civil society to establish a shelter for victims of trafficking and forced prostitution. UNIFEM, UNHCR, WHO and UNAMI Human Rights Office are cooperating under the leadership of UNFPA to develop Iraq's capacity to comhat violence against women. These agencies are working to enhance the government's capacity to develop national plans and programmes to combat violence against women; the ability of government institutions and civil society organisations to deal with survivors; and increase knowledge among community leaders, teachers, students and local communities on gender equality. UNDP is providing technical support to the Directorate for Tracing Violence against Women and the Family Protection Unit. UNIFEM accelerated its activities in post-war Iraq, documenting gender violence, convening seminars, publicising rules of war and conventions against torture and fostering an Iraqi women journalist network and a Voice of Women Arabic language radio station (Carapico, 2014). UNDP is working together with the Ministry of Interior, Ministry of Labour and Social Affairs and civil society organisations to finalise the shelter policy and draft a database tracking violence against women. Technical support is also being provided to the Kurdistan Regional Government with the development of its Domestic Violence Bill.

Summary

Iraq faces one of the worst ever humanitarian crisis in the history of the world. Continued war and sanction regime imposed by the external powers devastated the country and inflicted heavy sufferings to the masses.Women and children were the most affected group in this category. Women were the victims in of the crisis in multiple ways. This range from loss of life, liberty, property, dignity and even their existence were also challenged. Human rights violations in many cases are evident in Iraq in various phases of history. This chapter briefly portraid these violations. They also lost their kith and kins during war and post-invasion phase.The post-war political arrangemets are also inadequate to protect the life and dignity of the women community in Iraq.

Notes

1. Barlow (2008). It is impossible for countries under occupation-Palestine, Iraq-to published in journal of Middle East Women's Studies,128. The U.S. invasion of Iraq and the occupation of Palestinian territories threatens women's rights. The draft which was put into act in 2008 has been met with criticism by international experts. Countries such as Iraq and the Palestinian territories remain under foreign occupation. In the Middle East women lack proper health and education and are severely under represented in the public and political sphere. Available online at www.e-ir.info/human-rights-in-the-middle-east-questions-of-compatib. (www. nobelwomensinitiative.org).
2. Iraq: Women forced to give up their jobs, marriages, a service of the UN Office for the Coordination of Humanitarian Affairs. IRIN (Integrated Regional Information Networks) Humanitarian news and analysis. Available online at http://www.irinnews.org/report/72451/iraq-women-forced-to-give-up-their-jobs-marriages.
3. Pina, Aaron D (2005) Women in Iraq: Background and Issues for U.S. Policy, Congressional Research Service, the Library of Congress CRS Report for Congress. Received through the CRS Web Order Code RL32376. http://fpc.state.gov/documents/organization/50258.pdf.Amnesty International, "Decades of suffering, now women deserve better", Available online at http: //www.amnestyusa.org/women/document.do?id=9E865CC-4FD535B2880256F73005E4047.
4. Yifat Susskind, "One Year Later Women's Human Rights in 'Liberated' Iraq", MADRE is a International Women's Organisaton. Spring 2004. Available online at http //madre.org//articles/me/womensrights.html.
5. Iraq: Unemployment bad and getting worse, Iraq's security situation improves, its employment situation is lagging behind, according to a report compiled by the United Nations and other, non-governmental agencies. Babylon and beyond. Observations from Iraq Iean, Israel, the Arab world and beyond. Available online at http://latimesblogs.latimes.com/babylonbeyond/2009/ 02/iraq-iraq-unemp.html.
6. Mark Peplow, "Iraq Faces Growing Health Crisis" News@nature.com 13 October 2004. Available online at http://www.nature.com/news/2004/041011/pf/041011-8_pf.html.
7. Raga Habib Khuzai and Songul Chapouk, 'Iraq's Women's are Ready to Lead Absent Voices,' *New York Times*, December4, 2003. CRS Report for Congress. http //fpc.state.gov/documents/organization/50258.pdf.
8. Aron D.Pina, Backgrounder on Women in Iraq. The GFIW grew to play a significant role in implementing state. updated March 13, 2006. For more details available online athttp //www.cpa-iraq.org/regulations/CPAORD1.pdf.

9. A.D.Pina,(2006),Women in Iraq Background and Issues for US Policy. Available online athttp //wwwoccupationwatch.org.article.php?id=3503.
10. President, Mrs Bush Mark Progress in Global Women's Rights, March12, 2004, Available online at http://www.whitehouse.gove/news/releases/2004/ 03/200403 12-5.htm.
11. Annia Ciezadlo, 'A Religious Awakening,' *Newsday*, February 19,2004.A rise in popular religious activism has called into question the future, signed by the Iraqi Governing Council in March 2004 included many matters.fpc. state.gov/documents/organization39339.pdf.
12. Lynne Amowitz, et.al, Human Rights Abuses and Concerns about Women's Health and Human Rights in Southern Iraq, '*Journal of American Medical Association* 291(2004).
13. Ghali Hassn, 'Iraqi Women under Occupation'. Since the invasion of Iraq women have been denied their human right including the right to health, education etc. Available online at http //www.countercurrents.org/iraq-hassan090505.htm.
14. See Reports on. Girls Education in Iraq 2010, UNICEF. Dr Griffiths, Matthew. A Situational Analysis of Girls Education in Iraq. With recommendations for the Government of Iraq and for UNICEF Iraq in their support for the Government in the development of girls' access to good quality education.
15. Nagel, Joane and Lindsey Feitz (2007) Deploying *Race, Gender and Class*, and Sexuality in the Iraq War. When the U.S. attacked Iraq in March, 2003 another longstanding feature of military demography was changing. 14 (3-4).28-47. Race, Gender & Class Available online at www.suno.edu/ sunorgc/.
16. Deneitz Kandiyoti, "Between the Hamner and the Anvil: Post conflict Reconstruction, Islam and Women's Rights," *Third World Quarterly*, 28(3):2007, 503-517. Wrote, The invocation of Women's Rights for Political expediency in the context of the "war on terror' has tended to breed skepticism, if not outright resistance."
17. Huda Ahmed elicited strong but varied opinions reported in "women in the Shadows of Democracy," *Middle East Report*, 239 (2006) 24-26.
18. NCCI was established in 2003 by NGOs working in Iraq and has a membership of many local and international NGOs that work with humanitarian projects throughout the country.
19. "Iraqi Women Meet Paul Bremer," Women Without Borders, 11 May2004, last accessed 21.07. 2004, ohne-grenzen.org/frauen-ohne-grenzen.asp? loc=&pg=&id=723.
20. United Nations Iraq Assistance strategy 2008-2010, United Nations Country Team - Mission Statement *to strengthen Iraq to implement the NDS / ICI and meet the needs of the most vulnerable by being a trusted proactive*

partner, accountable for high quality tangible results, and focusing on agreed outcome areas.

21. See Hammurabi Human Rights Organization (HHRO), *Report of visiting women' prison in Baghdad*, 10 October 2012, http://www.hhro.org/hhro/reports_en.php?lang=en&art_id=592; Amnesty International follow-up conversations with members of HHRO.

Conclusion

Human rights are the basic rights and freedom that belongs to every person everwhere in the world. These rights and freedom based on the core principles like dignity, equality and respect-inspired a wide range of international and regional human rights treaties. Human rights are moral principles or norms that describe certain standards of human behaviour, and are regularly protected as legal rights in national and international law. Human rights are commonly understood as inalienable fundamental rights 'to which a person is inherently entitled simply because she or he is a human being,' and which are "inherent in all human beings" regardless of their nation, location, language, religion, ethnic origin or any other status. It is applicable everywhere and at every time in the sense of being universal, and egalitarian in the sense of being the same for everyone. Human rights require empathy and the rule of law and impose an obligation on persons to respect the human rights of others. Human rights should not be taken away except on specific circumstances, and require freedom from unlawful imprisonment, torture, and execution.

The doctrine of human rights has been highly influential within international law, and further in global and regional institutions. Actions by states and non-governmental organisations form a basis of public policy worldwide. The idea of human rights suggests that "if the public discourse of peacetime global society can be said to have a common moral language, it is that of human rights". The strong claims made by the doctrine of human rights continue to provoke considerable doubt and debates about the content, nature and justifications of human rights till this day. The precise meaning of the term right is controversial and is the subject of continued philosophical debate; while there is consensus that human rights encompasses a wide variety of rights such as the right to a fair trial, protection against enslavement, prohibition of genocide, free speech or a right to education, there is disagreement about which of these particular rights should be included within the general framework of human rights; some thinkers suggest that human rights should be a minimum requirement to avoid the worst-case abuses, while others see it as a higher standard.

The modern concept of human rights is mainly concerned with international, moral and legal norms that aspire to protect all people everywhere from severe political, legal, and social abuses. Globalisation has adversely affected human rights throughout the world, and its impact is felt more particularly in developing world. State has responsibility to protect citizens. State follows the law of international human rights and it is mainly concerned with the regulation of public power in the form of the state. The modern human rights movement emerged during the latter half of the twentieth century. Individuals need their private lives to be protected from the misuse by the state and non-state power from inside and outside. Each country tries to balance its need for security and individual freedom. The principle of universality of human rights is the cornerstone of international human rights law. This principle, as first emphasised in the Universal Declaration on Human Rights in 1948, had been reiterated in numerous international human rights conventions, declarations, and resolutions. Through the last decades of the twentieth century, human rights and Universal Declaration followed the two International Covenants on Civil and Political Rights and on Economic, Social and Cultural Rights. The idea of human rights enters into rival political agendas; it requires more attention and analysis than when it became the slogan of our hopes. Whatever the conceptual and practical problems of human rights be faced by human beings around the world, it has been of great benefit for the humankind. The concept was stressed and clarified universally and was hammered upon continuously for almost half a century. Human rights are in the central position to the contemporary understandings of justice and equality, and it has crucial bearing on the ability to assess and respond to emerging technological, economic, social, and political issues. Yet the codification of human rights into laws has evolved over time as we discover more about the human suffering and abuse that still exist around the world. Human rights evolve over time, because we become more sensitive to the emerging needs of humanity.

Iraq witnessed one of the worst ever human rights violations and abuses in modern history. The continuous military interventions and occupation and Western imposed sanction regime against the country inflicted suffering to the innocent masses, especially women and children. Iraq's social structure was destalised by the transition in the first half of the twentieth century. At the same time, because of its foreign roots, the Iraqi political system suffered from a severe legitimacy crisis. Beginning with its League of Nations Mandate in 1920, the British government had laid out the institutional framework for Iraqi government and politics. Britain imposed a Hashimite (also seen as Hashemite) monarchy, defined the territorial limits of Iraq with little correspondence to natural frontiers or traditional tribal and ethnic settlements. Britain also influenced the writing of a constitution and the structure of parliament. By the Iraqi government's own admission, national reconciliation is out of reach. In fact, Iraq is a divided country, with Kurds controlling the north, Sunnis controlling some central and western regions, and Shiites controlling the rest. Between 1918 and 1958 British policy in Iraq had far reaching effects. Professional and middle class largely fled the country. Turkey was threatening attacks against Kurdish rebels in the north. Iran was influencing Shiite policy and contributing money and weaponry to the cause.

Since Iraq's independence in 1932 monarchy ruled the country between attempted coups. Britain tried to reoccupy the country from 1941 to 1947. In 1958, a coup instituted military-method dictatorship, gradually Saddam Hussein took power in the late 1960s. Democracy and political institutions were never part of Iraq's culture and history. Before 1958 Iraqi rulers used secrecy and power to control the people. Even after 1958 people of Iraq did not fully engage in political process. Since Iraq lacked strong political institutions and conventions, a small elite groups monopolise the political power. Often they were found by close family and tribal ties. After 1958 there were a series of conspiracies, coups, countercoups, and fierce Kurdish uprisings. Saddam Hussein waged the war on Iran in 1980 and invaded Kuwait in 1990.

The officials in the U.S. government planned to remove Saddam Hussein from power since the conclusion of the Gulf War. This plan was postponed for eight years during the Clinton Administration, but shortly after the election of George W. Bush, the plan was revitalised. Plans were made to remove Saddam Hussein from power during the early months of the Bush administration. The U.S. government worked to build a case for war convicting Iraq as a threat to the U.S. Evidence was shaped to coincide with the government's desire to invade Iraq, and consequently, much of the evidence was faulty and found to be unjustifiable. Because the war began under faulty pretences, it is important to consider why the U.S. chose to engage in this war at this particular time in history, while there are not definite answers. An unexpected channel occurred when terrorist attacked U.S. on 11th September 2001. The U.S. desired for revenge and the residual emotion of 9/11 provided a perfect window of opportunity for the Bush Administration to advance its military and political agenda for Iraq. While the US was never able to prove a definitive connection between Saddam Hussein, terrorism and 9/11, the Bush administration influenced and justified their foreign policy decisions and to advance an aggressive agenda against Iraq. It was one of the main causes behind occupation in Iraq. The human rights situation in post-war Iraq was no better, than it was before the war. It is merely different. Sectarian killings by Sunni and Shiite militias continued in 2006 and 2007. Victims usually showed signs of torture. Allegations of torture was leveled against the Iraqi interior ministry, which runs the nation's prison system. U.S. occupation authorities holded the Iraqis prisoners, without charge or legal representation.

The direct or physical violence was evident throughout the war against Iraq. At the beginning and end of the war in 1991 and in 2003, the term fear and terror developed throughout the war. Iraqis feared about the attack, particularly constant bombing campaign and Iraqis made a consequent effort to target the airplanes carrying bomb. This continuous violence worsened the medical field and the country failed to rebuild the healthcare system due to this war. Around eighty per cent of pregnant women were anaemic. Diarrhoea and acute respiratory infections, further compounded by malnutrition, accounted for about two-thirds of deaths amongst the under-five population. Two thousand physicians got murdered since 2003. Many missing cases were also reported. Nearly ten thousand people are missing from that period. This is the most visible after-effect of war. Death certificates were issued by other local agencies. Many unidentified bodies were found in those four years, and thousands of Iraqis got killed since 2003 without being identified by their relatives. They were buried in special cemeteries called unidentified body cemeteries. But before the war, the higher education, especially the scientific and technological institutions, was of an international standard, staffed by high quality personnel. Attacks on universities, by the occupation troops or others, have driven away students from continuing their studies. Iraqi non-governmental organisations reports estimate that the number of university Professors killed since 2003 is over three hundred. On 27th July 2007, UNICEF and the UNHCR issued a joint appeal, warning that a generation of Iraqis could grow up uneducated and alienated. So far there is no sign of any improvement in this sector. The U.S. armies have done many human rights violations against Iraqi people. In the whole world America cannot act as judge, especially in the case of democracy and in human rights. Junior Bush has done the biggest illegitimate activities in terms of human rights. At the same time the U.S. civilians are guilty because of supporting and selecting him as their President. The U.S. administrators chased a policy of suppression towards Saddam Hussein's Iraq subsequent to the first Gulf War. The United Nations inspectors were seeking for weapons of mass destruction and sanctions against Saddam which leads to the enormous toleration for the Iraqi ordinary people. It was clear that, the removal of Saddam Hussein and his regime from power was a part of U.S. foreign policy.

The Iraq war was not mainly about saving the Iraqi people from mass slaughter. The Bush administration's dominant remaining that justification for the war is that Saddam Hussein was a tyrant who deserved to be overthrown- is an argument of humanitarian intervention. The imperative of stopping or preventing genocide or other systematic slaughter can sometimes justify the use of a military force. The capacity to use military force is finite. Encouraging military action to meet to lesser abuses may mean lack of capacity to intervene when atrocities are most severe. The invasion of a country, especially without the approval of the U.N. Security Council, also damages the international legal order which itself is important to protect rights. War being waged in itself is a threat to human security. It challenges the framework of international human rights and humanitarian law. The world will not accept inhuman treatment under any context, and such a treatment will tarnish even legitimate security operations. Under such situations it is necessary to restore the balance between liberty and security reasserting the human rights framework, which provides for legitimate and effective efforts to respond to terrorist attacks. Failure to respect universal human rights norms not only undermines shared values, but also undermines the international operations and public support.

Violations happened in Iraq not only as a communal conflict, but also contains an important element of nationalist insurgency. The most challenging problem of our times is the realisation of human rights for all people both as individuals and in groups. Human rights are mainstream concern today and also an essential part of good governance. We are in the age of human rights; it has toddy become common language of humanity. The Universal Declaration of Human Rights symbolised a significant movement of arrival when human kind came to knowledge the 'reason of rights'. The United Nations Organisations transformed human rights into something with an official international paradigm. It even began an obligation by member state to modify their foreign policy accordingly. The central focus of the human rights has been the essential failure on the part of government's in the protection human rights and prevention its abuses. In neo-conservative eyes, the Iraq war was not about terrorism, it was about pivotal relationship between Saddam Hussein and the assertion of U.S. power. Fear of terrorism provided the necessary platform for influencing public opinion and the Bush Administartion cleverly used this occasion to manipulate US public support for the US intervention. The Administration officials gradually built an assumption in to the critical consciousness of the U.S. polity and project the linkages between war on terror and war to convince the US Cogress and the public.

A great nation has the capacity to pursue ambitious objectives but also to reconsider the costs involved in the pursuit of those objectives as well as to handle adversity and take compensating measures to reduce the consequences of adversity. In the case of Iraq, producing a decent Iraq would be great achievement worth enormous sustained effort, while failure would have serious consequences. The ways of producing a new Iraqi provisional government are also in flux and the subject of intense debates in Iraq and Washington. Military and civil officials have become less effusive about ambitious political goals for the new Iraq. These changes flow less from success and more to the realisation of lack of control in Iraq and need for greater flexibility. The concerns mostly raised by an early U.S. departure from Iraq focus on the psychological encouragement to terrorism, loss of U.S. prestige in the Arab world, instability in Iraq leading to major disorder or even civil war, and a broader reluctance to rely on U.S. commitments. In these areas disagreement will be great and depends not only on the information and analysis but on the way one thinks the world works. Great determination is of course, important; in pursuing difficult tasks and hesitation and doubt usually do not further the goal. Success is the ultimate arbiter but the costs could be great. Successful or not, Iraq has added some poison to our national life, particularly over the origins and wisdom of the war and the capabilities and integrity of our intelligence system.

Administration statement on the purpose of the Iraq war has covered the warfront. Emphasis have moved from Iraq's WMD, a connection to terrorist and violation of U.N. resolutions to a humanitarian intervention to an emphasise that, invasion would spur radical change in the Middle East. U.S. posses an underlying faith that dismantling Saddam's regime will ultimately incite regime change or hanged behaviour in other unsavory states. While the U.S. removal of Saddam reduced the military threat to Israel, so far there is little evidence that it is changing attitudes in the Middle Eastern and the Arab-Israeli conflict, including those in Iraq or that if it has much promise of doing so in the future. Indeed many Arabs apparently feel that the U.S. has its priorities wrong, that going after Saddam was a diversion from dealing with what was much more on their mind and more political potent for them, the Arab-Israeli conflict. Whether it was right or wrong the Administration tried to keep pace with demands for a quicker Iraqi sovereignty. There is no great confidence anywhere that the U.S. can produce a stable, desirable and durable political outcome in Iraq. U.S. forces in Iraq largely concentrated on their efforts in hunting down and killing insurgents. The idea of such operations is to erode the enemy's strength by killing fighters more quickly than the recruitement of replacements. Stephen Biddle says that the U.S. does not have the leverage to achieve needed compromises over the fundamental issues that divide Iraq: the constitutional structure, the distribution of oil revenues and security. A truly international mediation process in Iraq should be carefully planned, designed and coordinated. Three different civil wars raging in Iraq: the first between U.S.-led coalition forces and anti-government insurgents, the second between the Kurds and other communities in northern Iraq, and the third between Sunni Arab and Shitte Arabs in the centre of the country. The last is the most important because it represents the greatest potential for humanitarian disaster as well as for long-term instability in Iraq in the region.

The torture, abuse and inhuman treatment of Iraqi detainees held in Abu Gharib and other U.S. detention facilities proved the human rights violations of the occupation forces. The Bush administration always said that the hostile states were backing international terrorism, and especially those states that were actively pursuing nuclear weapons or other WMD to get international support. At the same time, women suffered the consequences of political repression. Female education may be the best way to advance the status of women. During the difficult decade of the 1990s, school enrollment rates for girls in Iraq declined significantly, making Iraq one of the few countries in the world today where mothers are better educated than their daughters. Although reliable literacy figures are hard to come by, most observers agree that Iraq has now one of the worst gender literacy gaps in the world.

While urging adherence to existing human rights and humanitarian standards in the fight against terrorism and raising the alarm about how the 'war on terrorism' is being waged, one should not ignore the challenges posed by transnational networks of persons willing to engage in acts of mass destruction. Nor is it suggested that any adjustment of the existing normative structure is inappropriate. There are opportunities for cooperative, multilateral approaches to this challenge. For example, expanding the jurisdiction of the International Criminal Court to cover a broader range of attacks on civilians would be a positive development. In Iraq, three years of counter-insurgency has stimulated more terrorism than it has suppressed. But if Iraq's sectarian wars were ended, ordinary Iraqi Sunni's might not have come to a realisation that the greatest threat to their well-being is not Iraqi Shittes but foreign jihadist in their midst. Perhaps they would begin to work at restoring the order in their country. The U.S. people must believe that the war is not worth the sacrifice, in lives, and treasure. The Iraqi people must believe that their government offers them a better life than the insurgents do, and they must think that the government will prevail.

The scale of death, destruction, systematic human rights violations and oppression, increased with the invasion of 2003. Iraqis lost their basic healthcare, education, drinking water and adequate sanitation. The rights and situation of women and children are totally vulnerable. The systematic abuse, mistreatment and torture continued in addition to the killing of victims. Iraq still faces a growing humanitarian emergency. The right for life and security are the basic human rights. These are the main concerns of the Iraqi civilians along with the unprecedented increase in poverty and unemployment. In Iraq, there is a wide range of corruption everywhere. Before the invasion, the Iraqi state never knew such an extreme phenomenon called corruption. More than 500 Iraqi intellectuals were assassinated during the past five years. All these are part of the consequences of the invasion and occupation. Civilians believed that U.S. force regularly violate the norm of non-combatant immunity. There are numerous estimates of civilian casualties in Iraq, all of which are problematic. By the end of 2006, the actual number of death of Iraqi civilian was approximately closer to 0.6 millions, and no one should underestimate the dreadful bloodshed in Iraq. The overall scale of civilian deaths is a reflection of the U.S. government's failure to plan the post-invasion contingencies, which allowed chaos to emerge in the wake of regime change. The number of deaths attributed to U.S. forces and crossfire also provides evidence that Iraqi civilians are at high risk of death and injury. Iraqi authorities are detaining thousands of Iraqi women illegally and subjecting many of them to torture and ill-treatment, including the threat of sexual abuse. Iraq's weak judiciary, plagued by corruption, frequently bases convictions on coerced confessions, and trial proceedings fall far short of international standards. Many women were detained for months or even years without any charge before consulting a judge. These were the vulnerable impact of the occupation in Iraq.

For Iraq Human Rights Ministry, a special parliamentary committee for human rights and dozens of organisations monitor the country's human rights situation. Yet practical results of these efforts are painful. Iraq still ranks very high, among global human rights violators in the case of torture in prisons, freedom of expression and journalist safety. The World Report in 2013, Human Rights Watch (HRW) documented numerous cases of torture, arbitrary arrests and other human rights violations in Iraq. They described the overall human rights situation in the country as "poor." The most affected by human rights violations in Iraq are women. Thousands of Iraqi women had been arrested and detained illegally, and many have suffered torture and rape. Corruption was rampant in the Iraqi judiciary to promote human rights on the ground, since there's no serious will to do so from the part of the political administration or the ruling coalition. In addition, the major world powers are not interested in pressuring the Iraqi government to improve its performance in this area.

Iraqi women and their children had been taken as detainees by U.S. forces. The repression that all Iraqis suffered under Saddam's regime, as well as the consequences of this wars, applied to the female as well. After the disastrous eighty years Iran-Iraq war, Saddam's regime moved away from Arab socialist ideals and moved closer to traditional interpretations of Islam in the region, including less tolerance for female autonomy in the public realm. Even the U.S. force is violating the international law, by taking Iraqi women hostages through force and compelling their male relatives to surrender. Iraqi women were arrested, detained, abused and tortured not because of anything they have done, but to save their close relatives like spouses, sons and brothers to collaborate with the occupation and to inform against the resistance. As a result of the U.S. dismantling of the Iraqi state, many women lost their jobs. Unemployment among Iraqi women is more than seventy per cent and it is on a rise today. The dismantling of the Iraqi security and police led to increase in violence and crimes against women. Women are no longer leaving their homes unaccompanied by relatives. The Bush administration's promotion of religious fundamentalism and sectarianism give the worst for Iraqi women rights. The miseries of the Iraqi people have doubled in the last few years, and Iraqis viewed the occupation as the cause of their miseries. In addition to the crimes of sexual abuse, torture and rape committed by U.S. soldiers against Iraqi women, all other aspects of Iraqi women's rights have also deteriorated. Women health and women education have fallen significantly. Unemployment, prostitution and malnutrition, have increased dramatically. Right from the beginning of the U.S. occupation, there has been a dramatic increase in sexual assaults and violations of women's rights by U.S. forces in Iraq. In Iraq there are additional challenges in addressing crimes of a sexual nature. In many parts of the country when a woman or girl loses her sexual cleanliness, she will be subjected to imprisonment or even death, if she cannot prove herself. Many women have been taken hostages, tortured, and sexually abused even in Abu Ghraib prison. Sexual violence and abuse committed by U.S. troops go far beyond a few isolated cases. Many people feel it is due to the ongoing terror wrought in their land that brings so much oppression to women. Prior to the arrival of forces in Iraq, Iraqi women were free to wear whatever they liked and go wherever they chose. The Iraqi constitution of 1970 gave equality and liberty to women in the Muslim world, but since the invasion, women's rights have fallen to the lowest in Iraqi history.

Since the invasion in 2003, Iraqi women have been brutally attacked, and kidnapped in the Iraqi society. War and occupation have cost Iraqi women their legal standing and their everyday freedom of dress and movement. Arising from their fear of being raped and harassed, women have to wear not only the veil, but must also to wear the black dress in order to avoid attention. Iraqi women's lives had become immeasurably worse, with rapes, burnings and murders. In addition to torture and sexual violence perpetuated by U.S. occupation forces, a great number of Iraqi women and girls are kept locked up in their homes by a very real fear of abduction and criminal abuse. Since the invasion in Iraq, Iraqi women have denied their human right, including the right to health, education and employment. Prior to the 1991 U.S. war and the 13 years of the genocide sanctions, Iraqi women enjoyed unquestionable quality rights to education and health. Iraqi women had the most progressive human rights in the region and they were the first Arab women to hold high positions in academic, law, medicine and government. Before the U.S. invasion and occupation of Iraq, Iraqi women made up forty per cent of the public-sector work force. Men and women received equal pay for work; education and healthcare were free at all levels. In today's Iraq, crimes and abuse against women were back to the levels of before independence. The crime of rape was capital offence under Iraq's Constitution. The miseries of the Iraqi people have more than doubled in the last two years, and Iraqis viewed the occupation as the cause of their miseries. Unemployment, prostitution and malnutrition, have increased dramatically, and are now widespread among Iraqi women today. In Baghdad, none of them had running water, guaranteed electricity, or adequate medical supplies etc. In the contemporary world, everyone should always be the honest and courageous advocates and defenders of the human dignity for every human being man, woman, or child,

Muslim or non-Muslim, related to any land, race or ethnicity. Humankind is in no need of much talk about 'globalism,' 'new world order' and 'post-modernism,' but it badly needs a 'qualitative' change in its thinking and practices.

Major Findings of the Study

- U.S. intervention in Iraq was against all international norms and laws and violated the provisions of the UN Charter. Economic and strategic priorities of the US in the post cold war era was the major reason for the war and occupation of Iraq. The United States also failed to justify the war or its allegation of the Iraqi possession of weapons of mass destruction.
- The war and occupation worsened the human rights situation in Iraq and it created the destruction of the Iraq's basic infrastructure mainly sanitation, water supply and electricity.
- Conservative social structures and religious fundamentalism were the obstacles of the development of women rights in Iraq.
- The war and occupation seriously affected almost all sectors of Iraq including: education, public health, employment, economic development, infrastructure development etc.
- State and other governmental institutions failed to take effective initiatives for the betterment of women.
- Lack of women's participation in politics led to the degrdation of women's life in iraq.
- The lack of infrastructure, the rise of Islamic sectarian groups, insecurity and fear had turned the majority of Iraqi women to prisoners in their own house.
- Most of the women had not received any humanitarian assistance since U.S. occupation. Widows do not receive a pension and sometimes they were forced to go into temporary marriage with one of the bureaucrats who distribute the funds. In the sense, it is a flourishing of sex exploitation of Iraqi women.
- Displaced families in Iraq headed by women could not find employment. At the same time single mothers faced social

stigmas and were treated inhumanely whenever they tried to get an employment or additional educational opportunities.

- Decreased literacy rate affected the development of Iraqi women.
- Equality is not yet achieved by Iraqi women.
- The state failed to provide basic needs such as food, water supply, and medical care.

The sensitivity of the research topic, geographical spread and in particular, financial constraints inhibited the execution of an in-depth exposition of violation as originally conceived. This research will therefore rely on a review of the literature and conceptual analysis. It is possible to ascertain that physical violence has been employed most times to impose violations because its application sometimes will leave behind blemishes and contusions. The obvious limitation with the research is that there is not one definitive answer to the research question, to what extend the U.S. intervention is responsible for the torture and sufferings of the Iraqi people and Iraqi women. In absence of a sustainable democracy movement shaped from down to up by the people and not by the governing regimes, one cannot anticipate what will happen in Iraq. The extend of how much the civil society is powerful, and how much the people will participate in the process of rebuilding state and society is still not clear. History will allow more valued insight into the answers, but absence of an official statement by the U.S. Government, left to answer to the question by collecting the evidence and drawing conclusions based on an assessment of the evidence. However, it is not so easy to ascertain mental, psychological or emotional problems except with the aid of an expert. Practices of violations in front of our eyes can easily see. However, this may not be so apparent about the violations perpetrated behind the closed doors in secrecy or in a custodial arena.

Suggestions for Further Study

- This study can be made more comprehensive by taking into account the historical roots of human rights violations with specific reference to the origin of conflict and the changing nature of conflicts.

- More case study approach can be taken into account and studied deeply, viz., the situation of Political Prisoners, Actions against minorities with emphasis on Kurds and the changing international climate of terror.

Bibliography

Abdullah, Thabit A. J. (1989): *Dictatorship, Imperialism and Chaos IRAQ since 1989*, New York: Fernwood Publishing.

Afkhami, Mahnaz (1995): *Faith and Freedom Woman is Human Rights in the Muslim World*, New York: Syrause University Press.

Agosin, Marjorie (2002): *Women, Gender and Human Rights; A Global Perspective*, Washington: Library of Congress Cataloguing Publication Data.

Ahmed, Leila (1992): *Women and Gender in Islam*, New Haven: Yale University Press.

Aijmer, Goran, and Jon Abbink (2000): *Meanings of Violence: A Cross Cultural Perspective*, Oxford: Berg.

Akberzadeh, Shahram and Benjamin Mac Queen (2008): *Islam and Human Rights Practice-Perspectives across the Ummah*, New York: Routledge.

Al-Ali, Nadje (2000): *Secularism, Gender and the State in the Middle East*, Cambridge.

Al-Ali, Nadje Sadig (2007): *Iraqi Women Untold stories from the 1948 to the Present*, London: Zed Books.

Al-Ali, Nadje and Nicola Pratt (2008): *What kind of Liberation. Women and the Occupation of Iraq*, London: University of California Press. Ltd.

Allan, T.R.S. (2001): *Reader in Legal And Constitutional Theory*, Cambridge: University of Cambridge.

Allawi, Ali A. (2007): *The Occupation of Iraq: Winning the War, Losing the Peace*, New Haven, CT: Yale University Press.

Alnasrawi, Abbas (1994): *The Economy of Iraq: Oil, Wars, Destruction of Development and Prospects, 1950–2010*, United States of America: Greenwood Press.

Anastasiou, Harry and Robert Gould (2007): "Securing Human Rights Through War and Peace: from Paradox to Opportunity," in Gail M. Presbey (ed.), *Philosophical Perspectives on the "War on Terrorism,"* New York: Amsterdom.

Anderson, Pamela Sue and Beverley Clack (2004): *Feminist Philosophy of Religion: Critical Readings*, London: Routledge.

Anderson, Terry H. (2011): *Bush's Wars*, New York: Oxford University Press.

Arebi, Saddeka (1994): *Women and Words in Saudi Arabia Politics of Literary Discourse*, New York: Columbia University Press. Available online at http: //www.goodreads.com /book/show/ 2427765.Women-and-Words-in-Saudi-Arabia.

Armitage, David (2007): *The Declaration of Independence: A Global History*, America: Harvard University Press.

Azam, J. Kousar (2001): *Rediscovering America: American Studies in the New Century*, New Delhi: South Asian Publishers.

Azhary, M.L. (1984): *The Iran–Iraq War: an Historical, Economic, and Political Analysis*, New York: Routledge.

Bacevich, J. Andrew (2005): *The New American Militarism*, New York: Oxford University Press.

Bacevich, J. Andrew (2005): *The New U.S. Militarism*, New York: Oxford University Press.

Bajwa, S.G. (1997): *Human Rights in India,* New Delhi: Anmol Publications.

Balaghi, Shiva (2005): *Saddam Hussein: A Biography (Greenwood Biographies)*, United States of America: Greenwood Press.

Barakat, Sultan (2008): Reconstructing Post-Saddam Iraq: an Introduction, New York: Routledge.

Barberet, Rosemary (2014): *Women, Crime and Criminal Justice: A Global Enquiry*, New York: Routledge.

Baretto, Manuel Jose (2013): *Human Rights from a Third World Perspective: Critique, History and International Law*, Cambridge: Cambridge Scholars Publishing.

Barton, Frederick and Bathsheba Crocker (2004): *Progress or Peril? Measuring Iraq's Reconstruction, the Post-Conflict Reconstruction Project*, Washington: DC.

Barzilai, Gad (2003): *Communities and Law Politics and Cultures of Legal Identities*, Greene Street: Ann Arbor University of Michigan Press.

Batatu, Hanna (1978): *The Old Social Class and Revolutionary Movements of Iraq: A Study of Iraq's Old Landed and Commercial Classes and Communists, Baathists, and Free Officers*, New Jersey: Princeton University Press.

Baxi, Upendra (2007): *Human Rights in Post-Human World*, New York: Oxford University Press.

Baxi, Upendra (2008): *The Future of Human Rights*, New York: Oxford University Press.

Benjamin, Daniel and Steven Simon (2003): *The Age of Sacred Terror*, New York: Random House Publishers.

Bercovitch, Jacob (2010): *Unraveling Internal Conflicts in East Asia and the Pacific Incidence, Consequences, and Resolution*, Lanham: Rowman and Littlefield Publication Group.

Berlin, I. (1958): *Two Concepts of Liberty*, Oxford: Oxford University Press.

Bertram, Christopher (2004): *Rousseau and the Social Contract*, London: Routledge Taylor and Francis Group.

Bigong, Dino (1997): *The Political Ideas of St. Thomas Aquinas*, Simon and Schuster.

Bilmes, Linda and Joseph Stiglitz (2011): "The Long-Term Costs of Conflict: The Case of the Iraq War," in Derek L. Braddon and Keith Hartley (eds.), *Handbook on the Economics of Conflict*, UK: Edward Elgar Publishing.

Black, Eric (2013): *Neo-Conservatism and The Iraq War: Their View then and Now 10 Years Later.* Available online at http://www.minnpost.com/eric-black-nk/2013/03/neocons-and-iraq-war-their-view-then-and-now-10-years-later accessed on 15.03.2013.

Bodansky, Yossef (2004): *Secret History of the Iraq War*, New York: Harper Collins.

Boerefijn, Ineke (2008): *Changing Perceptions of Sovereignty and Human Rights: Essays in Honour of Cees Flinterman*, Antwerp: Intersentia.

Borgohain, Bani (1999): *Human Rights, Social Justice and Political Challenges*, New Delhi: Kanishka Publishers.

Boucher, David and Paul, Kelley (2009): *Political Thinkers. From Socrates to the Present*, Oxford: Oxford University Press.

Bourdieu, Pierre (1994): "Structures, Habitus, Power: Basis for a Theory of Symbolic Power," in N.B. Dirks, G. Eley and S.B. Ortner, *Culture, Power, History: A Reader in Contemporary Social Theory*, Princeton: Princeton University Press.

Braude, Joseph (2003): *The New Iraq Hardcover*, New York: Amazone Best Basic Books.

Brennan, Jasson, (2012): *Libertarianism: What Everyone Needs to Know*, Oxford: Oxford University Press.

Bromley, Simon, (1991): *Oil and American Hegemony*, United States: Pennsylvania State University Press.

Brooke, Christopher (2012): *Philosophic Pride: Stoicism and Political thought from Lipsius to Rousseau*, New Jersey: Princeton University Press.

Brown, Alan (1986): *Modern Political Philosophy Theories of the Just Society*, England: Penguin Books.

Brown, Chris (2013): "Human Rights and Human Nature," in Cindy Holder and David Reidy (eds.), *Human Rights-The Hard Questions*, Cambridge: Cambridge University Press.

Bunch, C. (2006): "Women's Rights as Human Rights", in B. Lockwood (ed.), *Women's Rights: A Human Rights Quarterly Reader*, Baltimore: Johns Hopkins University Press.

Burgess, Hazel and Mark Philip (2010): *Thomas Paine: A Collection of Unknown Writings*, Basingstoke, Hants: Palgrave MacMillan.

Burke, Roland (2010): *Decolonisation and the Evolution of International Human Rights*, United States: University of Pennsylvaniavania.

Burns, J. H. (ed.) (1991): *The Cambridge History of Political Thought 1450-1700*, New York: Cambridge University Press.

Byrne, J.O. Darren (2003): *Human Rights: An Introduction*, New Delhi: Pearson Education Ltd.

Cameron, Fraser (2002): *US Foreign Policy after the Cold War*, London: Routledge Taylor and Francis Group.

Campos, Joseph H. (2007): *The State and Terrorism: National Security and the Mobilisation of Power*, England: Ashgate Publishing Ltd.

Carapico, Sheila (2014): *Political Aid and Arab Activism-Democracy Promotion, Justice and Representation*, Cambridge: Cambridge University Press.

Cardwell, Curt (2014): "The Cold War," in Frank Costigliola and Michael J. Hogan (eds.), *America in the World*, Cambridge: Cambridge University Press.

Cassese, Antonio (1990): *Human Rights in a Changing World*, Cambridge: Polity Press.

Chand, Attar (1985): *Politics of Human Rights and Civil Liberties: A Global Survey*, New Delhi: UDH Publishers.

Charvet, John and Elisa Kaczynska (2008): *The Liberal Project and Human Rights: The Theory and Practice of a New World Order*, New York: Cambridge.

Chauhan, O.P. (2004): *Human Rights: Promotion and Protection*, New Delhi: Anmol Publications Pvt. Ltd.

Chowdhury, Azizur Rahman (2010): *An Introduction to International Human Rights Law*, Leiden: Brill.

Churchill, R. P. (2006): *Human Rights and Global Diversity*, New Jersey: Pearson Prentice Hall.

Cirincione, Joseph (2004): *WMD in Iraq evidence and implications*,Washington: Massachusette Avenue.

Clapham, Andrew (2007): *Human Rights: A Very Short Introduction*, Oxford: Oxford University Press.

Clark, Anne Marie (2001): *Diplomacy of Conscience: Amnesty International and Changing Human Rights Norms*, United States: Princeton University Press.

Clark, Ian and Iver B. Neuman (eds.) (1996): *Classical Theories Human Rights*, London: Macmillan Press Ltd.

Clark, Meghan J. (2014): The Vision of Catholic Social Thought: The Virtue of Solidarity and the Praxis of Human Rights, Fortress Press.

Clark, Wesley (2003): *Winning Modern Wars*, New York: Public Affairs.

Cleminson, Ronald (2003): *What Happened to Saddam's Weapons of Mass Destruction?*, Washington: Arms Control Association.

Cleveland, William L. and Martin P. Bunton (2000): *A History of the Modern Middle East*, United States: Westview Press.

Cole, Juan R.I. (2006): *The Ayatollahs and Democracy in Iraq*, U.S.: Amsterdam University Press.

Collier, P., Elliot, *et. al.*, (2003): *Breaking the Conflict Trap: Civil War and Development Policy*, Washington: Oxford University Press.

Colson, Elizabeth (1992): "Conflict and Violence" in Carolyn Nordstrom and Jo Ann Martin (eds.), *The Paths to Domination, Resistance and Terror*, Oxford, England: University of California Press.

Conway, Moncure Daniel (ed.) (2010): *The Writings of Thomas Paine*, New York: G. P. Putnam's Sons.

Cook, Miriam (1996): *Women and the War Story*, London: University of California Press Ltd.

Cox, Michael and Dough Stokes (2008): *U.S. Foreign Policy*, New York: Oxford University Press.

Cranston: Maurice, (1973): *What Are Human Rights?*, New York: Talinger Publishing Company.

Croft, Stuart (2006): *Culture, Crisis and America's War on Terror*, Cambridge: Cambridge University Press.

Cryer, Robert, Hakan Friman, Darryl Robinson, Elizabeth Wilmshurst (2010): *An Introduction to International Criminal Law and Procedure*, New York: Cambridge University Press.

Daalder, Ivo H. and James M. Lindsay (2005): *America Unbound: The Bush Revolution in Foreign Policy*, Hoboken, NJ: John Wiley and Sons, Inc.

Davis, Eric (2005): *Memories of State: Politics, History, and Collective Identity in Modern Iraq*, London: University of California Press.

Dawisha, Adeed (2009): *Iraq a Political History from Independence to Occupation*, New Jersey: Princeton University Press.

Denselow, James (2009): "Securing the state: the US and post-war Iraqi border security dynamics," in David Ryan and Patrick Kiely (eds.), *America and Iraq Policy-Making, Intervention and Regional*

Politics, New York: Routledge Taylor and Francis Group.

Dickson, Julie (2001): *Evaluation and Legal Theory*, Oxford: Hart Publishing.

Diller, C. Daniel (1990): *The Middle East*, Washington: Congressional Quarterly Inc.

Dobbins, James (2009): *Occupying Iraq: A History of the Coalition Provisional Authority*, New York: Library of Congress.

Dodge, Toby (2003): *Inventing Iraq: The Failure of Nation Building and a History Denied*, New York: Columbia University Press.

Donnelly, Jack (2003): *Universal Human Rights in Theory and Practice,* Ithaca and London: Cornell University Press.

Doyle, William (2001): *The French Revolution: A very short Introduction*, Oxford: Oxford University Press.

Dunne, Tim and Nicholas J. Wheeler (ed.) (1999): *Human Rights in Global Politics*, United Kingdom: Cambridge University Press.

Dupre, Louis (2004): *The Enlightenment and the Universal Human Rights in Theory and Practice Intellectual Foundations of Modern Culture*, New Haven: Yale University Press.

Edmundson, W. (2004): *An Introduction to Rights*, Cambridge: Cambridge University Press.

Efart, Moshe and Jacob Bercovitch (1991): *Superpowers and Client States in the Middle East*, New York: Routledge.

Ehrenbery, John, J. Patrice McSherry and Jose Ramon Sanchez (2010): *The Iraq Papers*, New York: Oxford University Press.

Elsheshtawy, Yasser (2002): *Planning Middle Eastern Cities*, Routledge: Taylor and Francis.

Engdhal, William (2004): *A Century of War: Anglo American Oil Politics and the New World Order*, London: Pluto Press.

Enloe, Cynthia (2004): *The Curious Feminist-Searching for Women in a New Age of Empire*, United States: University of California Press.

Evans, Tony (1999): *Trading Human Rights: In Global trade and global social issues*, edited by A. Taylor and C. Thomas, *et al.*, London: Routledge.

Fabian, George (2011): *Karl Marx-Prince of Darkness*, United States of America: Library of Congress.

Falk, Richard A. (2008): *Human rights at the U.N. the Political History of Universal Justice*, USA: Indiana University Press Bloomington and Indianapolis.

Farer, Tom J. (2004): "The Interplay of Domestic Politics, Human Rights and U.S. Foreign Policy", in Weiss, Thomas G, Margaret E. Crahan and John Goering (eds.), *Wars on Terrorism and Iraq, Human Rights, Unilateralism and U.S. Foreign Policy*, New York: Routledge.

Farnham, Dave (2014): *Gandhi's Teachings for Troubled Times*, MTB.

Farrelly, Collin (2004): *Contemporary Political Theory*, New Delhi: Sage Publication Pvt. Ltd.

Fattah, Hala Mundhir (2009): *A Brief History of Iraq*, New York: An Imprint of Infobase Publishing.

Fawn, Rick and Raymund Hinnebush (2006): *The Iraq War: Causes and Consequences*, Colorado: Lynne Rienner Press.

Feinberg, Joel (1980): *The Nature and Value of Rights, Rights, Justice and the Bounds of Liberty* (ed.), Princeton: Princeton University Press.

Ferguson, James (1990): *The Anti-Politics Machine: "Development", Depoliticisation, and Bureaucratic Power in Lesotho*, Minneapolis: University of Minnesota Press.

Finnis, John (1998): *Aquinas: Moral, Political, and Legal Theory*, Oxford: Oxford University Press.

Finnis, John (2011): *Natural Law and Natural Rights*, Oxford: Oxford University Press.

Fisk, Robert (2006): *The Great War for Civilisation: The Conquest of the Middle East*, New York: Vintage Book.

Fontan, Victoria (2008): *Voices from Post- Saddam Iraq: Living with Terrorism, Insurgency, and New Forms of Tyranny*, Briton: British Library Cataloging.

Foot, Rosemary (2000): *Rights beyond Borders*, New York: Oxford University Press.

Forsythe, P. David (1991): *The Internationalisation of Human Rights*, Lexington, Mass: Lexington Books.

Forsythe, P, David (2000): *Human Rights and Comparative Foreign Policy*, New York: U.N. Press.

Fox, Jonathan (2008): *A World Survey of Religion and the State*, New York: Cambridge University Press.

Fraser, Cary (2009): "The Middle East and the Persian Gulf as The Gateway to Imperial Crisis: The Bush Administration in Iraq," in David Ryan and Patrick Kiely (eds.), *America and Iraq Policy-Making, Intervention and Regional Politics*, New York: Routledge Taylor and Francis Group.

Freeman, Michael (2002): *Human Rights: An Interdisciplinary Approach*, Cambridge: Polity.

Friedman, Lawrence M. (2011): The Human Rights Culture: A Study in History and Context, New Orleans, Louisiana: Quid Pro Books.

Fromm, Erich (1981): *Marx's Concept of Man*, Open Road Media.

Fukuyama, Francis (2006): *America at the Crossroads: Democracy, Power, and the Neoconservative Legacy*, New Haven: Yale University Press.

Galtung, Johan (1996): *Peace by Peaceful Means: Peace and Conflict, Development and Civilisation*, Oslo and London: International Peace Research Institute and Sage Publications.

Gayur, Paul (2002): "Kant's Deduction of the Principles of Right," in Mark Timmons (ed.), *Kant's Metaphysics of Morals: Interpretative Essays*. New York: Oxford University Press.

Gibson, Bryan (2010): *Covert Relationship: American Foreign Policy, Intelligence, and the Iran-Iraq War, 1980-1988*, New York: Praeger.

Girling, S; L, John (1980): *America and the Third World*, USA: Routledge and Kegan Paul.

Glass, Charles (2004) : *The Northern Front: A Wartime Diary*, London: Saqi Books.

Gordon, Michael R., and Bernard E. Trainor (2006): *Cobra II: The Inside Story of the Invasion and Occupation of Iraq*, New York: Pantheon.

Gould, Carol C. (2004): *Globalising Democracy and Human Rights*, Cambridge: Cambridge University Press.

Gould, Carol C. (2013): "The Human Right to Democracy and its Global Import," in Cindy Holder and David Reidy (eds.), *Human Rights-The Hard Questions*, Cambridge: Cambridge University Press.

Grant, Ruth W. (2010): *John Locke's Liberalism*, Chicago:University of Chicago Press.

Grossman, Dave (1995): *On Killing: The Psychological Cost of Learning to Kill in War and Society*, Boston: Little, Brown.

O'Hanlon, Michael E. (2005): *Defense Strategy for the Post-Saddam Era*. Washington, D.C.: Brookings Institution Press.

Hannum, Hurst (2006): *The Concept of Human Rights International Human Rights Problems of Law, Policy, and Practice*, United States: Aspen Publishers.

Heller, Mark A. (2000): *Continuing and Change in Israeli Security Policy*, London: Oxford University Press for the International Institute of Strategic Studies.

Hershberg, James G, and James B. Conant (1993): *Harvard to Hiroshima and the Making of the Nuclear Age*, Stanford: Stanford University Press.

Hesse, Carla and Robert Post (1999): *Human Rights in Political Transitions: Gettysburg to Bosnia*, New York: Zone Books.

Heyns, Christof H. and Frans Viljoen (2002): *The Impact of the United Nations Human Rights Treaties on the Domestic Level*, Netherland: Kluwer Law International.

Heywood, Andrew (2002): *Politics*, New York: Palgrave Foundations.

Hill, Matthew Alan (2012): *Democracy, Promotion and Conflict based Reconstruction: The United States and Democratic Consolidation in Bosnia, Afghanistan and Iraq*, New York: Routledge.

Hogan, J, Michael (1995): *America in the World. The Historiography of American Foreign Relations since 1941,* United States: Library of Congress Cataloging Publication Data.

Horowitz, Revital, and Shira Atik (2011): *Daughters of Iraq*, Washington: Smashwords.

Hume, David (1965): A Treatise of Human Nature by David Hume Sheba Blake Publishing.

Hunt, Courtney (2005): *The History of Iraq*, United States of America: Greenwood Press.

Hunt, Lynn (2007): *Inventing Human Rights*, New York: W.W. Norton and Company.

Hunter, T., Shireen and Huma Malik (2005): *Islam and Human Rights - advancing a U.S.-Muslim Dialogue,* Washington: Library of Congress Cataloging Publication Data.

Hussein,Yasmine Al Jawaheri (2008): *Women in Iraq*, London: Lynne Rienner Publishers.

Ibezim, Felicia Okeke (2006): *Saddam Hussein: The Legendary Dictator*, USA: Ekwike Books.

Isaiah Berlin (1969): *Four Essays on Liberty*, Oxford: Oxford University Press.

Ishay, R., Micheline (2004): *The History of Human Rights, From Ancient Times to the Globalisation Era*, London: University of California.

Jackson, Robert and Soresen, George (2007): *Introduction to International Theories and Approaches*, New York: Oxford University Press.

Joanne, McWilliam, Barnes Timothy. D, Michael A. Fahey and Peter Slater (1992): *Augustine: From Rhetor to Theologian*, Canada: Wilfrid Laurier University Press.

Jones, Peter (2013): "Groups and Human Rights," in Cindy Holder and David Reidy (eds.), *Human Rights–The Hard Questions*, Cambridge: Cambridge University Press.

Kamp, M. (2003) "Organizing Ideologies of Gender, Class and Ethnicity: The Pre-Revolutionary Women's Movement in Iraq," in S. Zuhur (ed.), *Women and Gender in the Middle East and Islamic World Today*, Berkeley: University of California Press.

Karsh, Efraim (2002): *The Iran-Iraq War 1980-1988*, London: Osprey Publishing.

Keene, Edward (2005): *International Political Thought*, United States: Polity Press.

Keddie, Nikkie and Beth Baron (1991): *Women in the Middle East History: Shifting Boundaries in Sex and Gender*, New Haven: Yale University Press.

Keys, Mary M. (2008): *Aquinas, Aristotle and the Promise of the Common Good*, Cambridge: Cambridge University Press.

Kinsella, David and Craig L. Carr (2008): *The Morality of War*, New Delhi: Viva Books.

Kiely, Patrick (2009): "Through Distorted Lenses: Iraq and Balance of Power Politics 1969-1979," in David Ryan and Patrick Kiely (eds.), *America and Iraq Policy-Making, Intervention and Regional Politics*, New York: Routledge Taylor and Francis Group.

Knights, Michael (2005): *Cradle of Conflict: Iraq and the Birth of Modern U.S. Military Power*, United States: Naval Institute.

Kolakowski, Leszek (1983): Marxism and Human Rights, *Daedalus-American Academy of Arts and Science*, 112(4): 81.

Kriner, Douglas L. and Francis X Shen (2010): *The Casuality Gap: The Causes and Consequences of Amercian Wartime Inequalities*, Oxford: Oxford University Press.

Krivenko,Yahayaoui, Ekaterina (2009): *Women, Islam and International Law*, United States: Library of Congrss Cataloging Publication Data.

Kumar, Aravind (1998): *Encyclopaedia of Human Rights, Violence and Non-Violence*, New Delhi: Anmol Publications.

Leckie, Scott and Anne Gallanger (2006): *Economic, Social and Cultural Rights: A Legal Resource Guide*, Philadelphia, U.S.A.: University of Pennsylvania Press.

Li, Quan (2006): "*Political Violence and Foreign Direct Investment. In Research in Global Strategic Management*," *Regional Economic Integration*: Oxford: Elsevier.

Lockwood, Bert B (2006): *Women's Rights: A Human Rights Quarterly Reader*. Baltimore: Johns Hopkins University Press.

Longrigg, Stephen (1953): *Iraq: 1990-1950*, New York: Oxford University Press.

Luciani, Giacomo and Ghassan Salame (1998): *The Politics of Arab Integration*, New York: British Library Cataloging Publication Data.

Lynch, Marc (2006): *Voices of the New Arab Public Iraq, al-Jazeera, and Middle East Politics Today*, New York: Columbia University Press.

Lynch, Michael (1992): *Scotland: A New History*, U.K.: Pimlico.

Lynch, Timothy J., and Robert S. Singh (2008): *After Bush: The Case for Continuity in American Foreign Policy*, New York: Cambridge University Press.

MacCormick, N. (1982): *Legal Right and Social Democracy*, Oxford: Oxford University Press.

MacKey, Sandram (2003): *The Reckoning: Iraq and the Legacy of Saddam Hussein*, New York: W. W. Norton and Company.

MacLean, J., Sandra (2004): "*Globalisation and the New Inequalities: Threats and Prospects for Human Security*," Department of Political Science, Simon Fraser University. Centre for Global Political Economy. Canada.

MacMillan, John (2005): "Introduction: The Iraq War and Democratic Politics" in Alex Danchev and John MacMillan (eds.), *The Iraq War and Democratic Politics*, Routledge.

Maguire, Peter H. (2013): *Law and War: International Law and American History*, New York: Columbia University Press.

Makiya, Kanan (1998): *Republic of Fear: The Politics of Modern Iraq*, California: University of California Press.

Mansfield, Peter (2003): *A History of the Middle East*, London: Penguin Books.

Marcuse, Herbert (1998): *Technology, War and Fascism: The Collected Papers of Herbert, Marcuse*, Vol. 1. Ed. Douglas Kellner, New York: Routledge.

Martin, Rex (1993): *A System of Rights*, Oxford: Clarendon Press.

Matthews, Rupert (2012): *On Liberty: With Full Text*, by John Stuart Mill and Modern Introduction, Smashwords: Bretwalda Books.

Mayer, Ann Elizabeth (2007): *Islam and Human Rights Tradition and Politics*, United States: Westview Press.

McBride, Cillian (2005): *Deliberative Democracy and the Politics of Recognition*, Institute of Governance: Queen's University. Available online at http://works.bepress.com/cillian_mcbride/2.

McCresken, Trevor B. (2009): "George W. Bush, American exceptionalism and the Iraq War," in David Ryan and Patrick Kiely (eds.), *America and Iraq Policy-Making, Intervention And*

Regional Politics, New York: Routledge Taylor and Francis Group.

McNaughton, Neil (1996): *Success in Politics*, London: John Murray Publishers.

Mearsheimer, John J. (2001): *The Tragedy of Great Power Politics*, New York: W.W. Norton.

Mendelson, Oliver and Baxi, Upendra (1994): *The Rights of Subordinated Peoples*, Walton Street: Oxford University Press.

Mernissi, Fatima (1991): *The Veil and the Male Elite: a Feminist Interpretation of Women's Rights in Islam*, New York: Addison Wesley Publishing Company.

Mertus, A., Julie and Jeffrey W. Helsing (2006): *Human Rights and Conflict-Exploring the Links between the Rights, Law and Peace Building*, United States: Library of Congress Cataloguing Publication Data.

Messer-Davidow, Ellen (2002): *Disciplining Feminism from Social Activism to Academic Discourse*, Durham, N.C.: Duke University Press.

Michline, R., Ishay (1997): *The Human Rights Reader: Major Political Essays, Speeches and Documents from the Bible to the Present*, New York: Routledge.

Mill, John Stuart (2005): *Utilitarianism*, New York: Start Publishing LLC.

Mill, John Stuart (2008): *Utilitarianism and on Liberty: Including 'Essay on Bentham' and Selections from the Writings of Jeremy Bentham and John Austin*, NJ: Wiley. Uses the 1871 edition of *Utilitarianism*, the last to be published in Mill's lifetime. Includes selections from Bentham and John Austin, the two thinkers who most influenced Mill. Introduction written by Mary Warnock, a highly respected figure in 20th-century ethics in her own right.

Mishra, Santap Sanhari (2007): *Human Rights: An Introduction*, Hyderabad: The ICFAI University Press.

Moghadam, M. Valentine (1993): *Modernizing Women: Gender and Social Change in the Middle East*, London: Lynne Renner Publishers.

Moghadam, M. Valentine (2007): *From Patriarchy to Empowerment. Women's Participation, Movements and Rights in the Middle East, North Africa and South Asia*, New York: Syrause University Press.

Mogi, Sobei (1989): *The History of Political Theory*, New Delhi: Anmol Publications.

Mohanthy, Biswaranjan (2010): *Dynamics of Political Theory: The Current Analysis*, New Delhi: Atlantic Publishers.

Mojab, Shahrzad (2006): *Women, War, Violence and Learning*, New York: Routledge.

Momen, Moojan (1985): *An Introduction to Shiite Islam*, London:Yale University Press.

Morgenthau, J. H. (1960): *Politics among Nations. The Struggle for Power and Peace*, New York.

Morgenthau, Hans J. (1973): *Politics Among Nations*, United States: Library of Congress Cataloguing in Publications Data.

Morrissey, John (2009): "The Geoeconomic Pivot of the Global War on Terror: US Central Command and the War in Iraq," in David Ryan and Patrick Kiely (eds.), *America and Iraq Policy-Making, Intervention And Regional Politics*, New York: Routledge Taylor and Francis Group.

Morrow, John (2005): *History of Western Political Thought*, New York: Palgrave Macmillan.

Murray, Williamson and Robert H. Scales (2003): *The Iraq War-A Military History*, Cambridge: Harvard University Press.

Nashat, Guity (1982): *Women in the Ancient Middle East, in Restoring Women to History*, Bloomington, Indiana : Organisation of American History.

Neff, Stephen C. (2005): *War and the Law of Nations: A General History*, New York: Cambridge University Press.

Neier, Aryeh (2012): *The International Human Rights Movement: A History*, Princeton University Press.

Ness, Peter Van, and Nikhil Aziz (1999): *Debating Human Rights: Critical Essays from the U.S. and Asia*, London: Routledge Publication.

Nordstrom, Carolyn, and JoAnn Martin (1992): "The Culture of Conflict: Field Reality and Theory," in *The Paths to Domination, Resistance and Terror*, C. Nordstrom and J. Martin, (eds.), Berkeley: University of California Press.

Nordstrom, Carolyn (2004): *Shadows of War: Violence, Power, and International Profiteering in the Twenty-First Century*, Berkeley: University of California Press.

Norman, Jesse (2013): *Edmund Burke: The Visionary Who Invented Modern Politics*, New York: Harper Collins.

Norrlof, Carla (2010): *America's Global Advantage. U.S. Hegemony and International Cooperation*, United Kingdom: Cambridge University Press.

Northcott, Michael (2004): *An Angel Directs the Storm. Apocalyptic Religion and American Empire,* New York: I. B. Tauris.

Nylan, M. and T.A. Wilson (2010): "*Lives of Confucius,*" New York: Doubleday.

Nozick, Robert (1974): *Anarchy, State, and Utopia*, New York: Perseus Book Group.

O'Driscoll, Cian (2008): *Renegotiation of the Just War Tradition and the Right to War in the Twenty-First Century*, New York: Palgrave Macmillan.

O'Hanlon, Michael E., Jason H. Campbell, and Ian Livingston (2007): *Iraq Index: Tracking Variables of Reconstruction and Security in Post-Saddam Iraq*, Washington DC: Brookings Institution.

Okawa, Ryuho (2013): *The Just Cause in the Iraq War: Did Saddam Hussein Possess Weapons of Mass Destruction?*, Japan: IRH Press Co. Ltd.

Paffenholz, T. and C. Spurk (2010): *Civil Society and Peace Building-a Critical Assessment*, London: Lynne Rienner Publishers, INC.

Paine, Thomas (2004): *The Rights of Man*, Raleigh, N.C: Alex Catalogue Publishing.

Pangalangn, Raul, C. (2002): *Sweatshops and International Labour Standards: Globalising Markets, Localizing Norms Globalisation and Human Rights*, California: University of California Press.

Parisi, Laura (2013): "Gender Mainstreaming Human Rights: A Progressive Path for Gender Equality," in Cindy Holder and

David Reidy (eds.), *Human Rights- The Hard Questions*, Cambridge: Cambridge University Press.

Pauls, Carmen (1999): Report from the Field, Mennonite Central Committee News Service.

Paya, Ali (2011): "Islamic democracy: a valid concept or an oxymoron?," in Ali Para and John L. Esposito (eds.), *Iraq, Democracy and the Future of the Muslim World*, New York: Routledge Taylor and Francis Group.

Pearson, Graham S. (2000): *The UNSCOM Saga*, New York: Palgrave Macmillan.

Perlmutter, Amos, Michael I. Handel, and Uri Bar-Joseph (2003): *Two Minutes over Baghdad*, London: Frank Cass. Peter, Baer. R. (2001): *Human Rights Universality in Practice*, New York: Palgrave Publication.

Peter, Baer. R. (2001): *Human Rights Universality in Practice*, New York: Palgrave Publication.

Peters, Julie (1995): *Women's Rights, Human Rights: International Feminist Perspectives*, New York: Routledge Publications.

Peterson, V. S. and Runyan, A. S. (1999): *Global Genders Issue*, Boulder, Westview Press.

Pilger, John (2002): *The New Rulers of the World*, London: Verso.

Pitt, William R. (2002): *War On Iraq: What Team Bush Doesn't Want You to Know?*, New York: Context Books.

Polk, William R. (2005): *Understanding Iraq*, New York: Harper Collins.

Pollis, Admanita and Peter Schuab (1980): *Human Rights: Cultural and Ideological Perspectives*, New York: Praeger.

Preston, Samuel H., Patrick Heuveline, and Michel Guillot (2001): *Demography: Measuring and Modeling Population Processes*, London: Basil Blackwell.

Rajwat, Mamta (2001): *Burning Issues of Human Rights*, New Delhi: Kalpaz Publications.

Ranstorp, Magnus and Wikinson, Paul (2009): *Terrorism and Human Rights*, New York: Routledge Taylor and Francis Group.

Rawls, John (1971): *A Theory of Justice*, Cambridge, MA: Belknap Press of Harvard University Press.

Rawls, John (1999): *A Theory of Justice*, Oxford: Oxford University Press.

Record, Jeffrey and Andrew Terrill (2004): *Iraq and Vietnam: Differences, Similarities, and Insights*, Strategic Studies Institute Carlisle Barracks: U.S. Army War College.

Rehma, Javaid and Susan Carolyn (2007): *Religion Human Rights and International Law: A Critical Examination of Islamic State Practices*, Netherlands: IDC Publishers.

Reichert, Elizebeth (2006): *Understanding Human Rights*, London: Sage Publications.

Rejali, Darius M. (2009): *Torture and Democracy*, Princeton, N.J.: Princeton University Press.

Repetto, David (2010): *Social Problems-Selections from CQ Researcher*, New Delhi: Sage Publications.

Ripstein, Arthur (2007): *Ronald Dworkin*, New York: Cambridge University Press.

Roberts, David (2008): *Human Insecurity Global Structures of Violence*, New York: Zed Books.

Rogan, L. Eugene and Avi Shlaim (2001): *The War of Palestine Rewriting the History of 1948*, U.K: Cambridge University Press.

Romano, David (2006): *The Kurdish Nationalist Movement*, New York: Cambridge University Press.

Roper, Jon (2009): "The Imperial Presidency Redux: presidential power and the war in Iraq," in David Ryan and Patrick Kiely (eds.), *America and Iraq Policy-Making, Intervention and Regional Politics*, New York: Routledge Taylor and Francis Group.

Rosenau, James N. (2003): *Distant proximities: Dynamics beyond Globalisation*, Princeton: Princeton University Press.

Ryan, David (2009): "From the 'Tilt' to the Unintended 'Transformation': the United States and Iraq, 1975-1992," in David Ryan and Patrick Kiely (eds.), *America and Iraq Policy-Making, Intervention and Regional Politics*, New York: Routledge Taylor and Francis Group.

Sabine, H., George (1993): *A History of Political Theory*, New Delhi: Oxford and IBH Publishing Co.

Sacino, Sherry (2012): *A Commentary on the United Nations Conventions on the Rights of the Child*, United States: Library of Congress Cataloguing in Publications Data.

Sada, Georges, and Jim Nelson Black (2006): *Saddam's Secrets: How an Iraqi General Defied and Survived Saddam Hussein*, Brentwood, TN: Integrity Publishers.

Said, Edward W. (2004): *From Oslo to Iraq and the Road Map*, New York: Pantheon Book.

Salit, Siraj and Hilary Lim (2006): *Land, Law and Islam: Property and Human Rights in the Muslim World*, New York: U.S. Cataloguing Publication Data.

Sanlon, Peter T. (2014): *Augustine's Theology of Preaching*, Minneapolis MN: Fortress Press.

Salman, Emad (2000): *Sanctions from an Iraqi Perspective*, Cambridge: Cambridge University.

Scarre, Geoffrey (1996): *Utilitarianism*, London: Routledge.

Schmidt, Bettina E., and Ingo W. Schroder (2001): *Anthropology of Violence and Conflict*, New York: Routledge.

Schopenhauer, Arthur (2012): *On Human Nature*, New York: Start Publishing LLC.

Schwartz, Michael (2008): *War Without End: The Iraq War in Context*, Chicago: Haymarket Books.

Shay, Jonathan (1994): *Achilles in Vietnam: Combat Trauma and the Undoing of Character*, New York: Simon and Schuster.

Shepard, Mark (2004): *Mahatma Gandhi and His Myths: Civil Disobedience, Nonviolence, and Satyagraha in the Real World*, Olympia, Wash.: Shepard Publications.

Shields, Charles J. (2005): *Saddam Hussein: Major World Leaders*, China: Chelsea House Publishers.

Shirazi, Faegheh (2010): *Muslim Women in War and Crisis*, USA: University of Texas Press.

Shlaim, Avi (2001): *The Iron Wall Israel and the Arab World*, New York: W.W. Norton and Company.

Shwartz, Michael (2008): *The War without End: The Iraq War Context*, Chicago, Haymarket Books.

Simons, Geoff (2004): *Iraq: from Summer to Post-Saddam,* New York: Palgrave Macmillan.

Snyder, Sarah B (2011): *Human Rights Activism and the End of the Cold War: A Transnational History of the Helsinki Network (Human Rights in History)*, Cambridge: Cambridge University Press.

Solaro, Erin (2006): *Women in the Line of Fire Common-Sense look at Women in Arm*, United States: Seal Press.

Soros, George (2004): *The Bubble of U.S. Supremacy*, London: Weidenfeld and Nicolson.

Spencer, Dr. William (1994): *The Middle East*, United States of America: The Dushkin Publishing Group.

Stewart, Pamela J. and Andrew Strathern (2002): *Violence: Theory and Ethnography*, London and New York: Continuum.

Stiehm, Judith (1989): *Arms and the Enlisted Woman*, Philadelphia: Temple University Press.

Stiglitz, Joseph, and Linda Bilmes (2008): "Hidden Wounds and Accounting Tricks: Disguising the True Costs," in Miriam Pemberton and William D. Hartung (eds.), *Lessons From Iraq: Avoiding the Next War*, USA: Penguin Publishers.

Stiglitz, Joseph E. and Linda J. Bilmes (2012): "Estimating the Costs of War: Methodological Issues, with Applications to Iraq and Afghanistan." in Michelle R. Garfinkel and Stergios Skaperdas (eds.), *Oxford Handbook of the Economics of Peace and Conflict*, UK: Oxford University Press.

Strathern, Paul (2012): *Kant: Philosophy in an Hour*, New York: Harper Collins.

Sumner, L.W. (1987): *The Moral Foundation of Rights,* Oxford: Clarendon Press.

Susskind, Yifat (2007): *Promising Democracy, Imposing Theocracy: Gender-Based Violence and the U.S. War on Iraq*, —: MADRE Publication.

Teague, Don and Rafraf Barrak (2010): *Saved by Her Enemy: An Iraqi Woman's Journey from the Heart of War to the Heartland of America*, New York: Simon and Schuster.

Teeple, Gary (2005): *The Riddle of Human Rights*, Aurora: Garamond Press.

Teixeira, Nuno Severiano (2011): *The International Politics on Democratisation*, New York: Routledge.

Tenet, George and Bill Harlow (2007): *At the Centre of the Storm: My Years at the CIA*, New York: Harper Collins.

Teson, F. (2005): *Humanitarian Intervention: An Inquiry into Law and Morality*, Ardsley, New York: Transnational.

Terrill, Andrew W. (2003): *Nationalism, Sectarianism, and the Future of the U.S. Presence in Post-Saddam Iraq*, Honolulu Hawaii USA: University Press of the Pacific.

Tripp, Charles (2010): *A History of Iraq*, United States: Cambridge University Press.

Twiss, Sumner B. (2004): *Human Rights, History and Globalisation*, Mexico: Jose Luis Martinez.

Verma, S.B. (2005): *Status of Women in Modern India*, New Delhi: Deep and Deep Publiccations.

Vizard, Polly (2006): *Poverty and Human Rights: Sen's Capability Perspective' Explored*, London: Oxford University Press.

Volo, James M. (2010): *A History of War Resistance in America*, California: Greenwood.

Waluchow, W.J. (1994): *Inclusive Legal Positivism*, Oxford: Clarendon Press.

Wasleker, Sandeep (1991): *The New World Order*, New Delhi: Onark Publishers.

Watkins, Susan (2006): *Selections from New Left Review*, Calcutta: Seagull Books Private Limited.

Webster, Donovan (1996): *Aftermath: The Remnants of War*, New York: Random House.

Weiss, Thomas G. (ed.) (2004): *War on Terrorism and Iraq. Human Rights, Unilateralism and U.S. Foreign Policy*, New York: Routledge Publication.

Weissbrodt, David S. and Connie De La Vega (2007): *International Human Rights Law-An Introduction*, Philadelphiya: University of Pennsilvaniya.

Welchman, Lynn (2007): *Women and Muslim Family Laws in Arab States: A Comparative Overview of Textual Development and Advocacy*, Amsterdom: Amsterdom University Press.

West, Bing and General Ray L. Smith (2003): *The March Up: Taking Baghdad with the first Marine Division*, New York: Bantam Books.

Wilshire, Howard Gordon, Jane E. Nielson, Richard W. Hazlett (2008): *The American West at Risk: Science, Myths, and Politics of Land Abuse and Recovery*, New York: Oxford University Press.

Wilson, Ashby, Richard (2005): *Human Rights in the War on Terror*, New York: Cambridge University Press.

Wolff, Robert Paul (1977): *Understanding Rawls: A Reconstruction and Critique of A Theory of Justice*, Princeton, N.J.: Princeton University Press.

Wolosky, S. (2013): "The Jewish Annotated New Testament," in Amy-Jill Levine and Marc Zvi Brettler (eds.), *Common Knowledge*, Duke University Press. Accessed on May 11, 2013.

Woods, Kevin M., Williamson Murray, Elizabeth A. Nathan, Laila Sabara, and Ana M. Venegas (2011a): "Saddam's Generals". D-4121. Alexandria, VA: *Institute for Defense Analyses.*

Woods, Kevin, David D. Palkki, and Mark E. Stout, (eds.) (2011b): *The Saddam Tapes: The Inner Workings of a Tyrant's Regime, 1978-2001*, Cambridge, UK: Cambridge University Press.

Wood, R., Charles (1999): *The Old Testament,* U.S: Kregel Publications.

Yacoub, Sameer (2010): "Changing of the Guard at Last U.S. Run Prison," Burlington, Vermont: Burlington Free Press.

Yildiz, Kerim (2004): *The Kurds in Iraq- The Past, Present and Future*, London: Pluto Press.

Yusuf, Abdulqwai A. (2013): *Human Rights: a Third World Perspective*, Italy: European University Press.

Zaborowski, Holger (2012): *Natural Moral Law in Contemporary Society*, United States: Catholic University of America Press.

Zagorin, Perez (2009): *Hobbes and the Law of Nature*, New Jersey: Princeton University Press.

Zalewski, Marysia (2013): "Searching for the Hard Questions about Women's Rights," in Cindy Holder and David Reidy (eds.), *Human Rights-The Hard Questions*, Cambridge: Cambridge University Press.

Articles

Abdel-Fadil M. (2003): "Issues of economic reconstruction of Iraq, in ESCWA," *Report on the Workshop on Iraq and the Region after the War, Beirut*, 9(11): 25-37.

Abirafeh, Lina (2003): "The Role of Religion in the Lives of Women in the New Afghanistan," *Critical Half, Annual Journal of Women for Women International*, 1(1): 36.

Addis, Adeno (2003): "Economic Sanctions and the Problem of Evil", *Human Rights Quarterly*, 25(3): August 573-623.

Afary, Janet and Kevin B. Anderson (2005): "Seductions of Islamism: Revisiting Foucault and the Iranian Revolution," *Human Rights Global Focus*, 2(1).

Ahram, Ariel I. (2002): "Iraq and Syria: The Dilemma of Dynasty," *Middle East Quarterly*, 9(2): 33-42.

Al-Ali, Nadje (2005): "Reconstructing Gender: Iraqi Women between Dictatorship, War, Sanctions and Occupation," *Third World Quarterly*, 26(4-5): 739-758.

Al-Ali, Nadje and Nichola Pratt (2006): "Women in Iraq: Beyond the Rhetoric," *Middle East Report*, 239: 18-23.

Al-Araji A (2001): "Iraqi Doctors Appeal for Help from Doctors in other Countries," *British Medical Journal*, 323(7303): 53.

Al-Khateeb, Mukdad A, Nadhir Al-Ansari, Sven Knutsson (2014): "Sustainable University Model for Higher Education in Iraq," *Scientific Research-an Academic Publisher*, 5(5): 318-328.

Ali, Miriam (2012): "Iraqi Women Face Workplace Discrimination," *Al-Monitor*, http://www.al-monitor.com/pulse/originals/2014/02/iraq-human-rights-situation-bad-hrw.html.accessed on 21.08.2013.

Ali, Miriam (2014): "Human Rights Watch Condemns Situation in Iraq," *Al-Monitor*, http://www.al-monitor.com/pulse/originals/2014/02/iraq-human-rights-situation-bad-hrw.html.accessed on 07.02.2014.

Ali, Mohamed M and Iqbal H. Shah (2000): "Sanctions and Childhood Mortality in Iraq," *The Lancet*, 355(9218): 1851-57.

Alkhuzai, A.H., Ahmad I. J., Hweel M. J. and Ismail T. W. (2008): "Violence-Related Mortality in Iraq from 2002 to 2006," *The New England Journal of Medicine* 358 (5): 484-493.

Amowitz, Lynn L., Glen Kim, Chen Reis, Jana L. Asher and Vincent Iacopino (2004): "Human Rights Abuses and Concerns about Women's Health and Human Rights in Southern Iraq," *JAMA* (*Journal of American Medical Association*) 291(12):1471-1479.

Andersen, Margaret L. (2005): "Thinking about Women: A Quarter Century's View," *Gender and Society*, 19(4) 437-455.

Apodaca, Clair (2001): "Global economic patterns and personal integrity rights after the Cold War," *International Studies Quarterly*, 45 (4): 587-602.

Apodaca, Clair and Michael Stohl (1999): "United States Human Rights Policy and Foreign Assistance," *International Studies Quarterly*, 43(1): 185.

Aral, Berdal (2004): "The Idea of Human Rights as Perceived in the Ottoman Empire," *Human Rights Quarterly*, 26(2): 454-482.

Arat, Zehra F. (1999): "Human Rights and Democracy: Expanding or Contracting," *Polity*, 32(1): 119-144.

Arat, Zehra F. (2002): "Analyzing Child Labour as a Human Rights Issue: Its Causes, Aggravating Policies and Alternative Proposals," *Human Rights Quarterly*, 24(1): 177-204.

Ariany, Bnar (2013): "The Conflict between Women's Rights and Cultural Practices in Iraq," *The International Journal of Human Rights*, 17(4): 530-566.

Arkin, William M. (2001): "America Cluster Bombs Iraq," *Common Dreams News Center*, Electronic document, Available online at http://www.com mondreams.org/views01/0226-06.htm, accessed on 15/02/2006.

Ascherio, Alberto, Robert Chase, Tim Cote and Godelieave Dehaes (1992): "Effect of the Gulf War on Infant and Child Mortality in Iraq," *The New England Journal of Medicine*, 327: 931-936.

Assadi, Muzaffer (2011): "Discourse on Human Rights: Narratives Beyond Political," *The Indian Journal of Political Science*, LXXII (2): 378.

Avineri, Shlomo (1993): "Israel and the End of the Cold War: The Shadow has faded," *The Brookings Review*, 11(2): 26-31.

Azarva, Jeffrey (2009): "Is U.S. Detention Policy in Iraq Working?," *Middle East Quarterly*, 16(1): 5-14.

Azinge, E. (1992): "Millstone Decision on Human Rights" in (ed.) A. U. Kalu and Y. Osinbayo, *Perspective on Human Rights II*, 12: 197.

Bahgat, Gawdat (2005): "Saddam Hussein's Legacy: a Preliminary Assessment and its Implications," *SAIS Review of International Affairs*, 25(2): 93-103.

Barakat, Sultan (2005): "Post-Saddam Iraq: Deconstructing a Regime, Reconstructing a Nation," *Third World Quarterly*, 26(4/ 5): 571-591.

Bari, H. M. Fazlul (2013): "Feminist Approach in Human Rights: An Appraisal," *Human Rights Monitor*, April 13.

Barker, Isabelle and Jasbir Kaur Puar (2002): "Feminist Problematisation of Rights Language and Universal Conceptualisation of Human Rights," *International Journal of Theology*, 608-616.

Barlow, Rebecca (2008): "The First International Conference of the Nobel Women's Initiative: Women Redefining Peace in the Middle East and Beyond," *Journal of Middle East Women's Studies*, 4(1): 125-131.

Beattie, Peter M. (2011): "A Poverty of Rights: Citizenship and Inequality in Twentieth-Century Rio de Janeiro," *The Americas*, 67(4): 574-575.

Beetham, David (2000): "Democracy and Human Rights," *International Affairs*, 76(4):863.

Bellamy, Alex. J. (2004): "Ethics and Intervention: The 'Humanitarian Exception' and the Problem of Abuse in the Case of Iraq", *Journal of Peace Research*, 41(2) March 131-147.

Bengio, Ofra (2003): "Iraqi Kurds: Hour of Power?," *Middle East Quarterly*, 10(3): 39-48.

Benomar, Jamal (2004): "Constitution- Making after Conflict: Lessons for Iraq," *Journal of Democracy*, 15(2): 81-95.

Betts, Paul (2012): "Socialism, Social Rights, and Human Rights: The Case of East Germany," *An International Journal of Human Rights, Humanitarianism and Development*, 3(3): 407-426.

Biando, Julie and Stephan P. Edwards (2008): "Culture and the New Iraq: The Iraq National Library and Archive, "Imagined Community," and the Future of the Iraqi Nation", *Libraries and Cultural Record* 43(3), 327-342.

Binion, Gayle (1995): "Human Rights: A Feminist Perspective," *Human Rights Quarterly*, 17(3): 509-526.

Bloom, Mia (2010): "Deaths Becomes Her: Women, Occupation and Terrorist Mobilisation," *Political Science and Politics*, 43(3): 445-450.

Bonds, Eric (2009): "Strategic Role Taking and Political Struggle: Bearing Witness to the Iraq War", *Symbolic Interaction*, 32(1), Winter 1-20.

Booth, Ken (1995): "Human Wrongs and International Relations," *International Affairs*, 71: 103-126.

Borshchevskaya, Anna (2010): "Sponsored Corruption and Neglected Reform in Syria," *Middle East Quarterly*, 17(3):41-50.

Brands, Hal (2011): "Inside the Iraqi State Records: Saddam Hussein, 'Iron gate,' and the United States," *Journal of Strategic Studies*, 34(1): 95-118.

Brekert, George G. (1986): "Marx and Human Rights," *Journal of the History of Philosophy*, 24(1): 55-77.

Brett, Annabel (2002): "Natural Right and Civil Community: the Civil Philosophy of Hugo Grotius," *The Historical Journal*, 45(1): 31-51.

Briggs, Bill (2013): "Unemployment among post-9/11 Veterans still Running Heavy," NBC News contributor, Friday Mar 8.

Brooks, Thom (2003): "T. H. Green's Theory of Punishment," *History of Political Thought*, 24 (4): 685-701.

Brown, Lucy and David Romano (2006): "Women in Post-Saddam Iraq One Step Forward or Two Step Back?," *Journal of NWSA*, 18(3): 51-70.

Brown, Michael E. (1979): "The Nationalisation of the Iraqi Petroleum Company," *International Journal of Middle East Studies*, 10(1): 107-124.

Bruner, Whitley (1990): "Soviet New Thinking and the Middle East: Gorbchev's Arab-Israeli Options," *Comparative Strategy*, 9(4): 385-401.

Brunham, Liam, Patricia Lee, and Andrew Pinto (2003): "Medical Students not mum on Iraq," *Canadian Medical Association Journal*, 169(6): 541.

Bunch, Charlotte (1990): "Women's Right as Human Rights: Towards a Re-Vision of Human Rights," *Human Rights Quarterly*, 12: 486-498.

Bunting, Annie (1993): "Theorizing Women's Cultural Diversity in Feminist International Human Rights Strategies," *Journal of Law and Society*, 20(1): 6-22.

Bunting, Annie (2005): "Stages of Development: Marriage of Girls and Teens as an International Human Rights Issue," *Social and Legal Studies*, 14(1): 17-38.

Burkle, Frederick M., Jr, Bradley A. Woodruff and Eric K. Noji (2005): "Lessons and Controversies: planning and executing immediate relief in the aftermath of the war in Iraq," *Third World Quarterly*, 26(4/5): 797-814.

Burnham, Gilbert; Riyadh Lafta, Shannon Doccy and Less Roberts, (2006): "Morality after the 2003 Invasion of Iraq: A Cross-Sectional Cluster Sample Survey," *The Lancet*, 368(9545): 1421-1428.

Buzzell, Emily and Samuel H. Preston (2007): "Mortality of American Troops in the Iraq War," *Population and Development*, 33(3): 555-566.

Byman, Daniel (2001): "Iraq after Saddam," *The Washington Quarterly*, 24(4): 151-162.

Byman, Daniel (2004): "*Insecuring Iraq*," *The National Interest*, 76: 15-18.

Cardenas, Sonia and Andrew Flibbert (2005): "National Human Rights Institutions in the Middle East," *Middle East Journal*, 59(3): 411-436.

Carroll, Katherine Blue (2011): "Tribal Law and Reconciliation in the New Iraq", *The Middle East Journal,* Winter.

Chamberlin, Paul Thomas (2011): "Rethinking the Middle East and North Africa in the Cold War," *International Journal of Middle East*, 43(2): 317-319.

Champagne, Duane (2013): "UNDRIP (United Nations Declaration on the Rights of Indigenous Peoples): Human, Civil, and Indigenous Rights," *Wicazo Sa Review*, 28(1): 9-22.

Chibi, Andrew A. (1998): "The social and Regional Origins of the Henrician Episcopacy," *The Sixteenth Century Journal*, 29(4): 955-973.

Clark, Tillman (2010): "Human Rights and Radical Social Change: Liberalism, Marxism and Progressive Populism in Venezuela," *The International Student Journal Student Pulse*, 2(3): 1-11.

Coleman, Isobel (2006): "Women, Islam, and the New Iraq," *Foreign Affairs*; 85 (1): 24.

Collins, Dana, Sylvann Falcon, Sharmila Lodhia and Molly Talcott (2010): "New Directions in Feminism and Human Rights," *International Feminist Journal of Politics*, 12(3): 298-318.

Cooks, Bridget R. (2009): "Civil Rights Memorials and the Geography of Memory," *American Studies*, 50(1/2): 248-249.

Corm, G (2003): "Identifying the main economic and reconstruction issues in Iraq, in ESCWA," *Report on the Workshop on Iraq and the Region after the War, Beirut*, 9(11): 13-21.

Cotter, David A., Joan M. Hermsen, Seth Ovadia, and Reeve Vanneman (2001): "The Glass Ceiling Effect," *Social Forces*, 80(2): 655-682.

Court, C. (1995): "Iraq Sanctions Lead to Half a Million Child Deaths," *British Medical Journal*, 311: 1523.

Cox, Michael (2009): "Why did We Get the End of the Cold War Wrong?," *The British Journal of Politics and International Relations*, 11(2): 161-176.

Craner, Lorne (2006): "Will U.S. Democratisation Policy Work? Democracy in the Middle East," *Middle East Quarterly*, 13(3): 3-10.

Crook, John R. (2005): "Human Trafficking Proposal to Criminalize the Patronisation of Prostitutes by U.S. Service Members," *The U.S. Journal of International Law*, 99(1): 264-265.

Cunningham, Steve and Michael Lavalette (2004): "Active Citizens, or Irresponsible Truants? School Students Strikes against War," *Critical Social Policy*, 24(2): 255-269.

Davis, Jessica (2013): "Evolution of the Global Jihad: Female Suicide Bombers in Iraq," *Studies in Conflict and Terrorism*, 36(4): 279-291.

Davies-Netzley, Sally Ann (1998): "Women above the Glass Ceiling Perceptions on Corporate Mobility and Strategies for Success," *Gender and Society*, 12(3): 339-355.

Dawisha, Adeed (2003): "Requiem for Arab Nationalism," *Middle East Quarterly*, 10(1): 25-41.

Denny, Frederick (1977): "Umma in the Constitution of Medina," *Journal of Near Eastern Studies* 36(1): 44.

Dobbins, James (2007): "Who Lost Iraq," *Foreign Affairs*, 86(5).

Dobbs, Michael (2000): "Josef Korbel's Enduring Foreign Policy Legacy," *The Washington Post*, December 28, accessed on 4.9.2009.

Downes, Alexander. B. (2006): "More Borders, Less Conflict? Partition as a Solution to Ethnic Civil Wars", *SAIS Review*, 26(1), Winter-Spring 49-61.

Dreher, Axel (2006): "Does globalisation affect growth? Evidence from a new index of Globalisation," *Applied Economics* 38(10): 1091-1110.

Dreze, Jean and Haris Gazdar (1991): "War, Sanctions and Human Well-Being in Iraq," *Economic and Political Weekly*, 26(50): 2866-2867.

Duelfer, Charles (2004): "Comprehensive Report of the Special Advisor to the Director of Central Intelligence on Iraq's Weapons of Mass Destruction," *Biological Warfare*, September 13: 21.

Eckel, Jan (2010): "Human Rights and Decolonisation: New Perspectives and Open Questions," *An International Journal of Human Rights, Humanitarianism, and Development*, 1(1): 111-135.

Eckert, Amy E. (2005): "Philosophical Theory and the Universal Declaration of Human Rights," *University of Toronto Quarterly*, 74(1): 320-322.

Efrati, Noga (2008): "Competing Narratives Histories of the Women's Movement in Iraq, 1910-58," *International Journal of Middle East Studies*, 40(3): 445-446.

Eisenberg, L. (1997): "The Sleep of Reason Produces Monsters - Human Costs of Economic Sanctions," *New England Journal of Medicine*, 336(17): 1247-1250.

Eland, Ivan (2005): "The Way out of Iraq: Decentralizing the Iraqi Government," *International Journal on World Peace*, 22(1): 39-81.

El-Khawas, Mohamed A. (2008): "Nation Building in a War Zone: The U.S. Record in Iraq, 2003 to 2007," *Mediterranean Quarterly*, 19(1): 42-62.

Encarnacion, Omar G. (2005): "The Follies of Democratic Imperialism," *World Policy Journal*, 22(1): 47-60.

Enloe, Cynthia and Elizabeth Miklya Legerski (2006): "Taking Women seriously makes Us Smarter about the U.S. War in Iraq," *Social Thought and Research*, 27: 3-25.

Erik and Paul R. Brewer (2006): "Public Opinion, the War in Iraq, and Presidential Accountability", *The Journal of Conflict Resolution*, 50(6): December 809-830.

Evers, Erin (2014): "Women's Rights under Threat in Iraq," *Human Rights Watch*, Available online at http://www.hrw.org/news/2014/03/26/women-s-rights-under-threat-iraq accessed on 26.03.2006.

Farer, Tom (2008): "Un-Just War against Terrorism and the Struggle to Appropriate Human Rights," *Human Rights Quarterly*, 30(2): 356-403.

Farhud, D. D., H. Sadighi, H. Pour-Jafari and A. M. Sheibani (1998): "Aging coefficient in different religious groups in Iran," *Iranian Journal of Public Health*, 27: 1-8.

Field, Osgood, John (1993): "From Food Security to Food Insecurity: The Case of Iraq, 1990-91", *Geo Journal*, 30(2), June 185-194.

Filkins, Dexter (2007): "Iraq-Kanan Makiya - Saddam Hussein-The New York Times". Available online at http://www.nytimes.com/2007/10/07/ magazine/07MAKIYA-.html?. accessed on 02.09.2009.

Fineman, Martha Albertson (2013): "Feminist Perspectives on Transitional Justice from International and Criminal to Alternative Forms of Justice," *Gender and Law*, 13: 360.

Finkelstein, Norman (1992): "Reflections on Palestinian Attitudes during the Gulf War," *Journal of Palestine Studies*, 21(3): 54-70.

Foot, Rosemary (2005): "Collateral Damage: human rights consequences of counterterrorist action in the Asia-Pacific," *Journal of International Affairs*, 81(2): 411-425.

Forsythe, David P. (2012): "Human Rights in the Twentieth Century," *Journal of Interdisciplinary History*, 42(3): 444-445.

Forsythe, David P. (1991): "Human Rights in a Post-Cold War World," *Journal of International Law*, 15(2): 55-69.

Freedman, Lawrence D. (2010): "Decoding the Cold War, 20 Years Later," *Foreign Affairs*, 89(2): 136.

Freeman, Gunnar (1994): "Peace in the Middle East: A Window of Opportunity," *International Challenge*, 14(2): 32-40.

Frenk, J. (2010): "The global health system: strengthening national health systems as the next step for global progress," *Plos Medicine*, 7(1): 3 Available online at http://www.ncbi.nlm.nih.gov/pmc/articles/PMC2797 599.

Furber, Andrew S. and Paul Johnstone (2004): "Rebuilding Health Care in Iraq," *Journal of Epidemiology and Community Health*, 58(11): 890-892.

Gaines, Brian J., *et.al.,* (2007): "Same Facts, Different Interpretations: Partisan Motivation and Opinion on Iraq," *The Journal of Politics*, 69(4): 957-974.

Galtung, Johan (1969). "Violence, Peace, and Peace Research," *Journal of Peace Research*, 6(3): 167-191.

Gardam, Judith (1997): "Women and the Law of Armed Conflict Why the Silence?," *The International and Comparative Law Quarterly*, 46(1): 55-80.

Garfield, Andrew (2007): "The U.S. Counter-propaganda Failure in Iraq," *Middle East Quarterly*, 14(4): 23-32.

Gelleny, Ronal D. and Matthew McCoy (2001): "Globalisation and government policy independence: The issue of taxation," *Political Research Quarterly*, 54(3): 509-29.

Gelpi, Christpher Peter D. Feaver and Jason Reiffer (2006): "Success Matters: Causality, Sensitivity and the War in Iraq", *International Security*, 30(3).

Genot, Cecile (2010): "International NGO in Iraq: Actors or Witnesses in the Evolution of the Iraqi NGO Sector," *NCCI* (NGO Coordination Committee for Iraq). Available online at http://southsudanngoforum.org/wp-content/uploads/ 2011/05/NCCI-Survey-INGOs-Iraqi-NGOs-Draft-2.pdf.

Ghabra, Shafeeq, N. (2001): "Iraq's Culture of Violence," *Middle East Quarterly*, 8(3): 39-49.

Gilchrist, Andy (2003): "Workers' Rights in the Firing Line," *International Union Rights*, (10) 4: 22-23.

Glick, F, Thomas (2011): "Her Day in Court: Women's Property Rights in Fifteenth-Century Granada," *Enterprise and Society*, 12(3): 685-686.

Gordon, David (2003): "Iraq, War and Morality," *Economic and Political Weekly*, 38(12/13): 1117-1120.

Goodwin, Jason (2003): "Iraq from Sumer to Saddam," *The Wilson Quarterly*, XXVII (2), Spring.

Gree, Michael Steven (2005): "Legal Realism as Theory of Law," *William and Mary Law Review*, 46(6): 1917-2000.

Grewal, Inderpal (1999): "Women's rights as human rights': Feminist Practices, Global Feminism, and Human Rights Regimes in Transnationality," *Citizenship Studies*, 3(3): 337-354.

Gross, Leo (1948): "The Peace of Westphalia, 1648–1948," *American Journal of International Law*, 42(1): 20-41.

Guernica (2007): "First Victims of Freedom," *Magazine of Arts and Politics*, May 1.

Hadar, Leon. T. (1996): "America's Moment in the Middle East," *Current History,* January: 1-6.

Halliday, Denis J. (1999): "The Impact of The U.N. Sanctions on People of Iraq," *Journal of Palestine Studies*, 28(2): 29-37.

Hamad, Wadood (2005): "Unraveling Iraq: The Socio-political and Ethical Dimensions of Resistance," *New Politics*, X-2(38).

Hamza, Khidhir and Jeff Stein (2001): "Saddam's Bombmaker: The Terrifiying inside Story of the Iraqi Nuclear and Biological Weapons," *Scribner,* June 24.

Hannum, Hurst (2006): "Human Rights in Conflict Resolution: The Role of the Office of the High Commissioner for Human Rights in UN Peacemaking and Peace building," *Human Rights Quarterly*, 28(1): 1-85.

Hargaden, Kevin (2013): "Karl Marx and the Trouble with Rights," *The Other Journal*, Available online at http://theotherjournal.com/2013/ 05/16/karl-marx-and-the-trouble-with-rights/ accessed on 16.05.2013.

Hargreaves, Sally (2003): "Questions Remain over Lack of U.N. Role in Humanitarian Aid in Iraq," *British Medical Journal*, 326(7392): 729.

Harland, Christopher (2000): "The Status of the International Covenant on Civil and Political Rights (ICCPR) in the Domestic Law of State Parties," *Human Rights Quarterly*, 22(1).

Harutyunyan, Satenik (2010): "Nation within a Nation: Kurdistan in Iraq," *Prospect Journal of International Affairs at University of California, San Diego*, Available online at http://prospectjournal.org/2010/11/27/nation-within-a-nation-kurdistan-in-iraq/ accessed on 27.11.2010.

Hassan, Ghali (2005): Iraqi Women under US Occupation, *Centre for Research and Globalisation*, 16 June, Global Research.

Heidenrich, J. G. (1993): "The Gulf War: How Many Iraqis Died?," *Foreign Policy*, 90 (Spring).

Herring, Eric and Glen Rangwala (2005): "Imperialism and Global Governance", *Third World Quarterly*, 26(4/5), 667-683.

Hewitt, A, Nancy (2012): "Recasting Women's Activism in the Nineteenth Century," *Reviews in American History*, 40(3): 444-451.

Hayes, Danny and Matt Guardino (2011): "The Influence of Foreign Voices on U.S. Public Opinion", *American Journal of Political Science*, 55(4), October 831-851.

Heyns, H.C. and Frans Viljoen (2001): "The Impact of the United Nations Human Rights Treaties on the Domestic Level," *Human Rights Quarterly*, 23(3): 483-535.

Hitchens, Christopher (2005). "Sticking up for Saddam - *Slate Magazine*". Available online at http://www.slate.com/id/2131405. accessed on 02.09.2009.

Hobbs, Hadden (2004): "Divine Feminine: Theosophy and Feminism in England, and: Radical Spirits: Spiritualism and Women's Rights in Nineteenth-Century America," *NWSA Journal*, 16(2): 221-225.

Hosseini, Mir, Zib (2006): "Muslim Women's Quest for Equality Between Islamic Law and Feminism," *Critical Enquiry*, 32 Summer 12-24.

Howard, John (2009): "2009 Menzies Lecture by John Howard," *The Australian* (News Limited) accessed on 14.09.2009.

Hudnall, C. Amy (2003): "Feminists Protest War with Iraq," *NWSA Journal, (National Women's Studies Association)*, 15 (2): 99-110.

Hunt, Swanee and Cristina Posa (2004): "Iraq's Excluded Women Building Democracy in Iraq," *Foreign Policy*, July 21.

Ismael, Jacqueline S. (2014): "Iraqi Women in Conditions of War and Occupation," *Arab Studies Quarterly*, 36(3): 260-267.

Isamel, Shereen T. (2004): "Dismantling the Iraqi Social Fabric: From Dictatorship through Sanctions to Occupation," *Journal of Comparative Family Studies*, 35(2), Spring.

Ismael, Tareq Y. and Jacquelines S. Ismael (2005): "Whither Iraq? Beyond Saddam, Sanctions and Occupation," *Third World Quarterly*, 26(4-5): 610.

Jervis, Robert (2003): "Understanding the Bush Doctrine," *Political Science Quarterly*, 118(3): 365-388.

Jones, Peter (2000): "Human Rights and Diverse Cultures: Continuity or Discontinuity," *Critical Review of International Social and Political Philosophy*, 3 (1):27-50.

Jones, Vivian C. (2004): "Iraq's Trade with the World: Data and Analysis," *The Library of Congress Congressional Research Service*, accessed on September 10, 2014.

Jordan, Carole, E. and John Briere (2004): "Violence against Women, Outcome Complexity and Implications for Assessment and Treatment," *Journal of Interpersonal Violence*, 19(11): 1252-1276.

Jordan, Eason (2003): "The News We (CNN) kept to Ourselves," *The New York Times,* 04/11/03.

Kahl, H. Collin (2007): "In the Crossfire or the Crosshairs. Norms, Civilian Casualties and U.S. conduct in Iraq," *International Security*, 32(1): 7-46.

Kalantry, Sital (2010): "Enhancing Enforcement of Economic, Social and Cultural Rights using indicators: A Focus on the Right to Education in the ICESCR," *Human Rights Quarterly*, 32(2): 253-310.

Kalyvas, Stathins N. and Mathew Adam Kocher (2007): "Ethnic Cleavages and Irregular War: Iraq and Vietnam," *Politics and Society*, 35(2): 183-223.

Karr, Longfield Susan (2011): "The History of Human Rights: From the Ancient Times to the Globalisation Era," *Journal of World History*, 22(3): 582-585.

Khakhar, Priyan and Hussain Gulzar Rammal (2013): "Culture and business networks: International business negotiations with Arab managers," *International Business Review*, 22(3): 578-590.

Khalouzadeh, Saeed (2011): "Iran-Iraq War: Legal and International Dimensions," *Iran Review* Saturday, *University of Tehran Faculty Member and Expert on European Studies.* October 8, 2011.

Khashan, Hillel (2001): "Arab Christians as Symbol: Disappearing Christians of the Middle East," *Middle East Quarterly*.

Kiani, Shirin (2010): "The Iranian Population is Graying: Are we ready?," *Archives of Iranian Medicine*, 13(4): 333-339.

King, Laury (2007): "Iraq: A Look Back," *Orbis*, 51(1).

Knapp, Patrick (2014): "Iraq's Lessons on Political Will," *Middle East Quarterly*, 21(1): Winter.

Korieh, Chinma H. (2007): "Imperialism and Human Rights: Colonial Discourses of Rights and Liberties in African History," *African Studies Review*, 50(3): 191-192.

Kozyrev, Andrei Vladimirovich and Gennadii Mikhailovich Gatilov (1990): "The UN peace-making system: problems and prospects," *International Affairs*, 12: 79.

Krist of, D. Nocholas (2003): "Missing in Action: The Truth About Iraqi Arms," *New York Times*, 5 July.

Kutter, Glen (2007): "U.S. Military Fatalities in Iraq in Perspective," *Orbis*, 51(3).

Kwiatkowski, Karen (2007): "Making Sense of the Bush Doctrine," Lew Rockwell.com, accessed on 18. 09.2008.

Lambert, Jennifer (2011): "Political in Qatar: Participation, Legitimacy and security," *Middle East Policy Council*, XVIII (1): 1-6.

Lanctot, J, Catherine (2012): "Lucretia Mott's Heresy: Abolition and Women's Rights in Nineteenth-Century America, and: Elizabeth Cady Stanton: An American Life," *The Journal of the Civil War Era,* 2(1): 88-90.

Langille, Chris (2008): "Political and Moral Myths in American Foreign Policy: The Neoconservative Question," *International Journal of Contemporary Iraqi Studies*, 2(3): 321-336.

Lapkin, Ted (2004): "Does Human Rights Law Apply to Terrorists?," *Middle East Quarterly*, 11(4): 3-13.

Lattimer, Mark (2007): "Freedom Lost," The *Guardian*, December.

Laughlin-Schultz, Bonnie (2009): "From Abolition to Equal Rights for All: The Making of a Reform Community in the Nineteenth Century," *American Studies*, 50(1/2): 161-162.

Layne, Christopher (1991): "Why the Gulf War Was Not in the National Interest," *The Atlantic Monthly*, 268(1): 55-81.

Leland, John (2013): "Iraqi Women Are Seeking Greater Political Influence," *New York Times*, accessed on 10.05.2013.

Leung, Kwong Tang (2000): "The Leadership Role of International Law in Enforcing Women's Rights: The Optional Protocol to the Women's Convention," *Gender and Development*, 8(3): 65-73.

Levenstein, Lisa (2006): "Rethinking the Origins of Woman's Rights: Gender and Nineteenth-Century Political Culture," *Reviews in American History*, 34(1): 28-33.

Lewis, Jonathan Eric (2003): "Iraqi Assyrians: Barometer of Pluralism," *Middle East Quarterly*, 10(3):49-57.

Libal, Kathryan (2007): "The Politics of Refugee Advocacy and Humanitarian Assistance," *Middle East Report*, 37(277).

Liberman, Peter (2007): "Punitiveness and U.S. Elite Support for the 1991 Persian Gulf War," *The Journal of Conflict Resolution*, 51(1): 3-32.

Long, Douglas (1990): 'Utility' and the 'Utility Principle': Hume, Smith, Bentham, Mill," *Utilitas*, 2: 12-39.

Luft, Gal (2005): "Reconstructing Iraq: Bringing Iraq's Economy Back Online," *Middle East Quarterly*, 12(3): 25-32.

MacDonald, Chris (2005): "The Origins of Justice: The Evolution of Morality, Human Rights, and Law," *University of Toronto Quarterly*, 74(1): 312-314.

Macklin, Ruth (2005): "Yet another Guideline- UNESCO Draft Declaration," *Developing World Bioethics*, 5(3): 244-250.

Makar, Ragi N. (1998): "New Voices for Women in the Middle East," *The Journal of Middle East Librarian Association*, 1: 65-66.

Makiya, Kanan (2003): "A Model for Post-Saddam Iraq," *Journal of Democracy*, 14(3): 5-12.

Malekafzali, H. (2004): "Population control and reproductives health in the Islamic Republic of Iran," *Arch Iranian Medicine,* 7(4): 247-250.

Malone, David (2006): "Iraq Awaits," *The World Today*, 62(8/9): 32-34.

Mandelabum, Michel (1996): "Foreign Policy as Social Work," *Foreign Affairs*, February: 16-32.

Manique, O, John (1992): "Development and Human Rights Law," *Human Rights Quarterly*, 14(3).

Mark, Heller (2000): "Continuing and Change in Israeli Security Policy," *International Institute of Strategic Studies*, 87-115.

Mark, (2007): "Trauma-related infections in Battlefield casualties from Iraq," *Annals of Surgery, A Monthly Review of Surgical Science*, 245(5): 803-811.

Marr, Pbebe (2005): "Occupational Hazards-Washington's Record in Iraq," *Foreign Affairs*, 84 (4): 180-186.

Marshall, Jill (2009): "Feminist Reconstructions of Universalism and the Discourse of Human Rights," *International Journal of Law in Context*, 5(1): 87-92.

Martone, Gerald (2003): "Correspondence from Abroad: Water and Health in Iraq," *The American Journal of Nursing*, 103(11): 46-47.

Mason, Michael (2007): "Iraq's Medical Meltdown-Thousands of Iraqis Die Needlessly in a Crumbling Health-Care System,"

Science For The Curious Discover, July Issue 17, Available online at http://discovermagazine.com/ 2007/aug/iraq2019s.

Matthews, C, Wledon (2011): "The Kennedy Administration, Counterinsurgency and Iraq's first Ba'thist Regime," *International Journal of Middle East Studies*, 43(4): 635-653.

Maupin, Lara (2006): "The Decision to Go to War in Iraq," *OAH Magazine of History*, 20(3): 35-41.

Mazaheri, Nimah (2010): "Iraq and the Domestic Political Effects of Economic Sanctions", *The Middle East Journal*, 64(2), Spring 253-268.

McCutcheon, Richard (2006): "Rethinking the War against Iraq," *Anthropologica*, 48(1): 11-28.

McDonnell, Michael A. (2006): "Class War: Class Struggles during the American Revolution in Virginia," *William and Mary Quarterly*, 63(2): 305-344. Accessed on 30.01.2012.

Megret, Frederic and Florian Hoffmann (2003): "The U.N. as a Human Rights Violator? Some Reflections on the United Nations Changing Human Rights Responsibilities," *Human Rights Quarterly*, 25(2): 314-342.

Miller, Jim; Celeste Riendeau; Jessica Rosen (2013): "Lessons in Academic Rescue: An International Higher Education Response in Post-war Iraq," *Science and Diplomacy* 16 September 2(3).

Mingus, Matthew S. (2012): "Progress and Challenges with iraq's Multilevel Governance," *Public Administration Review*, 72(5): 678-686.

Mitchell, Neil, and John McCormick (1988): "Economic and political explanations of human rights violations," *World Politics* 40(4): 476-98.

Moghadam, Val (1988): "Women, Work and the Ideology in the Islamic Republic," *International Journal of Middle East Studies*, 20: 221-243.

Moni, Lal (2011): "Human Dignity and Suffering: Some Considerations," *Economic and Political Weekly*, XLVI (36): 23-26.

Monshipouri, Mahmood (2009): "Human Rights Matters: Local Politics and National Human Rights Institutions," by Julie A. Mertus,

Review by Mahmood Monshipouri, *Human Rights Quarterly*, 31(3): 830-834.

Monshipouri, Mahmood (2011): "Can Globalisation Promote Human Rights," *Human Rights Quarterly*, 33(2): 568-575.

Monten, Jonathan (2005): "The Roots of the Bush Doctrine," *International Security*, 29(4): 112-156.

Morton, Michael Quentin (2011): "The Abu Dhabi Oil Discoveries," *GEO Expro article*, 8(3).

Muravchik, Joshua (2006): "The Foreign Policy Memorandum: Operation Comeback," *Foreign Policy*, October 10, 19(6).

Narveson, Jan (1991): "Collective Rights?," *Canadian Journal of Law and Jurisprudence*, 4(2): 329-345.

Nayar, Kaladhara (1980): "Human Rights and Economic Development: The Legal Foundations," *Universal Human Rights*, 2(3):55-81.

Neier, Arayeh (1996): "The New Double Standard," *Foreign Policy*, 105(winter): 91-103.

Newman, Richard (2009): "From Abolition to Rights for All: The Making of a Reform Community in the Nineteenth Century," *Journal of Social History*, 43(2): 469-471.

Niaz, A. Shah (2006): "Women's Human Rights in the Koran: An Interpretive Approach," *Human Rights Quarterly*, 28(6): 868-903.

Nick Ayers (2008): "Ghost Martyrs in Iraq an Assessment of the Applicability of Rationalist Models to Explain Suicide Attacks in Iraq," *Studies in Conflict and Terrorism* 31: 862-864.

Noorbaksh, Mehdi (2005): "Shiism and Ethnic Politics in Iraq," *Middle East Policy Council*, XV(2).

Noorbaksh, Mehdi (2008): "Shiism and Ethnic Politics in Iraq," *Middle East Policy*, June.

Osgood, Charles (2005): "Iraqi Women Fear Setback in Civil Rights Because New National Assembly is Predominately Shi'i," *The Osgood File*, February 16.

Otterman, Sharon (2004): "Iraq: The Interim Government Leaders," Council on Foreign Relations, June 2, Available online at http://www.cfr.org/iraq/iraq-interim-government-leaders/p7664. accessed on 14.11.2014.

Pagden, Anthony (2003): "Human Rights, Natural Rights, and Europe's Imperial Legacy," *Political Theory*, 31(2): 171-199.

Pan, Esther and Sharon Otterman (2005): "Iraq: The Transitional Government," *Council on Foreign Relation*, April 7, Available online at http://www.cfr.org/iraq/iraq-transitional-government/ p. 8078.

Papagianni, Katia (2005): "Transitional Politics in Afghanistan and Iraq: Inclusion, Consultation, and Public Participation", *Development in Practice*, 15(6): November 747-759.

Parasiliti, T. Andrew (2003): "The Causes and Timing of Iraq's Wars: A Power Cycle Assessment," *International Political Science*, 24(1): 151-165.

Parke, Sam (2009): "Is Iraq Back-Current History," *Journal of World Affairs*, 108(722): 429.

Parver, C. and R. Wolf (2008): "Civil Society's Involvement in Post Conflict Peacebuilding," *International Journal of Legal Information*, 36(1): 50-79.

Patnaik, J.K. (2004): "Human, Rights: The Concept and Perspectives: A Third World View," *The Indian Journal of Political Science*, 65(4): 499-514.

Payman, Salamati (2013): "Mortality and Injuries among Iranians in Iraq-Iran war: A Systematic Review," *Archives Iranian Medicine*, 16(9): 542-550.

Pease, S., Kelley-Kate and David, P., Fosyth (1993): "Human Rights, Humanitarian Intervention and World Affairs," *Human Rights Quarterly*, May: 290-314.

Perry, E. Glenn (2006): "Imperial Democratisation: Rhetoric and reality," *Arab Studies Quarterly* 28(3/4): 55.

Perry, Thomas D. (1977): "A Paradigm of Philosophy: Hohfeld on Legal Rights," *American Philosophical Quarterly*,14(1):41-50.

Pilger, John (2000): "Squeezed to Death," The Guardian Professional Network, March 4, Saturday. Available online at http:// www.theguardian.com/theguardian/ 2000/mar/04/ weekend7.weekend9.

Pipes, Daniel (2011): "Iraq-A Province of Iran," *The Washington Times*, May 12.

Poe, Steven, and C. Neal Tate (1994): "Repression of human rights to personal integrity in the 1980s: A global analysis," *American Political Science Review*, 88(4): 853-72.

Pollack, K. M. (2004): "After Saddam: Assessing the Reconstruction of Iraq," *Analysis Paper I*, 36(1), (Washington, DC: Saban Center for Middle East Policy, Brookings Institution).

Post, Jerrold M. (1990): "Explaining Saddam Hussein: a Psychological Profile," presented to the *House Armed Services Committee* December.

Pratt, Nicola and Nadje Al Ali (2008): "Women's Organizing and the Conflict in Iraq since 2003," *Feminist Review*, 88: 74-85.

Puram, Sidhanth (2002): "U.S. Sanctions on Iraq: The Persistence of Failed Policy," *Breakthrough*, XI (1): 37.

Qureshi, Shazia (2012): "Feminist analysis of Human Rights Law," *Journal of Political Studies*, 19(2): 41-55.

Rabet, Delphine (2009): "Human rights and globalisation: The myth of corporate social responsibility?," *Journal of Alternative Perspectives in the Social Sciences*, 1(2): 463-75.

Rangel, Javier Trevin (2006): "The Human Rights Movement and the Torture Debate," *A Journal of Social Justice*, 18(2): 227-235.

Raphaeli, Nimrod (2004): "Understanding Muqtada al-Sadr," *Middle East Quarterly*, 11(4): 33-42.

Raphaeli, Nimrod (2007): "Culture in Post-Saddam Iraq," *Middle East Quarterly*, 14(3): 33-42.

Rhodes, Edward (2003): "The Imperial Logic of Bush's Liberal Agenda," *Survival*, 45(1): 131-54.

Rizer, K. R. (2001): "Bombing Dual-Use Targets: Legal, Ethical, and Doctrinal Perspectives," *Air and Space Power Chronicles*, May 1.

Roberts, Les, Rriyadh Lafta, Richard Garfield, Jamal Khudhairi and Gilbert Burnham (2004):. "Morality before and after the 2003 Invasion of Iraq: Cluster sample Survey," *The Lancet*, 364(9448): 1857-1864.

Ron, James and Oskar N. T. Thomas (2007): "Do Human Rights Violations Cause Internal Conflict," *Human Rights Quarterly*, 29(3): 674-705.

Ross, M., Ellen (2012): "Lucretia Mott's Heresy: Abolition and Women's Rights in Nineteenth-Century America," *Quaker History*, 101(1): 37-38.

Roth, Kenneth (2004): "Setting the standard: justifying humanitarian intervention," *Harvard International Review*, 26(1): 58-62.

Roth, Kenneth (2005): "Was the Iraq War a Humanitarian Intervention," *Journal of Military Ethics*, 5(2): 84-92.

Roug, Louise (2006): "War in Iraq- Decrepit healthcare adds to toll in Iraq," November 11. A once enviable system lacks doctors, medicine and key equipment. Despite U.S. funding, no cure seems imminent. Available online at http://iraq-war.ru/article/108687.

Rubin, Barry (2006): "Arab Liberals Argue about America," *Middle East Quarterly*, 13(1): 49-58.

Rubin, Barry (2007): "Arab Politics- Back to Futility," *Middle East Quarterly*, 14(1): 53-62.

Rubin, Judith Colp (2008): Women in the New Iraq, *Middle East Review of International Affairs* 12(3): September.

Rubin, Michael (2001): "Sanctions on Iraq: A Valid Anti-American Grievance," *Middle East Review of International Affairs*, 5 (4): 100-115.

Saad, Rasha (2003): "Women's Fate," *Al-Ahram Weekly*, 19-25 June.

Saadawi, Nawal, EI. (2008): "War Against Women and Women Against War Waging War on the Mind," *The Black Scholar*, 38 (2/3): 27-32.

Said, K. Aburish (2003): "The Survival of Saddam: Secrets of his Life and Leadership," See PBS Frontline (2003).

Sams, Victoria (2013): "Imagining Human Rights in Twenty-First Century Theatre: Global Perspectives by Becker, Florian N., Paola S. Hernández, and Brenda Werth," *College Literature*, 40(3): 183-186.

Santisteban, Agustín Velloso De. (2005): "Sanctions, War, Occupation and the De-Development of Education in Iraq", *International Review of Education*, 51 (1): January 59-71.

Satia, Priya (2007): "Developing Iraq: Britain, India and the Redemption of Empire and Technology in the First World War," *Oxford Journals of Past and Present*, 197 (1): 211-255.

Saul, Mathew (2011): "The Normative Status of Self-Determination in International Law: A Formula for Uncertainty in the Scope and Content of the Right," *Human Rights Law Review*: 11(4): 609-613.

Schleifer, Ron (2005): "Reconstructing Iraq: Winning the Propaganda War in Iraq," *Middle East Quarterly*, 12(3): 15-24.

Schlesinger, Arthur (1979): "Human Rights and the American Tradition," *Foreign Affairs*, 57(2): 503-526.

Schneller, Rahul (2010): "Iraq and the U.S. Pullout: Separate we Must," *World Today*, 18.

Scholvin, Soren (2011): "The failure of Iraq's Future in Iraq," *World Affairs*, 15(3): 48-71.

Schonsteiner, Judith, Alma Beltrany Puga and Domingo A. Lovera (2011): "Reflections on the Human Rights Challenges of Consolidating Democracies: Recent Developments in the Inter-American System of Human Rights," *Human Rights Law Review*, 11(2): 362.

Schwartz, Michael (2010): "War: Causes and Consequences War Without End," *Contemporary Sociology*, 39(4): 399-402.

Schwenninger, Sherle R. (2003): "Revamping American Grand Strategy," *World Policy Journal*, 20(3), November 1.

Segal, D. and Segal, M (2004): "America's Military Population," *Population Reference Bureau*, 59(4).

Seymour, Michael (2004): "Ancient Mesopotamia and Modern Iraq in the British Press, 1980-2003," *Current Anthropology*, 45(3), June.

Shah, A, Niaz (2006): "Women's Human Rights in the Koran: An Interpretive Approach," *Human Rights Quarterly*, 28(4): 868-903.

Shughart II, William F. (2006): "An Analytical History of Terrorism, 1945-2000", *Public Choice*, 128(1/2): July 7-39.

Simpson, Bradley R. (2013): "Self-determination, Human Rights and the End of Empire in the 1970s," *An International Journal of Human Rights, Humanitarianism, and Development*, 4(2): 239-260.

Smallwood, Peter D. and William T. Liimatainen (2011): "Securing WMD Expertise: Lessons Learned from Iraq," *Arms Control Today*, 41(6): 8-14.

Smidt, E. Corwin (2005): "Religion and American Attitudes toward Islam and an Invasion of Iraq," *Sociology of Religion*, 66(3): 243-261.

Smihula, Daniel (2009): "Definition of National Minorities in International Law," *Journal of U.S. China Public Administration*, 6(5): 45-51.

Smith, I. Jane (1979): "Women in Islam Equity, Equality and the Search for the Natural Order," *Journal of the American Academy of Religion*, 47(4): 517-537.

Sofer, Ken (2013): The Iraq War Ledger (2013 Update). A Look at the War's Human, Financial, And Strategic Costs. See also: The War in Iraq: A Timeline of Events, Online in *Centre for American Progress*.

Sovacool, Benjamin and Saul Halfon (2007): "Reconstructing Iraq: Merging Discourses of Security and Development", *Review of International Studies*, 33 (2): April 223-243.

Spagat, Michael (2010): "Truth and Death in Iraq under Sanctions," *Significance*, 7(3): 116-120.

Stafford, Jonathan (2010): "Comparisons in Nation Building: Korea and Iraq," *Small Wars Journals*, September 13.

Stansfield, R. V. (2003): "Politics and governance in the new Iraq: reconstruction of the new versus resurrection of the old," *Whitehall Papers*, 59: 67-89.

Steinberg, Gerald M. (2013): "Human Rights Watch Protects the Arab Tyrants," *Middle East Quarterly*, 20(3): 49-58.

Stein, Judith (2009): "Civil Rights and Political Space," *Dissent*, 56(2): 124-128.

Stockman, Farah (2005): "Talabani Calls Allegations of Torture 'Nonsense'," *The New York Times*, Monday, November 28.

Stoltman, Joseph P. and C. Sonia Wardley (1996): "Social issues relative to water," *Global Change and Environmental Issues*, 39(3): 299-309.

Stover, Eric, Hanny Megally, and Hania Mufti (2005): "Bremer's Gordian Knot: Transitional Justice and the U.S. Occupation of Iraq," *Human Rights Quarterly*, 27(3): 830-857.

Strauss, Mark (2002): "Attacking Iraq," *Foreign Policy*, 129: 14-19. Available online at http://www.jstor.org/stable/3183385, accessed on 01.03.2012.

Suzanne, Goldenberg (2008): Iraq war my biggest regret, Bush admits," London: Available online at www.guardian.co.uk, accessed on 02.12.2008.

Synovitz, Ron (2013): "Ten Years of Change since Invasion of Iraq," Radio Free Europe Radio Liberty, March 17, Available online at http://www.rferl.org/content/iraq-war-lynndie-ghraib/24930947.html, accessed on 14.11.2014.

Takeyh, Ray (2010): "The Iran-Iraq War: A Reassessment," *Middle East Journal*, 64(3): 365-383.

Taras, Ray (2006 December): "The Illogic of Intervention in Iraq. Sectarianism, Civil War and the U.S. Game Plan," *International Journal of World Peace*, XXIII(4).

Thahir, Aandrea Fischer (2010): "Competition, Cooperation and Resistance: Women in Political Field in Iraq," *International Affairs*, 86(6) December.

Thakur, Ramesh (2003): "Iraq, U.N. and Changing Bases of World Order", *Economic and Political Weekly*, 38(23): June 2261-2266.

Thomas, Daniel C. (2005): "Human Rights Ideas, the Demise of Communism and the End of the Cold War," *Journal of Cold War Studies*, 7(2): 110-141.

Townsend, Barbara K. (2003): Disciplining Feminism from Social Activism to Academic Discourse, *Journal of Higher Education*, 74(6): 715.

Udombana, N. J (2000): "The Third World and the Right to Development: Agenda for the Next Millennium," *Human Rights Quarterly*, 22: 753-787.

Verma, Priya, Carol Annie Douglas, Rachel Pleatman, Annsley Chapman, Angelita Manzano and Karla Mantilla (2005): "Iraq: U.S. Soldiers accused of Sex Assaults," *Off Our Backs*, 35(5/6): 7-8.

Vernon, Alex (2001): "The Gulf War and Postmodern Memory," *The Wilson Quarterly*, 25(1): 68-82.

Vidal, John (1992): "Cold Comfort on the Mountainside," *The Guardian Weekly*, January 26.

Voeten, Erik and Brewer Paul *R.* (2006): Public Opinion, the War in Iraq, and Presidential Accountability, *Journal of Conflict Resolution*, 50 (6): 809-830.

Walker, Martin (2003): "The Making of Modern Iraq," *The Wilson Quarterly*, 27(2): 29-40.

Wallace, Duncan (2014): "Trends in traumatic limb amputation in Allied Forces in Iraq and Afghanistan," *Journal of Military and Veterans' Health*, 20(2): 31-35.

Waltz, Susan E. (2001): "Universalizing Human Rights: the Role of Small States in the Construction of the Universal Declaration of Human Rights," *Human Rights Quarterly*, 23(1): 44-72.

Wall, Steven (2007): "Collective Rights and Individual Autonomy," *Ethics*, 117(2): 234-264.

Watenpaugh, Keith (2004): "Between Saddam and the American Occupation: Iraq's Academic Community Struggles," *Academe* 90(5): 18-24.

Wheeler, Nicholas (2003): "The Bush doctrine: the dangers of American exceptionalism in a revolutionary age," *Asian Perspective*, 27(4): 183-216.

Whelan, Daniel J. and Jack Donnelly (2007): "The West, Economic and Social Rights and the Global Human Rights Regime: setting the Record Straight," *Human Rights Quarterly*, 28(4): 908-949.

White, Jeffrey B. and Michael Schmidmayr (2003): "Resistance in Iraq," *Middle East Quarterly*, 10(4): 17-32.

Wilbanks, Mark and Efraim Karsh (2010): "How the "Sons of Iraq" Stabilised Iraq," *Middle East Quarterly*, 17(4): 57-70.

Wilcox, Clyde; Lara Hewitt and Dee Allso (1996): "The Gender Gap in Attitudes toward the Gulf War a Cross-National Perspective," *Journal of Peace Research*, 33(1): 67-82.

Winston, Morton (2011): "Human Rights and the Ethics of Globalisation," *Human Rights Quarterly*, 33(3): 893-895.

Winter, Bronwyn (2006): "The Great Hijab Coverup" Off Our Backs," *A Women's Newsjournal* 36(3): 38-40.

Wolf, Antenor Hallo De (2006): "Modern Condottieri in Iraq: Privatizing War from the Perspective of International and Human Rights Law," *Indiana Journal of Global Legal Studies*, 13(2): 315-356.

Yaphe, S. Judith (2003): "War and Occupation in Iraq: What Went Right? What Could Go Wrong?," *Middle East Journal*, 57(3): 381-399.

Yew, Kuan, Lee (2007): "The United States, Iraq and the War on Terror. A Singapore Perspective," *Foreign Affairs*, January 86(1).

Zaidi, S. and Fawzi, M. (1995): "Health of Baghdad's Children," *The Lancet*, 346(8988): 1485.

Zangana, Haifaa (2005): "Women of the New Iraq," *al-Ahram Weekly*, No.755.11-17.

Zizek, Slaver (2004): "Iraq's False Promises," *Foreign Affairs*, 140(1): 42-49.

Reports

Abdel, Fadil M. (2003): "Issues of economic reconstruction of Iraq, in ESCWA," *Report on the Workshop on Iraq and the Region after the War, Beirut* 9(11) July, 25-37 (New York United Nations).

Aftermath of War, Part II: The Plight of the Iraqi Kurds a Year Later, Staff report to the U.S. Senate Subcommittee on Immigration and Refugee Affairs, January 17, 1992, p. 1.

Al-Mesalla (2012): "Who we are". Available online at http://www.almesalla.net/ Default1.aspx?page=sitecontents&c=menu1whoweare accessed on 13.12. 2012.

Amnesty International (2014): Document - Iraq: Amnesty International calls on New Iraqi Prime Minister to uphold Rights. Public Statement.19 September 2014. Amnesty International today sent a letter to the new Iraqi Prime Minister, Dr Haider Al-Abadi, urging him to do his utmost to ensure human rights.

Aprim, Fred (2003): Aprim Strikes Back. Author and Historian, Discussion Forum. Posted by Jeff, on Tuesday, June 17, from. wideopenwest.com (69.14.196.62) on Tuesday, June 24,California. U.S.A. 04.04. 2003.

Belder, Bert D. (2007): War Crimes: Health Care in Iraq has Collapsed- After 4 years of occupation Iraq's health status is nothing short of disastrous, Global Research Report, April 06. Available online at http://www. globalresearch.ca/war-crimes-health-care-in-iraq-has-collapsed/ 5289.

Brahimi, Lakhdar (2004a): *The Political Transition in Iraq: Report of the Fact-Finding Mission*, Report annexed to S/2004/140 Letter from the UN Secretary General to the Security Council, 23.02.2004.

Brahimi, Lakhdar (2004b): *Statement of the Special Advisor to the Secretary-General, Lakdhar Brahimi, to the Security Council on the Political Transition Process in Iraq*, UN briefing, 27.04.2004.

Brian C. Schmidt and Michael C. Williams (2007): *The Bush Doctrine and the Iraq War: Neoconservatives vs. Realists*, Carleton University and University of Wales, Aberystwyth. Paper presented at the Annual Conference. British International Studies Association Cambridge U.K. 17-19 December 2007.

Brown, Nathan J. (2005): *Democracy and Rule of Law Project*, Debating Islam in Post-Baathist Iraq, Carnegie Endowment for International Peace.

CEGE Center for European Governance and Economic Development Research. Discussion Papers.

Charter of the U.N. 26 June 1945, Available online at http:// www.un.org/aboutun/ charted. accessed on 16.04.2012

Chicago Council of Foreign Relations, American Public Opinion Report (1995), Available online at http://www.uicdocs.lib.uic.edu/ ccfr/publications/ opinion-1995/2-3html.

Cingranelli, David L, and David L, Richards (2006): The Cingranelli-Richards (CIRI) human rights dataset 2006. Available online at http://www. humanrightsdata.org/ accessed on 27.09.2006.

Conetta, Carl (2004): "Disappearing the Dead: Iraq, Afghanistan, and the Idea of a "New Warfare," Project on Defense Alternatives.

Cortrig, David (ed.) (June 2003): Unproven the Controversy Over Justifying War in Iraq. Available online at http://.www.middle-eastreprence.org.uk/ iraqweapons.html.

Craviotto, Nerea (2012): Global Partnership for Effective Development Co-operation: A feminist perspective. Effective Development Co-operation Blog. Available online at http://devcooperation.org/

2014/06/12/global-partnership-for-effective-development-co-operation-a-feminist-perspective.

Dale, Catherine (2008): *Operation Iraqi Freedom: Strategies, Approaches, Results, and Issues for Congress.* CRS Report for Congress. Congressional Research Service. Prepared for Members and Committees for Congress.

D. J. Ravindran (2000): Circle of Rights. International Human Rights Internship Program and Asian Forum for Human Rights Development.

Donnelly, Jack (2009): "Human Dignity and Human Rights," Swiss Initiative to Commemorate the 60th Anniversary of the UDHR, Protecting Dignity: An Agenda for Human Rights, Research Project on Human Dignity.

Dreher, Axel; Martin Gassebner and Lars H.R Siemers (2010): Globalisation, Economic Freedom and Human Rights.

Dreher, Axel (2010): Globalisation, Economic Freedom and Human Rights. CEGE (Center for European Governance and Economic Development Research). Discussion Papers. Do Globalisation and Economic Freedom affect Human Rights. Available online at www.uni-goettingen.de/de/document/download/ 115_Dreher.pdf by A Dreher-2010-Cited by 16-Related articles Human Rights, Globalisation, Economic Freedom, Liberalisation. JEL-Codes:...

Dreher, Axel, Martin Gassebner and Lars H R Siemers (2010): "Globalisation, Economic Freedom and Human Rights," *Center for European Governance and Economic Development Research (CEGE)*, Discussion Papers, (115) October.

Furst, Barbara (2005): "Gertrude Bell and Iraq," American Diplomacy-Foreign Service Dispatches and Periodic Report on U.S. Foreign Policy. Available online at http://www.unc.edu/depts/diplomat/item/2005/0103/furst/furst_ bell.html.

Gibson, Bryan (2010): *Covert Relationship: American Foreign Policy, Intelligence, and the Iran-Iraq War, 1980-1988.* New York: Praeger; Cold War International History Project. The 1980-1988 Iran-Iraq War: A CWIHP Critical Oral History Conference.

Girls Education in Iraq (2010): UNICEF. Dr Griffiths, Matthew. A Situational Analysis of Girls Education in Iraq. With recommendations for the Government of Iraq and for UNICEF

Iraq in their support for the Government in the development of girls' access to good quality education.

Gorbechev, Mikhail (1988): Address to the U.N. General Assembly: Soviet News 6455 (1988). Available online at http://www.enotes.com/topics/mikhail-gorbachev-131323. Found in United Nations General Assembly, Provisional Verbatim Record of the Seventy-Second Meeting.

Governing Iraq (2013): "Make or Break: Iraq's Sunnis and the State," *International Crisis Group, Middle East Report*. 144 August 14.

Hassan, Husseinn D. (2007): Iraq: Tribal Structure, Social, and Political Activities, CRS Report, Congressional Research Service, the Library of Congress Prepared for Members and Committees of Congress.

Hendessi, Mandana (1986): "Fourteen Thousand Women Meet Report from Nairobi," *Feminist Review,* No. 23, 147-156.

Hopwood, Derek (2003): "British Relations with Iraq," BBC Homepage, Recent History, last updated in 2006. Available online at http://news.bbc.co.uk/ 2/hi/middle_east/1940050.stm

Human Development Reports, 1993 and 1994. United Nations Development Programme. 1993 and 1994. Human Development Reports, New York: Oxford University Press. Available online at http://www.nap.edu/ openbook.php?record_id=5513&page=25.

International Council on Human Rights Policy: 2002. Jouralism, Media and the Challenge of Human Rights Reporting. 48, Grand-Montfleury, POB 147, 1290 Versoix, Switzerland.

International Crisis Group (2005): "Unmaking Iraq: A Constitutional Process Gone Awry" *ICG Middle East Policy Briefing* 26 September.

Iraq Multiple Indicator Cluster Survey 2011: Childinfo.org. Available online at www.childinfo.org/files/MICs4_iraq_Preliminary_Report_Eng.pdf. Central Statistical Organisation (CSO). Kurdistan Regional Statistics Office (KRSO). Ministry of Health. Unicef. Unite For Children.

Iraq: Nine Years after Ouster of Saddam Hussein, Workers Still Toil under His Labor Law. Available online at *www.aflcio.org. AFL-CIO Now-Global Action.*

IRAQ 2012: Human Rights Report-US Department of State Available online at www.state.gov/documents/organisation/204572.pdf, accessed on 02.05.2013-other cruel, inhuman, or degrading treatment or punishment; harsh and life-threatening human rights; discrimination against and societal abuses of women and ethnic, religious, and racial... across 18 cities killed 113 persons and injured more than 250 Spillover from the conflict in Syria affected Iraq.

Jordan, Sea Dead (2006): *Iraqi Women's Rights and International law.* A High level Conference on Gender Rights in transitional justice and beyond. For the judges of the Iraqi high tribunal and Iraqi civil society and government leaders. Global Justice Centre Human Rights through the Rule of Law.

Katulis, Brian (2009): Democracy Promotion in the Middle East and the Obama Administration. A Century Foundation Report. Lise Rakner (Chr. Michelsen Institute), Alina Rocha Menocal (ODI) and Verena Fritz (ODI) (2007): Democratisation's Third Wave and the Challenges of Democratic Deepening: Assessing International Democracy Assistance and Lessons Learned. Working Paper 1. Good Governance, Aid Modalities and Poverty Reduction: Linkages to the Millennium Development Goals and Implications for Irish Aid Research Project (RP-05-GG) of the Advisory Board for Irish Aid.

Katzman, Kenneth (2004): Iraq: Transition to Sovereignty, CRS Report for Congress Received through the CRS Web, Foreign Affairs, Defense, and Trade Division.

Katzman, Kenneth (2009): "Iraq: Post-Saddam Governance and Security. Specialist in Middle Eastern Affairs," *CRS Report for Congress* 28.10. 2009.

Katzman, Kenneth (2014): Iraq: Politics, Governance, and Human Rights, Specialist in Middle Eastern Affairs, CRS (Congressional Research Service) Report, Prepared for Members and Committees of Congress.

Krug, Etienne G., Linda L. Dahlberg, James A. Mercy, Anthony B. Zwi and Rafael Lozano (2002): World Report on Violence and Health, Geneva: *World Health Organisation.*

Kubrusi, A (2003): "Strategies for Development Under Crisis Conditions, in ESCWA," *Report on the Workshop on Iraq and the Region after the War, Beirut* 9(11) July, 22-25, United Nations.

Kubrusi, A and Kadri, A (2003): "The economic consequences of the war on Iraq on the ESCWA region, in ESCWA," *Report on the Workshop on Iraq and the Region after the War, Beirut* 9(11) July 48-51, United Nations.

Lasky, Majorie P. (2006): Iraqi Women under Saddam, A Report by CODEPINK Women for Peace and Global Exchange. Alternatives International; Available online at http://www.alterinter.org/spip.php?article170.

Massoud Barzani, leader of the Kurdish Democratic Party, when asked recently what would happen if the Allied forces left the region, replied, "It's very simple. If there is no agreement with Saddam Hussein, there will be a new battle, the Iraqi army will return, we will resist, and people will flee again to the mountains." Michel Verrier, "Barzani: Pas Question de Proclamer un Etat Indépendant,=" *Libération*, May 16 and 17, 1992.

More Human Rights Watch reporting on Iraq Human rights conditions in Iraq remained extremely poor, especially for journalists, detainees, and opposition activists.

Parast, Sohofi M. (2008): *Iran Pension system, current and future situation*, in *International Conference on Insurance Industy*. Iran.

Paul, E, Darrel. The Siren Song of Geopolitics: Towards a Gramscian Account of the Iraq War. Available online at http://mil.sagepub.com. Accessedon 28.5.2012.

Prusher, Ilene R. (2003): "Five Women Confront a New Iraq," *Christian Science Monitor*, 16 July, Available online at http://www.csmonitor.com/2003/ 0716/p01s04-woiq.html

SCID (2000): Select Committee on International Development, International Responsibilities Task Force of the American Library Association's Social Responsibilities Round Table Alternative Resources on the U.S. War against Iraq Resources listed on this page do not necessarily reflect the views of IRTF, SRRT.

Schmidt, Brian C. and Michael C. Williams (2007): *The Bush Doctrine and the Iraq War: Neoconservatives vs. Realists*, Carleton University and University of Wales, Aberystwyth. Paper presented at the Annual Conference. British International Studies Association Cambridge, U.K. 17-19 December 2007.

Shalom, Stephen R. (2014): "The United States and Iran-Iraq War 1980-1988," in *Iran Chember Society* on 04.10.2014.

Simmang, Stephen (2013): "Operation desert shield and Desert Storm, Saddam Hussein," In Prezi.com on 11 January 2013.

Sunday, November 27, 2005 Posted: 1424 GMT (2224 HKT). CNN.com-Ex-PM: Abuse as bad Saddam era. Available online at www.cnn.com/2005/ WORLD/ meast/11/27/iraq.allawi/.

The International Council on Human Rights Policy (2007) was established in 1998. Catching the Wind-Human Rights. ICHRP. Kilim detail. Grand-Montfleury, P. O. Box 147, 1290 Versoix, Switzerland. *Catching the Wind-Human Rights*, 2007. International Council on Human Rights Policy. Versoix, Switzerland.

Unemployment, Female (Percent Of Female Labor Force) (Modeled ILO Estimate). The World Bank, Available online at http:// Data.Worldbank.Org/Indicator /Sl.Uem.Totl.Fe.Zs/Countries/1w-Iq?Display=Graph.

United Nations Division for the Advancement of Women, Department of Economics and Social Affairs, Short History of CEDAW Convention, Available online at http://www.un.org/womenwatch/ draw/cedaw/ history.htm accessed on 08.03.2011.

UNICEF (2013): Iraq Statistics, Available online at http:// www.unicef.org/ infobycountry/iraq_statistics.html accessed on 27.12.2013.

UNTC (2006): Human Rights. "Convention on the Rights of Persons with Disabilities," New York, Status At: 15.10.2014. Available online at https://treaties.un.org/Pages/ViewDetails.aspx?mtdsg_ no=IV-15&chapter= 4&lang=en, accessed on 13.12.2006.

"UN welcomes Iraqi ratification of Pact on Rights of Persons with Disabilities," Medicine magazine. Available online at http:// medicinezine.com/news/ welcomes-iraqi-ratification-pact-rights-persons-disabilities/, accessed on 30.01.2012.

U.N. Security Council (1999): Poverty: 1999 issued May 2003 Census. Poverty: 1999 Census 2000 Brief By…developed in the Social Security. It was adopted by the Council of Economic

Advisors, Available online at www.census.gov/prod/2003pubs/c2kbr.

United Nations Iraq Assistance strategy 2005-2007.

United Nations Development Assistance Framework 2015-2019. The Development Strategy of the National Authorities and People of Iraq and the Agencies, Funds and Programmes of the United Nations System.

Winning the Peace Conference Report: (2003), Findings and conclusions presented in the *Women's Role in Post-Conflict Iraq*, Woodrow Wilson International Center for Scholars, Proceedings of a Forum held on April 21-22, p. 4. United Nations Development Program (2005): Iraq Living Conditions Survey.

World Health Organisation (2000): *World Health Report 2000-Health systems: improving performance.* Geneva, WHO. Available online at http://www.who.int/whr/2000/en/index.html.

World Report (2013): Human Rights Watch, Human Rights conditions in Iraq. Available online at http://www.hrw.org/world-report/2013/country-chapters/iraq.

World Report Chapter: Iraq 2012 (PRF) Iraq at a Crossroads Iraqi Kurdistan's Silenced Spring.

Web Sites

News.Indict.2003-06-18. Available online at http://www.indict.org.uk/newsarticles. php?article=news180603. accessed on 02.09.2009.

BBC News, October 16, 2000: "Saddam Hussein executed in Iraq" BBC News, 2006-12.30.

Iraq Living Conditions Survey, *United Nations Development Program*, 2005.

John Pike. "Iran-Iraq War (1980-1988)". Available online at http://www.globalsecurity.org/military/world/war/iran-iraq.htm. accessed on 02.09.2009..

Jordan, Eason (April 11, 2003): "The News We (CNN) Kept To Ourselves". The New York Times. Available online at http://www.nytimes.com/2003/04/11/ opinion/11JORD.html.

http://www.hrw.org/reports/1995IRAQ955.htm, accessed on 17.09.2007 http://www.hrw.org/reports/1991/IRAQ913.htm, accessed on 15.09.2007

http://web.amnesty.org/ pages/iraq-article_6-eng accessed on 17.09.2007.

http://www.oxfordbibliographies.com/view/document/obo-9780199791279/obo-9780199791279-0137.xml.

Index

I

O

P

Q

R